CULTIVATION II

College Writers Analyzing the World through Words

GENERAL EDITOR, LAURIE CARTER

— ASSOCIATE EDITORS —

DARYL LYNN DANCE, ELIZABETH CUDDY, LAUREN DELACRUZ, JOYCE JARRETT, CRAIG WYNNE

Kendall Hunt

publishing company

Cover images © Shutterstock.com

Kendall Hunt
publishing company

www.kendallhunt.com
Send all inquiries to:
4050 Westmark Drive
Dubuque, IA 52004-1840

Published in the United States of America

CONTENTS

INTRODUCTION

We write for a variety of reasons: to express ourselves, to entertain, to exchange information, to persuade. And we do so in various social, academic, and professional contexts. Not surprisingly then, there are many different **genres** (kinds) of writing.

These are all quite different from one another in a great many ways. This is because each has a somewhat different purpose and intended reader. Hence their tone will vary. But there are other important contrasts too. Each is laid out differently on the page or screen, each is organized differently, and each employs certain approaches and strategies unique to that kind of writing. In short, each genre follows its own distinct formula. Over the years, these variations have evolved and become standard practice simply because they have proven to be what works best in each context.

If presented with examples of the various genres, most of us could easily identify which were which, even if we found the reasons behind our choices difficult to fully explain. This is because we're all experienced readers, and have therefore developed certain automatic—because subconscious—understandings and assumptions about each kind of writing. In order to be taken seriously, therefore, a writer must satisfy the reader's expectations. A business letter must look and "feel like" a business letter, a newspaper article must look and "feel like" a newspaper article, and so on. Certainly this is true of the academic essay, the main genre emphasized in college-level English courses. It's structured a certain way and includes a number of long-established features. Accordingly, this textbook—intended for use in first-year writing classes—focuses primarily on the academic essay, discussing several main modes of essay development, along with specialized applications such as essay exams, literary criticism, and research-based essays.

But the book goes beyond this principal emphasis to provide coverage of workplace writing as well, reflecting an ongoing trend in composition textbooks published in recent years. In truth, *Cultivation II* is not just about the kind of writing done in college; it's more than that, equipping you to write well even after graduation, when you'll be called upon to communicate on the job. Accordingly, there are revision checklists, model documents, and helpful exercises throughout, along with an appendix that identifies key strategies for improving your style and another that reviews the fundamentals of spelling, punctuation, and grammar.

In short, you will learn from this book. But how *much* you learn will depend primarily on your own efforts. You must attend class regularly, pay close attention to your professor's lectures, complete all assignments punctually, practice good time-management, and approach your English class—indeed, *all* your classes—with an enthusiastic, upbeat attitude. As with anything, a positive, goal-directed outlook gets the best results.

From *College English: The Basics, 2nd Edition* by George J. Searles. © 2017 by George J. Searles. Reprinted by permission of Kendall Hunt Publishing Company.

PART 1

The Most Basic Basics: Purpose, Audience, and Tone

Unless we're writing in a diary or personal journal, we usually write for one reason: to communicate with someone else. But the *specific* purpose of that communication, along with our relationship to the intended reader, greatly influences how the writing is done.

Our purpose may simply be to express ourselves. Sometimes the purpose is to make a request. Very often, the purpose is to provide information or to persuade, or both. Or perhaps the goal is just to amuse or entertain.

But the manner in which these objectives are pursued—singly or in combination—is determined by our audience. The writer and reader may be well-acquainted or may never have met. They may be equals (co-workers, for example) or not, as in the case of an employer and an employee. They may be in basic agreement about the topic or they may be in disagreement or even in conflict. So the "voice" or tone of the writing can vary greatly, from highly conversational to very formal indeed.

Certainly, awareness of these factors—purpose, audience, and tone—is crucial to good writing. The first part of this book explores these fundamental concerns, presenting an overview of the governing principles involved.

CHAPTER 1

Purpose

wavebreakmedia/Shutterstock.com

LEARNING OBJECTIVES

When you complete this chapter, you will be able to

▶ Determine your purpose for writing
▶ Apply the basic principles involved in self-expressive, informative, interrogative, persuasive, and entertaining writing

DETERMINING PURPOSE

The first step in the writing process is to understand that writing is done for a variety of different reasons, so it's crucial to determine your own objective. Ask yourself, "Summarized in one sentence, what am I trying to say and *why* am I saying it?" To answer, you must carefully consider your subject matter, focusing on its most important elements. A helpful strategy is to employ the "Five Ws" that journalists use to structure the opening sentences of newspaper stories: Who, What, Where, When, and Why. Just as they do for reporters, the Five W's will help you clarify your thinking and identify the key points in your communication.

For example, a probation officer composes a pre-sentencing report to convince the court to grant probation or impose a jail sentence. The officer may recommend either, and will provide supporting information, but the primary purpose of the report is to persuade. In such a case, the Five W's might function as follows:

<table>
<tr><td align="center">**WHO**</td><td align="center">**WHAT**</td><td align="center">**WHERE**</td></tr>
</table>

<u>Thomas Moran</u> should be <u>denied probation</u> and sentenced to <u>state prison</u>,

<table>
<tr><td align="center">**WHEN**</td><td align="center">**WHY**</td></tr>
</table>

effective <u>immediately</u>, because <u>he is a repeat offender</u>.

The Five W's are not magic. Any piece of writing would have to go far beyond a simple statement of five basic facts. But identifying those details helps you determine whether you are writing to express yourself, to provide or request information, to persuade, to entertain or—as is often the case—to achieve some combination of these goals. Once you decide on this, then and only then are you ready to move forward. But it's necessary to understand the strategies you can use. Let's consider each in some depth.

From *College English: The Basics, 2nd Edition* by George J. Searles. © 2017 by George J. Searles. Reprinted by permission of Kendall Hunt Publishing Company.

SELF-EXPRESSIVE WRITING

The main purpose of this kind of writing is to convey the writer's thoughts, feelings, emotions, attitudes, or opinions. Accordingly, self-expressive writing is nearly always phrased in the grammatical *first person* ("I did this," "I did that") and often provides an account of a lived experience the writer considers significant. Such writing typically includes information of a personal nature, and sometimes that material might be entertaining. But if the writer is attempting to defend or justify a particular belief, the narrative might employ strategies typical of persuasive writing.

Here's an example of self-expressive writing, the body of an e-mail from a student to her friend, complaining about a mutual acquaintance:

> I don't want you to think I'm being too impatient, but I've gotta tell you how upset I am with Alicia. She always says she'll be ready to go out when I get to her apartment, but when I get there she's never ready. She always has a million lame excuses and doesn't even apologize. So then we're late for whatever it is we're going to. Last night it happened again. We were supposed to go to an 8:00 movie at the mall, and we got there fifteen minutes late. If this keeps up I'm not gonna hang with her no more.

Since the student is expressing personal emotions—resentment and annoyance—she uses first-person narration, which is typical of e-mail exchanges (even those that are not essentially self-expressive). Her inclusion of the details about the movie lends credibility to her complaint, providing a concrete example to balance her rather overstated wording elsewhere ("always…never…always…a million"). Of course, her lapses into unconventional spelling ("gotta…gonna"), slang ("hang with"), and an ungrammatical double-negative ("not…no more") reflect the e-mail's conversational nature. But in self-expressive writing composed in response to college assignments, such informalities should not appear.

Dragon Images/Shutterstock.com

INFORMATIVE WRITING

The purpose of this kind of writing is simply to provide information desired or needed by the reader. Therefore, informative writing is usually phrased objectively, with emphasis on verifiable facts rather than on opinions or beliefs. It often includes statistics and other such data. Obviously, factual accuracy is crucial in informational writing. But if the writing uses information in an attempt to prove a point or promote a particular point of view, then it has become primarily persuasive rather than informational.

Here's an example of informative writing, taken from the *New York Safe Boating* manual:

> New York State law requires that all boats not exceed a speed of 5 miles per hour when within 100 feet of shore, a raft, a dock, or an anchored or moored boat. The only exception to this is when the boat is taking a skier from shore or landing a skier near the shore. On some specific bodies of water the 5 mph limit has been extended to 200 feet, and on several lakes there are daytime and nighttime speed limits. Local ordinances may further regulate the speed of boats operated within specific areas.

This manual is studied by persons enrolled in the state's comprehensive boating course, which teaches the fundamentals of safe boating operation. Clearly, all the information in the manual is needed by those readers.

With its precise identification of the various speed limits and distances, the above paragraph is representative of the manual's contents, and its objective tone and detailed wording are typical of most informative writing.

INTERROGATIVE WRITING

The purpose of this kind of writing is to request information desired or needed by the writer. First-person narration is often used, by way of explaining the writer's reasons for the inquiry. *Specificity* is the key to effective interrogative writing. The writer must ensure that the reader knows exactly what information is required, and in what degree of detail. Therefore, this kind of writing must not be vague or general. Instead, it must precisely "spell out," in all its particulars, what's being asked for and why.

Here's the body of an e-mail written by a newspaper reporter to the local police chief, requesting information about an arrest:

> It is our understanding that an Arlington resident, Mr. Alexander Booth, is the subject of an investigation by your department, with the assistance of the county district attorney. In keeping with the provisions of the state Freedom of Information Law, we're requesting information about Mr. Booth's arrest.
>
> This information is needed to provide our readership with accurate news coverage. *The Weekly News* prides itself on fair, accurate, and objective reporting, and we're counting on your assistance as we seek to uphold those standards.
>
> In particular, we need to know what charges are pending against Mr. Booth, and the sources of those allegations. In addition, we are requesting a dated chronological summary of the events leading to Mr. Booth's present situation.
>
> Because police records are by law a matter of public record, we anticipate your full cooperation.

This e-mail begins by providing some background, explaining the reasons for its request. But it becomes quite pointed in the third paragraph, where it details its exact requirements, just as all interrogative writing should. Notice also that the reporter has chosen first-person *plural* narration, using words like "we" and "our" rather than "I" and "my," thereby conveying a stronger sense of entitlement to the information. This is essentially a persuasive strategy intended to minimize any resistance on the reader's part. Of course, the e-mail clearly establishes the newspaper's right to the information by mentioning the laws governing such matters, but the first-person plural always suggests greater authority. Indeed, in olden times, kings and queens would employ the royal "we" when addressing their subjects.

PERSUASIVE WRITING

The purpose of this kind of writing is to convince the reader of something, or to urge the reader to adopt a particular stance toward something about which the reader and the writer already agree. At its most effective, persuasive writing is phrased objectively (like informational writing) rather than using first-person narration. To succeed, persuasive writing must adopt a reasonable tone, perhaps acknowledging opposing viewpoints before asserting its own. But its claims must be supported by solid evidence, not simply emotional appeals. And the writer must be careful not to stumble into other kinds of fallacy (faulty reasoning) as well. Persuasive writing is perhaps the most difficult kind to accomplish successfully, and is covered in depth in Chapter 7.

Here's a brief "letter to the editor," urging readers to vote for a particular mayoral candidate:

> Clearly, Judith Ayres deserves re-election as mayor of Derbyville. Her opponent, John Daly, is also a worthy candidate, but lacks experience and cannot match the mayor's track record. Now completing her first term in office, Ayres has reduced violent crime by 30%. In addition, she

has attracted three large new businesses to the town, thereby adding many thousands of dollars to the tax rolls and creating hundreds of new employment opportunities for local residents. Finally, her direct personal involvement has led to the recent opening of the Senior Citizens Center downtown, a project that the previous administration had been talking about for several years without taking any concrete steps to move it forward. In short, Judith Ayres obviously knows how to make things happen. She deserves your vote on election day next week!

Notice that the writer of this letter has created the appearance of objectivity by respectfully mentioning the opposing candidate before moving on to list the preferred candidate's credentials. And those accomplishments provide support for the letter's objective: to persuade readers to re-elect the mayor. Indeed, if this letter were expanded into a conventional college essay, the mayor's three main achievements—described in greater detail—would provide solid, highly persuasive content for the essay's body paragraphs. Notice also that the paragraph—like most persuasive essays—opens and closes with a firm statement of the writer's position.

ENTERTAINING WRITING

Usually the purpose of this kind of writing is to amuse. This is harder than it sounds, partly because today's media-saturated readers are accustomed to being entertained by professional comedians and commentators. To succeed, this kind of writing must make the reader laugh—or at least smile—by using the techniques perfected by the pros. Principal among these is *reversal of expectation*. All humor derives from unanticipated violation of norms, perhaps by comic exaggeration, or by presenting a familiar reality in a new and different light, or by simply poking irreverent fun at a widespread but questionable assumption. But too much humor relies heavily on crude (and often offensive) "cheap shots" that lack depth or sophistication. By contrast, the very best such writing is that which makes us *think* after we've stopped laughing.

This joke is a good example of entertaining writing:

jstudio/Shutterstock.com

A police officer is driving her patrol car when she notices a snail lying on the side of the road with its shell cracked and its hat knocked off. She quickly stops the car, jumps out, and runs to the snail's side to offer assistance. "Mr. Snail, what happened?" the officer asks. "Oh, it was terrible," the snail replies. "I was mugged by three turtles!" Taking out her pencil and notebook, the officer asks, "Three turtles. What did they look like?" And the snail moans, "I don't know. It all happened so fast."

In general it's a bit pointless to explain a joke. Either it's funny or not. But in this case we easily identify several basic features of writing that attempts to amuse. Most obviously, snails don't wear hats or get mugged, and they don't talk. Not so immediately apparent about this joke, however, is its underlying truth: the fact that all perception is subjective. To a snail (who literally moves "at a snail's pace") turtles *would* seem fast, even if they appear slow to the rest of us. So the joke is a subtle reminder about the relative nature of reality, and therein lies its deeper appeal.

But a piece of writing does not necessarily have to amuse in order to provide diversion. Sometimes entertainment is more sober in intention, seeking to deal with weightier issues. Indeed, much serious literature—poetry, fiction, drama—illustrates this. In the broadest sense, literature is certainly a form of entertainment. But it does not always make us smile or laugh. At its best, it makes us *think*. Therefore, it can sometimes sadden—maybe even make us weep. This autobiographical poem, by Belgrade-born former United States Poet Laureate Charles Simic, is a good example.

Old Soldier

By the time I was five,
I had fought in hundreds of battles,
Had killed thousands
And suffered many wounds
Only to rise and fight again.

After the bombing raids, the sky was full
Of flying cinders and birds.
My mother took me by the hand
And led me into the garden
Where the cherry trees were in flower.

There was a cat grooming herself
Whose tail I wanted to pull,
But I let her be for a moment,
Since I was busy swinging at flies
With a sword made of cardboard.

All I needed was a horse to ride,
Like the one hitched to a hearse,
Outside a pile of rubble,
Waiting with its head lowered
For them to finish loading the coffins.

Although playful on the surface, Simic's poem addresses very serious concerns, specifically the horrors of war and their negative, desensitizing effects on children. At the same time, it affirms the presence of certain reassuring constants in life: the survival instinct, the attentiveness of mothers, and the enduring resilience of the natural world.

As we have seen, the different kinds of writing—self-expressive, informative, interrogative, persuasive, and entertaining—are not always mutually exclusive, so a given piece of writing can serve two or more overlapping purposes simultaneously. But whether one or more than one purpose is being pursued, each kind possesses certain identifiable characteristics. Therefore, student writers wishing to improve their skills should familiarize themselves with those features, in order to produce writing that achieves its objectives in every kind of situation.

EXERCISES

1. Identify the purpose(s) of each of the following pieces of writing: a) to self-express; b) to provide information; c) to seek information; d) to persuade; or e) to entertain.

   ▶ business letter requesting payment of an overdue bill _____

   ▶ blog post joking about the writer's high school reunion _____

   ▶ e-mail asking about the status of a purchase order _____

   ▶ student's journal entry about meeting her boyfriend's parents _____

   ▶ newspaper story about a City Council meeting _____

2. Write two or three well-developed **self-expressive** paragraphs in which you discuss one decision or action of which you're especially proud. The subject matter can be something that happened fairly recently or longer ago.

3. Write two or three well-developed **informative** paragraphs in which you explain how to perform a particular procedure with which you are familiar. The procedure might be something job-related, or something you were taught by a friend or family member, or even something you figured out on your own. Be sure to present the steps in the procedure in the order in which they must be performed.

4. Write two or three well-developed **interrogative** paragraphs in which you ask your academic advisor for information about a course you're required to take next semester. Request specific details. You might inquire about the teacher, the textbook, the scheduled days and times, the subject matter and workload, or anything else that might help you know what to expect.

5. Write two or three well-developed **persuasive** paragraphs in which you defend a particular belief of yours. As always when writing persuasively, you must present good arguments for your assertions, rather than simply venting.

6. Write a well-developed **entertaining** paragraph in which you attempt to amuse the reader. You might approach this through the self-expressive avenue, perhaps by relating an embarrassing or otherwise comical experience, or you may choose to tell a joke. In any case, however, avoid X-rated or otherwise objectionable subject matter.

CHAPTER 2

Audience

LEARNING OBJECTIVES

When you complete this chapter, you will be able to

- ▶ Identify your intended audience
- ▶ Analyze that audience to understand needs and expectations
- ▶ Accommodate the demands of the communication hierarchy: upward, lateral, and downward interaction

Rawpixel.com/Shutterstock.com

AUDIENCE IDENTIFICATION

After you have determined your purpose in writing, you must then ask yourself, "Who will read what I have written?" Just as a writer has one or more purposes for writing, every reader has one or more reasons for reading. This is important for a writer to bear in mind, because different audiences have different needs and expectations. For illustration, consider these two examples. The first is a text message from a college student to his friend, and the second is the body of an e-mail from that student to his professor.

Example #1

Dude—u wouldn't belive how sick i was after got home from that keg party thursday nite. puked my guts out, no way i could get 2 english class at 8 in the AM. no big deal we never do nothing anyways just a lot of crap about writting

Example #2

Dear Professor,

Please excuse my absence from your 8:00 a.m. English class on Friday. I was not feeling well and was therefore unable to attend. With your permission, I will of course make up any missed work.

Respectfully,

Eric Cartman

Obviously, these are two very different messages indeed! The first is highly informal and quite poorly written. Like so many hastily composed text messages, it's been thrown together in a careless manner, is flawed by typos and mechanical errors, and is guilty of the TMI ("too much information") blunder. Moreover, it's crudely worded and disturbingly unconcerned about the serious problems of alcohol abuse, irregular attendance, and academic indifference. Clearly, Eric does not expect these shortcomings to bother his friend. In fact, he may even be deliberately exaggerating in a misguided attempt to impress his friend with how cool he is. The e-mail, on the other hand, has been composed with much greater care and attention, reflecting Eric's desire to create an entirely different impression. Here he has taken pains to consider his audience and adjust his tone, correctly assuming that his professor will be a far more judgmental reader. It should be noted, however, that in general we do ourselves a disservice when we write sloppily, regardless of who's on the receiving end. Such writing creates a negative impression. We all make mistakes occasionally, but it's worth the added effort to eliminate avoidable errors caused by simple carelessness.

AUDIENCE ANALYSIS

Matters of correctness aside, it's important to consider the audience when determining what should be included—or left out—in a piece of writing. These questions will help you decide:

▶ Is my audience one person or more than one?
▶ What does my audience already know about this topic?
▶ How much do they care about it?
▶ Why do they need this information?
▶ What do I want them to understand, believe, feel, or do after reading?
▶ What factors might influence their response? For example, how about their age, gender, sexual orientation, racial/ethnic background, education level, interests, and beliefs?

Because these questions are closely related, the answers will necessarily overlap. But by examining your readers this way, you come to see the subject of your writing from their viewpoint as well as your own. As a result, you're better able to provide necessary details while eliminating unnecessary ones, cite meaningful examples, and achieve the correct level of formality. This enables you to avoid giving offense, prevent misunderstandings, and achieve the desired outcome.

But audience analysis can be tricky. While it's true that age, gender, and other such considerations do play a part in determining a reader's responses, every reader is still a unique individual. It would be mistaken to imagine that persons who share a given set of demographic characteristics all think alike. Nevertheless, certain broad assumptions can be made. For example, if you were writing a highly detailed description of some aspect of computer programming, the readers' education and interests would be important considerations, while their age and gender would be irrelevant. Your readers would have no difficulty with technical terminology and concepts if those readers were trained specialists in that field. But if they were not, then the description would have to include more background and be phrased far more simply, using everyday vocabulary.

COMMUNICATION HIERARCHY

Another feature of audience analysis is the need to consider the nature of your relationship to the reader. Although most of us would prefer a more democratic arrangement, not all human interaction occurs between equals. While much writing *is* intended for readers at your own level of responsibility or authority within the hierarchy, sometimes your reader is at a higher or lower level. Clearly, these differences strongly influence the tone of any piece of writing, as discussed in greater depth in Chapter 3. But for now, it's enough to acknowledge that all communication, written and otherwise, falls into several broad categories:

► **Upward communication:** Intended for those above the writer in the hierarchy, upward communication should adopt a very courteous approach that reflects the reader's authority over the writer. (Example: the student-to-professor e-mail shown earlier.)

► **Lateral communication:** Intended for those at the writer's own level in the hierarchy, lateral communication can adopt a much more casual, conversational approach that reflects the relative equality of reader and writer. (Example: the student-to-student text shown earlier.)

► **Downward communication:** Intended for those below the writer in the hierarchy, downward communication commonly adopts a firmer, more instructive approach that reflects the writer's authority over the reader. (Example: a performance evaluation written by a supervisor to an employee.)

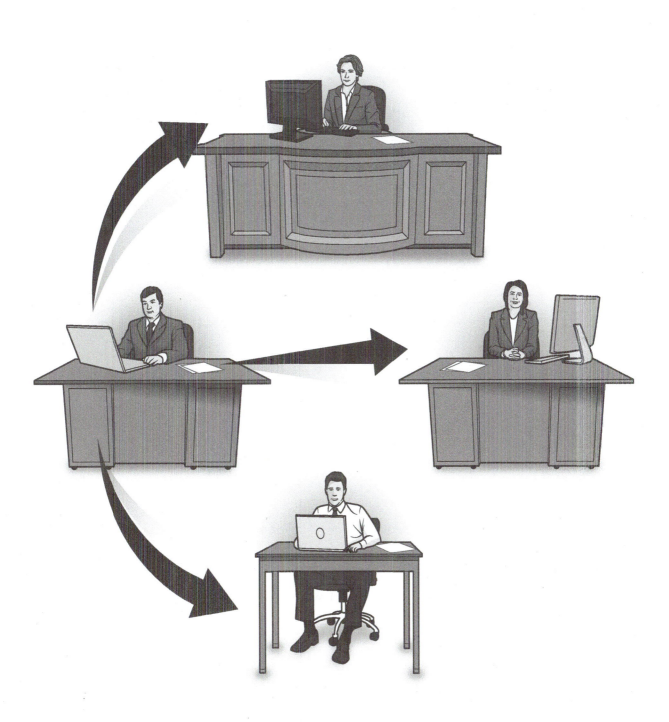

EXERCISES

1. Every newspaper, magazine, or other publication is aimed at a specific audience. Briefly identify the intended readers of the following periodicals. (If you're not familiar with these, you'll have to do some browsing in a library, at a magazine rack, or on the web.)

   Family Circle

   Maxim

   The New England Journal of Medicine

   The New York Review of Books

   The New Yorker

   The Onion

   PMLA

   Runners World

   USA Today

   Weekly World News

2. The following is an online restaurant review. Identify the writer's intended audience.

   Imagine my surprise when I was told at the door of this Barcelona restaurant that my footwear was unacceptable! I had arrived wearing a pair of black leather Teva sandals popular among tourists. The receptionist looked at my feet and declared that I could not enter. My husband and I stood there while a manager was called. He reluctantly agreed that we could be seated. As unwelcome as we had been made to feel, and as puzzled as we were when we noticed that many of the younger guests were also wearing sandals and in some cases running shoes, it would have been difficult to enjoy even an excellent meal. But this one was far from that. The food was expensive but totally unremarkable, and the service was rushed and unprofessional from beginning to end. We thought that every other restaurant we visited during our month in Spain was much, much better.

3. Your audience is the president of your college. Write three paragraphs in which you attempt to convince the president to adopt, modify, or abandon a specific policy that impacts the daily lives of students.

4. Your audience is an eleventh- or twelfth-grade student at the high school from which you graduated. Write three paragraphs in which you explain the principal differences between high school and college.

5. Your audience is a classmate in English 102. Write three paragraphs in which you recommend a particular restaurant or nightclub.

CHAPTER 3

Tone

LEARNING OBJECTIVES

When you complete this chapter, you will be able to

- ► Employ a tone appropriate to your audience
- ► Convey an upbeat, reader-centered perspective
- ► Understand the difference between denotation and connotation
- ► Avoid gender-biased and other offensive language

DenisProduction.com/Shutterstock.com

TONE AND AUDIENCE

In academic writing, your audience is of course your professor (and perhaps your classmates, if group discussion of student work is part of the course format). But at the first-year level most professors of English usually expect students to compose as if they were writing for someone they do not know—any reasonably intelligent and fairly well-informed stranger, though not necessarily a specialist in the topic area. Therefore, it's wise to pitch your writing that way unless your professor indicates otherwise. Maintain a fairly formal tone, avoiding overly conversational effects.

Elsewhere, however (on the job, let's say, or in your personal life), your actual relationship to your reader will determine your tone. But the tone of your writing—much like your tone of voice when you're speaking—is influenced by your purpose and also reflects your attitude toward the subject matter. This is especially true when writing about controversial issues, conveying bad news (the denial of a request from someone beneath you in the hierarchy, for example), or suggesting that someone should adopt some new or different procedure. Although writing in such situations can—indeed, *should*—be phrased in a firm, straightforward manner, a harsh, sarcastic, or belligerent approach is nearly always counterproductive. If your reader becomes defensive or resentful, communication breaks down. Therefore, don't try to sound tough or demanding when writing about sensitive issues. Instead, appeal to readers' best instincts, their sense of fairness and cooperation. Phrase sentences in a non-threatening way, acknowledging readers' potentially differing points of view while presenting enough concrete, factual detail to fully support your own position.

From *College English: The Basics, 2nd Edition* by George J. Searles. © 2017 by George J. Searles. Reprinted by permission of Kendall Hunt Publishing Company.

READER-CENTERED PERSPECTIVE

Also helpful is a reader-centered (rather than writer-centered) perspective. Here are examples of how to change a writer-centered perspective into a reader-centered one.

Writer-Centered	Reader-Centered
I am investigating the claim.	Your claim is being investigated.
We mailed the refund today.	Your refund was mailed today.
I assure you that…	You can be assured that…

Notice that using *you* and *your* rather than *I* and *we* personalizes the communication. Focusing on the reader this way is known as the "you" approach. Another important feature of reader-centeredness is the use of *please*, *thank you*, and other polite terms. Similarly, it's always best to strive for the most upbeat possible wording, especially when presenting unwelcome information. Here are examples of how to rephrase negative content in more positive, reader-centered terms.

Negative Wording	Positive Wording
We cannot complete your registration because the required deposit has not been received.	Your registration will be completed as soon as you submit the required deposit.
The restaurant is closed on Mondays.	The restaurant is open every day except Monday.
No children under the age of 12 are allowed in the hotel dining room.	Children age 12 and over are welcome in the hotel dining room.

What follows are two examples that illustrate these principles. Both e-mails have the same purpose—to change a specific behavior—and both address the same audience. But their tone differs greatly. The first adopts a writer-centered approach and is harshly combative. The reader-centered revision, on the other hand, is persuasively diplomatic and therefore much better. The first is almost certain to create resentment, whereas the second is far more likely to be well received.

Example #1

Date:	November 10, 2017
To:	All Students
From:	Dick Ketcham, Chief Campus Security
Subject:	Stolen Property

During the past couple of months my office has received a number of complaints about stolen purses, laptops, textbooks, and other items.

But it's become obvious that these events were the result of stupidity on the part of the so-called "victims." Trust me: If you leave stuff lying around in plain view and walk away for even a few minutes, it's going to grow legs. There are thieves all over the place on this campus.

And don't even get me started on burglaries of unlocked vehicles and dorm rooms. Come on, people—use your heads!

Example #2

Date: November 10, 2017

To: All Students

From: Dick Ketcham, Chief
           Campus Security

Subject: Protecting Your Property

Lately there have been increased reports of stolen purses, laptops, and other property.

For your own protection, never leave valuable personal belongings—including textbooks—unattended. In addition, always lock your vehicle and your dorm room. And if you see suspicious activity in the parking lots, dorms, or anywhere else on campus, please alert this office immediately.

With your help, my officers can continue to fulfill their mission: to serve and protect.

In most settings, you can adopt a somewhat more casual manner with your peers and with those below you than with those above you in the pecking order. Nevertheless, avoid an excessively conversational tone. Even if the situation isn't particularly troublesome or even when your reader is well-known to you, remember that writing is always somewhat more formal than speech, in part because it's more deliberate and far less impermanent. Although you need not sound stuffy, it's important to maintain a certain level of propriety. An especially polite tone is advisable when addressing those who outrank you, particularly when conveying unwelcome information or requesting assistance or cooperation from superiors. This can be achieved either through "softening" words and phrases (*perhaps, with your permission, if you wish*) or simply by stating outright that you fully understand that the decision is theirs. For example, consider these two e-mail messages.

Example #1

Date: November 11, 2017

To: Professor Sara Nac

From: Bud Weiser

Subject: Missed Class

Hey, Sara! You probably noticed that I blew off your class yesterday and wasn't there to hand in my essay assignment or take the quiz. No problem, I'll bring the paper to your office hours and take a make-up then. But don't bust my chops with penalties or any bull like that. Remember: My tuition pays your salary!

Example #2

Date: November 11, 2017

To: Professor Sara Nac

From: Bud Weiser

Subject: Missed Class

Hello, Professor. Please accept my apologies for missing class yesterday. I know there was an essay assignment due and also a quiz I missed. With your permission, I'll bring the paper to your office hours tomorrow. Would it be possible for me to make up the quiz then too? I realize there may be late penalties, but I'm hoping you might reconsider when I explain the reasons for my absence.

Although both deal with the same situation, the first is completely inappropriate in tone, so much so that it would likely result in negative consequences for the writer. With its far too-familiar salutation, its use of slang (*blew off…bust my chops…bull*), and its implication that the student, rather than the professor, can make the rules, it completely violates the norms of upward communication. By contrast, the second message is obviously much better because it's politely respectful, employs the "you" perspective, and properly reflects the nature of the relationship. In short, its courteous tone is far more likely to achieve the desired outcome.

DENOTATION AND CONNOTATION

In a related vein, all writers should understand the difference between denotation and connotation. The term *denotation* refers to the literal, dictionary definition of a word. *Connotation*, however, refers to the nuances and shades of meaning—the implications and associations—conveyed by a word. For example, *skinny* and *slim* mean essentially the same thing, but each of these terms has a different connotation, one negative and the other positive. To describe someone as skinny would be an insult, whereas describing someone as slim would be a compliment. It's important, therefore, to pay close attention to this aspect of wording. Connotation greatly affects the tone of a piece of writing and therefore influences the reader's responses. Consider, for example, the contrasting associations triggered by the following pairs of terms.

Positive or Neutral Connotation	Negative Connotation
athlete	jock
to object	to gripe
firm	stubborn
idealist	dreamer
inexpensive	cheap
reserved	aloof
thrifty	miserly
walk	swagger

BIASED LANGUAGE

Yet another important aspect of tone is the way in which writers handle gender issues. Since the 1960s we've come to understand that English (like most languages) tends to be male-oriented, as is the traditional view of society itself. However, men's and women's social roles have changed significantly. There are more women

than men attending college today. Title IX legislation has promoted women's participation in sports. Women are working in many jobs from which they would've been excluded in the past. And in general we're evolving toward a more sophisticated, less restrictive sense of the relationship between the sexes—and of the issue of gender identity and sexual orientation as well.

Certainly we should try to use language in a way that mirrors these realities. After all, language not only reflects social values but also reinforces them. Clinging to old-fashioned constructions only perpetuates outdated attitudes.

Here are four examples of gender-biased writing:

▶ Every student must sign his name on the log-in sheet before beginning his tutoring.
▶ Mr. Lopez, Miss Carter, and Mrs. Madden will teach this course in the fall.
▶ The college Kiddie Kampus requests that each child's mother help out at lunch at least once a month.
▶ It will require six workmen to complete this painting job on time.

Although all of these sentences are grammatically correct, each is sexist. The first, by twice using the word *his*, implies that all students are male—certainly not the case in today's world! But the bias can be removed simply by cutting or changing a few words.

Every student must sign the log-in sheet before beginning tutoring.

In the second example, we can assume that Madden is married and Carter is single. But Lopez's marital status remains undetermined, as it should; such matters have no relevance to a person's professional role. Equal consideration should be granted to all three professors by referring to both women as Ms. or by dropping such titles altogether. In addition, names should always appear in alphabetical order unless there's a valid reason for some other sequence; in this case, there's no apparent reason why the male name should automatically stand first. Here are two possible revisions:

Ms. Carter, Mr. Lopez, and Ms. Madden will teach this course in the fall.
Professors Carter, Lopez, and Madden will teach this course in the fall.

The third sentence implies that childcare is solely the responsibility of mothers. A far better phrasing would be to replace *mother* with *parent(s)*:

The college Kiddie Kampus requests that each child's parent(s) help out at lunch at least once a month.

And, by using the word *workmen*, the last sentence implies that only males (work<u>men</u>) could do the job. Avoid gender-biased terms like *workman, fireman, mailman, policeman,* and the like. Instead, use gender-neutral ones like *worker, firefighter, mail carrier,* and *police officer*. Here's an example of that kind of revision:

It will require six painters to complete this job on time.

In the interest of simple fairness, we must all develop the habit of nonsexist expression. And, of course, it should go without saying that any kind of crude or vulgar language is entirely inappropriate in academic writing, as are the acronyms and similar shortcuts typical of text messages and tweets. This is not to suggest that academic writing should sound stiff or artificial, but that it should display intelligence, maturity, and sophistication. Accordingly, disrespectful terms that victimize individuals on the basis of race, religion, ethnicity, age, gender identity, sexual orientation, and physical and/or mental challenges are totally offensive and have absolutely no place in twenty-first century discourse. For in-depth advice on avoiding *unintentionally* disparaging language, consult Sections 3.12 to 3.17 of the *Publication Manual of the American Psychological Association*, available in any college library and on the web (www.apaa.org).

EXERCISES

1. Here are two e-mails. Each deals with the same issue. Which one is more likely to get the desired results? Why? Be specific.

Date: January 12, 2018

To: All Employees

From: James Almas
     Physical Plant Supervisor

Subject: Filthy Break Room

The Employee Break Room on the third floor of the Main Building is disgusting! The whole place is filthy. Nobody ever cleans up after cooking, so the microwave is caked with burned-on food, the refrigerator is always filled with rotting food, the sink is always stained and slimy, there's always garbage all over the floor, and the tables are always covered with crumbs and debris.

If things don't improve you'd better bet I'll tell management to close the Break Room indefinitely until people are ready to take responsibility for keeping it clean. My staff shouldn't have to kill themselves with unnecessary work!

Date: January 12, 2018

To: All Employees

From: James Almas
     Physical Plant Supervisor

Subject: Our Break Room

We all appreciate the amenities available in the Employee Break Room on the third floor of the Main Building. It's convenient to be able to store lunches in the refrigerator, use the microwave, and so forth. But I think you'll agree that the room is not always clean.

Of course, it's the responsibility of my staff to provide basic maintenance, but you can help us greatly just by following a few simple procedures:

▶ Leave food in the refrigerator for no more than a few days
▶ Clean up any spills inside the microwave
▶ Rinse out the sink after using it
▶ Put all garbage into the waste receptacle
▶ Use dampened paper towels to wipe off the tables

Thanks for your cooperation, which will ensure a more pleasant atmosphere for us all!

2. In general, a positive tone is preferable to a negative one. Using the following example as a model, revise each of these sentences to create a more upbeat tone.

    <u>We close</u> at 5:30.   REVISION: <u>We stay open</u> until 5:30.
    negative   positive

    ▶   Your diploma cannot be mailed until you pay the graduation fees.

    _____

    ▶   This office is not open on Fridays.

    _____

    ▶   We have run out of the eggplant special. All we have off the menu is the fish fry.

    _____

    ▶   If the fire alarm bells ring, do not panic.

    _____

    ▶   No new purchases can be authorized until the budget is approved.

    _____

    ▶   Please don't forget to turn off your computer when you leave work.

    _____

    ▶   We have received your paperwork but are unable to respond until July 1.

    _____

    ▶   If you have any questions, don't hesitate to e-mail me.

    _____

3. Revise the following sentences to eliminate gender-biased language. (One is already correct.)

    ▶   Any man who wants to be well-informed about current events should read *The New York Times* every day.

    _____

    ▶   A student enrolled in college should understand the importance of completing all his assignments on time.

    _____

    ▶   An employee's job satisfaction is usually related to his interest in the work.

    _____

    ▶   Every American president has tried to surround himself with highly competent advisors.

    _____

► When a mailman approaches a residence, he should watch out for loose dogs.

_____

► I now pronounce you man and wife.

_____

► A motorcyclist must never ride with his kickstand extended.

_____

► In general, man-made materials are less expensive than natural ones.

_____

► Men who pursue law or medicine usually earn a substantial income.

_____

► A policeman should use his pistol only if he has no alternative.

_____

PART 2

The Writing Process: Pre-Writing, Drafting, Rewriting

More than thirty years ago, James C. Raymond, then a professor at the University of Alabama, published a book called *Writing Is an Unnatural Act*. Professor Raymond wasn't just joking around, trying to boost sales on the strength of a catchy title. He was onto something very fundamental: Writing is difficult and must be learned, mainly because it is indeed unnatural. If it were not, we'd each be born with ink in our index finger.

Granted, speech too is a learned activity. But the impulse to speak is instinctive. Writing, on the other hand, is quite different. It might almost be described as an artificial *substitute* for speech. As such, it's not instinctive. Rather, it's a highly conscious activity involving deliberate choices determined by principles and rules that must be gradually absorbed and then carefully applied. And, like anything requiring a learned skill (playing a sport or a musical instrument, for example) it must be practiced. Nobody can produce good writing without understanding this and putting in the necessary effort.

Because of reluctance to confront this very basic aspect of composition, many students attempt to write as if they were simply speaking aloud. As a result, their essays are unfocused, disorganized, and poorly developed. Not surprisingly, their grades are disappointing. Other students, though, get better results, earning a good grade on every assignment. Their secret? Somewhere along the way they've learned to accept the fact that writing is not natural and automatic. They know that it's instead a process, a three-step operation involving not only drafting (which is actually just the middle step) but also pre-writing and rewriting. To ignore this is like trying to make a sandwich without the bread. This section of the book explores each of the three steps and provides detailed recommendations.

From *College English: The Basics, 2nd Edition* by George J. Searles. © 2017 by George J. Searles. Reprinted by permission of Kendall Hunt Publishing Company.

CHAPTER 4

Pre-Writing

LEARNING OBJECTIVES

When you complete this chapter, you will be able to

▶ Use pre-writing strategies such as brainstorming, freewriting, topic mapping, and exploring outside sources
▶ Create an effective thesis statement
▶ Focus, organize, and outline your subject matter

WAYHOME studio/Shutterstock.com

PRE-WRITING STRATEGIES

Like a competitive runner performing a stretching routine before racing, a writer should warm up before attempting to compose. Just as the athlete employs a variety of exercises, the writer should also complete some preliminary activities. Foremost among these is simply thinking about the subject. Whether your professor has assigned a particular topic or allowed you to choose your own, you'll need to develop your ideas and begin to organize your approach. Time permitting, it's very helpful to consider the general subject for a day or two before actually picking up your pen or sitting down at the computer. Try to give the topic some thought while engaged in unrelated activities requiring little or no attention (taking a shower, folding the laundry, waiting for a bus). Then, when you do eventually attempt to write, you'll have something to bring to the table. This is much better than the discouraging predicament of facing the blank page or screen with an equally empty head. But there won't be much time for this preliminary thinking if you ignore the assignment until the night before it's due. Always get started as soon as possible.

Unfortunately, thinking is not always enough. Ideas may not occur to you as quickly as you'd like or you may have trouble coming up with any ideas at all. But *brainstorming, freewriting, idea mapping,* and *exploring outside sources* can be effective strategies to get your mental wheels turning and start the writing process.

Brainstorming

This involves putting pen to paper—or fingers to keyboard—without a plan and with as little conscious thought as possible. In the workplace, this is often done collaboratively by teams of employees as a way to solve problems or develop new approaches to familiar tasks. In academic settings it can be similarly used by students working on group projects. But in either environment it's equally helpful to the individual writer, as a way of breaking through whatever obstacles may be interfering with getting started.

From *College English: The Basics, 2nd Edition* by George J. Searles. © 2017 by George J. Searles.
Reprinted by permission of Kendall Hunt Publishing Company.

If you have no topic yet, you can begin with a random list of things you *might* want to write about. Don't analyze or judge ("this would be good…that's a dumb idea") at this point. Just quickly list, without evaluating, whatever comes to mind. You may discover one or two possible topics to explore further in another brainstorm or another pre-writing activity. If you do have a topic, or if you've just come up with a possibility, write it at the top of a blank sheet of paper or type it at the top of your screen. Then, in list format, write down whatever related words or phrases come to mind. Again, don't question or eliminate. Just jot everything down. In a few minutes, after you've run out of steam, look back over what you've got. Most likely you'll start to see things you can work with.

The brainstorm below is the result of a student's decision to explore her first job as a possible essay topic.

My first job

huge brick factory building	lots of laughs
noisy assembly line	line goes too fast
roaches in lockers	good pay in cash envelope
shoes not sandals	basketball courts next door
no air conditioning	luncheonette
summer heat	assembling parts
power tools	blind co-worker
loud machines	cafeteria for coffee, toast
dirty	two blocks to subway
can't figure out job	union walkout
cool co-workers, helpful	cross picket line?

You'll notice that some thoughts seem related and others do not. The list is basically a catalog of random details that came to mind when she began thinking about the experience. But it proved helpful because as she considered the list she discovered her focus. She realized that what she really wanted to write about was how that first job experience helped shape her attitudes toward labor unions. This might then lead to another pre-writing activity: *freewriting*.

Freewriting

Another way to generate material, this is not unlike brainstorming, in that you allow whatever comes to mind to appear on your paper or screen. But in freewriting you take a more headlong approach, writing sentences and phrases non-stop for a set period of time.

To freewrite, give yourself five minutes, set a timer, and write continuously until the five minutes are up. Don't erase, don't cross out, don't pause or stop to think. Don't worry about typos, grammar, spelling, or punctuation. (Remember: This writing is *free*.) Just keep moving. If your mind goes blank, write "I can't think of anything" or "I don't know what to write." You may surprise yourself when you see ideas emerge that you hadn't realized were there.

Freewriting can be done alone, as the only pre-writing for a given essay. Alternatively, it can be done in conjunction with other activities, to expand or find yet another path to the essay you want to write. The freewriting that follows was an outgrowth of the brainstorm above. Doing this other, different kind of pre-writing allowed the student to again explore the "first job" topic, but this time with an eye toward how it influenced her thoughts about unions.

That was really something, that walkout. I had no idea it was coming. Up from the subway one morning and there they were. All my co-workers in the street. Handmade signs, talking together, smoking, walking up and down. Like a picket line. Should I go in? Not a union member, just a summer employee. But these were the people who helped me out every day.

I was clueless about how to do the work. They helped me on the assembly line, did their work faster and then helped me with mine. Cheered me up. Warned me about the roaches. This day, they said, "Go on in! It's okay, you need the money for college." But I couldn't. Even though I knew my family wouldn't be happy about it—wouldn't look good, give up that day's pay. But something made me stay out. Stayed on the sidewalk. Hoped it would help. Solidarity? Maybe topic.

Although a jumble of thoughts and ideas, this second pre-writing still brought the student closer to the focus, organization, and development that would eventually emerge from the writing process.

Topic Mapping

This pre-writing strategy presents ideas within circles or ovals linked by lines or arrows, placing related thoughts near each other, showing the relationships among ideas. It's especially useful for visual learners, but can help any writer begin to organize thoughts.

One way to make a topic map is to write a topic in a circle or oval in the center of the page and begin to surround it with several others enclosing ideas you may want to discuss. Each of these can in turn be surrounded by yet another cluster identifying sub-points within the original ideas. Lines or arrows can reinforce the relationships among main ideas and supporting ideas. This approach not only helps you to generate ideas, but also begins to organize them, the next step in creating a rough draft.

Some writers prefer to enclose their ideas within squares, rectangles, or triangles rather than circles or ovals, but the example that follows is a more typical, oval-based topic map.

In this example, the student began with "my iPhone" as a possible topic for writing. Then he used ovals and connecting lines to lay out whatever ideas came to him. He didn't try to analyze them too deeply as he went, and he didn't worry about whether everything would be useful in the end. He simply put things down on the paper.

Through this mapping he discovered many related ideas that could lead to a variety of possible essays. Could he use all of these ideas in one 500–750 word paper? Obviously not. But from them he might begin to develop a descriptive essay about the iPhone's appearance, a process analysis about how to use iPhone features to stay in touch with friends, a research paper about the labor practices of Apple suppliers in China, or an exemplification essay about the reasons why company founder Steve Jobs was so important to the success of Apple products. The possibilities are many, and laying thoughts out in a non-linear way like this can make it easier for a writer to see them.

Exploring Outside Sources

This approach can also get your thoughts flowing, but it should not be confused with the type of formal research and documentation required when writing an in-depth, research-based term paper. Rather, it's an informal, "getting acquainted" process that can be useful when you have to write an assigned essay on an unfamiliar subject.

For example, let's say your professor has assigned the topic, "Dress Codes in the Workplace." It's not intended to be a research paper, but simply one in which you express your own point of view. But you may not have given this subject much thought before. You may not have firm opinions about it, even if you've worked jobs requiring the observance of such rules. In a case like this, it makes sense to consult outside sources. These may include people knowledgeable about the topic, newspaper or magazine articles, TV, radio, and other media, or—and this is of course the quickest and easiest source available—the Web. A Google search for this subject yields nearly three million hits. Not all are reliable, and no one could consult them all even if they were. But just by reading the headings of the links you can start to develop a better sense of the subject's range and complexity. For example, you might find information about restrictions on body modifications such as piercings and tattoos, and employers' responses to various circumstances requiring rule modifications or exceptions. Such angles may not have occurred to you before, but are now available for your use.

CREATING AN EFFECTIVE THESIS STATEMENT

Whatever pre-writing strategies you use, you'll eventually discover what you want to say by considering all the ideas that have surfaced. At that point you must formulate your *thesis statement*, one sentence that clearly identifies not only your topic but what you'll say about it. This is the "controlling idea" of the essay. Highly skilled writers sometimes employ an *implied* thesis, presenting it indirectly, especially when the topic is some sort of no-brainer. The writer of a paper about the absurdity of Holocaust denial, for example, can safely assume that readers will get the point without having it spelled out in the introduction. Indeed, in a

WAYHOME studio/Shutterstock.com

case like that, the very title of the piece has probably established the thesis already. Far more typically, however, there is a firmly phrased thesis statement, especially in a paper written to satisfy a college assignment.

Although it can appear elsewhere—sometimes even as the very first sentence—the thesis is usually positioned at the end of the introduction, after the reader has discovered your general topic. But it's the thesis itself that informs the reader about your focus and your point of view. Since your purpose is to communicate all of this to your readers, keeping their interest and earning their trust are essential. Different types of essays call for certain specific elements in a thesis, as you'll see in later chapters, but broad rules do apply.

Phrase your thesis as an assertion

It can be said that every piece of writing is an exercise in persuasion, in the sense that all writing tries to convince the reader to keep reading. Therefore, a good thesis statement is phrased as a reasonable assertion, a sentence that expresses a complete thought about the subject of your essay. It does not simply announce the topic ("This essay will attempt to prove that X is preferable to Y."). Instead, it makes a claim such as "X is preferable to Y because Z." Here are some examples of this approach:

- ▶ The electoral college should be abolished because it unnecessarily complicates the voting process.
- ▶ The drinking age should be lowered to eighteen nationwide because eighteen-year-olds are permitted to drive, marry, and serve in the military.
- ▶ Every college campus should be totally tobacco-free because this would result in health benefits for smokers and non-smokers alike.

Phrase your thesis in a reasonable, even-handed way

Although your thesis statement should be a firm expression of your intentions, *over*statement will alienate your readers rather than engage them. For example, consider these two thesis statements. Both are on the same topic and both are in fundamental agreement, but the second is much too aggressive

- ▶ Although some people are opposed to helmet laws for motorcyclists, all the evidence shows that helmets save riders' lives.

      NOT

- ▶ Anybody who's opposed to helmet laws for motorcyclists is a complete idiot.

Thanks to its more appropriate tone, the first of these thesis statements is far more likely to be taken seriously, even by readers who disagree.

Focus on only one thing

Since the thesis expresses a point of view, it must focus on only one aspect of the topic. For example, consider the topic of having a job while going to college. Are there both advantages and disadvantages to doing this? Surely so. But unless you're writing a comparison/contrast essay (see Chapter 8), you should focus on either one or the other, not both.

▶ Working while going to college is a bad idea for several reasons.

      OR

▶ Working while going to college helps students develop habits that will be useful to them for the rest of their lives.

      NOT

▶ There are advantages and disadvantages to working while going to college.

A narrower focus enables you to show your reader in greater depth and more specifically why it's good *or* why it's bad. You're not just providing information. As a writer, you have to decide what you want to communicate to your reader, what your focus is going to be, what your perspective is on this topic. Your thesis statement firms this up, and it's a key part of what makes your essay an essay.

Show how your essay will be developed

Essays can be developed in a variety of ways, as we shall see in later chapters. Part of the work of the thesis statement is to let your reader know from the beginning what type of development to expect. Will you tell a story? Define a term? Describe a place or person? Compare? Contrast? Explain a procedure? The thesis should make clear what approach your essay will take, whatever it is. "Renting a house at the Jersey Shore can be easy and affordable if you follow these steps" prepares the reader for an essay that explains a procedure, but "Renting a house at the Jersey Shore turned into a nightmare for my family" signals a very different kind of essay—one that tells a story.

Be prepared to revise your thesis as necessary

Your thesis is not necessarily permanent. It can be a work in progress. The essay may take you in unexpected directions as it unfolds. If that happens, don't resist. As the twentieth century British novelist E.M. Forster once asked, "How do I know what I think till I see what I say?" Let the discussion develop as it must. When you reach the rewriting stage, it's much easier to revise the thesis to match the essay than it would be to revise the essay to match the thesis.

FOCUSING, ORGANIZING, OUTLINING

Once you've completed your pre-writing and settled on a thesis, you must now begin the related tasks of focusing and organizing. Try to determine which ideas are closely related. Almost always, several will be. Combine them. This will make your job more manageable, by giving you fewer ideas to deal with. Next, rank-order your ideas: most important first, least important last. Then eliminate the last idea or two in the bottom of the rankings. Anything that unimportant to you is probably not worth mentioning. Besides, there won't be room for it. Now you'll have what you really need: several main ideas that will provide adequate content with which to support your thesis.

WAYHOME studio/Shutterstock.com

For the sake of illustration, let's say you're writing about the topic "What I'd Do If I Won a Million Dollars." Here's how your subject matter might evolve:

Stage 1	Stage 2	Stage 3	Stage 4
buy new car	car, house	debts, investments	debts, investments
buy new house	New York	New York	New York
visit New York City	debts, stocks	car, house	car, house
pay off school loans	family, church	family, church	family, church
pay off credit cards	Europe	Europe	
invest in stock market			
give $ to parents			
give $ to sister			
give $ to church			
travel to Europe			

Just as you used pre-writing strategies to determine which sub-points to cover in your essay about the larger topic, you must now go one step farther. Using those same strategies, assemble details about each sub-point so that the body paragraphs of your essay will be sufficiently developed. To illustrate once again, your "Million Dollars" subject might generate details like these:

Topics	Supporting Details
Debts	student loans (state college, community college): $10,000
	Master Card (unnecessary purchases): $5,000
	Visa (Spring Break): $3,000
Investments	stocks (G.E., Apple, Google): $50,000
New York City	shopping (clothes, jewelry, accessories), sightseeing (Empire State Bldg, Statue of Liberty, Ground Zero, Central Park, Metropolitan Museum, etc.): $35,000
Car	red Miata (six-speed, Pirellis): $35,000
House	mountain location, 10–12 acres, central air, game room, pool: $700,000
Family	parents (Florida vacation, retirement fund): $100,000
	sister (cash gift): $50,000
Church	social room renovations, parking lot blacktop: $10,000

You must now decide how to organize your essay. If your topic is chronological in nature (for example, "What I Did on New Year's Eve") this is fairly easy. You simply tell the story, after first deciding how to compress the events by determining which details to *leave out*—always a key decision when writing. But if your topic is not chronological (for example, "Three Reasons Why Extreme Fighting Should Be Outlawed"), you must identify the most effective sequence for your ideas. In general, the way to structure such an essay is to use *ascending order of importance*, following a "good/better/best" approach, saving your most convincing material for last. This pattern enables the paper to gain momentum as it moves along, building the interest level ever higher at each point along the way.

Non-chronological essays are typically structured in this ascending order because human psychology prefers that kind of progression. Almost everything in life operates accordingly. A fancy dinner starts with the appetizer, not the main dish. A rock concert opens with a lesser-known band before the headliners take the stage. And you can probably come up with many other examples on your own. A useful strategy for finding the best sequencing of ideas is to create an index card or sticky note for each. These can be physically arranged and rearranged until the ideal pattern emerges. Of course, many writers prefer to do this electronically, "cutting and pasting" on the computer to try out various possibilities.

Some students prefer (and many professors require) a working outline, an orderly system of headings and sub-headings that enable material to be organized in a highly visual way. Major headings are flush with the left margin and identified with Roman numerals, while sub-headings are identified with capital letters, Arabic numerals, and lowercase letters, in that order. Indenting is used to further reinforce the relationships among the headings. Here's how a working outline of the "Million Dollars" paper might look (see following page).

I – Introduction
II – Finances
    A. Debts
        1. Student loans
        2. Master Card
        3. Visa
    B. Stocks
        1. General Electric
        2. Google
        3. Apple
III – New York City Trip
    A. Shopping
        1. Clothes
        2. Jewelry
        3. Accessories
    B. Sightseeing
        1. Empire State Building
        2. Statue of Liberty
        3. Ground Zero
        4. Central Park
        5. Metropolitan Museum
IV – Car, House
    A. Car
        1. Mazda Miata
            a. Six-speed transmission
            b. Pirelli tires
    B. House
        1. Mountain location
        2. Two acres
        3. Central air-conditioning
        4. Fully-equipped game room
            a. pool table
            b. sound system
            c. electronic games

     5. Swimming pool

V – Parents, Sister, Church

  A. Parents

     1. Florida vacation

     2. Retirement fund

  B. Sister

     1. Shopping trip

     2. Cash gift

  C. Church

     1. Social room renovation

     2. Parking lot re-surfacing

VI – Conclusion

It's not always so easy to decide whether a given topic should be approached chronologically or not. Our "Million Dollars" essay is a case in point. It might depend on what the writer would actually do "in real life." But ascending order of importance would be helpful in making this somewhat routine topic as interesting as possible. Should the writer really follow the sequence shown in the above outline or would some other order be better? This may depend on what the thesis finally turns out to be. Indeed, the kind of deliberation that would be necessary for the writer to decide is an example of how writing is in many ways an exercise in decision-making. And it also illustrates the truth of E.M. Forster's comment that we don't really know what we think about something until we try to write about it. The very act of composition serves to clarify our thinking. It's not unusual for a writer to revise not only a thesis, but also a working outline to reflect changes as the essay evolves.

Of course, one writer's treatment of a given subject will differ greatly from another's. Every writer operates from a unique perspective. But regardless of the subject or your approach to it, the pre-writing activities discussed here will help. Time-consuming as they may seem, they will make the drafting stage of the process much easier and will actually *save* you time then.

EXERCISES

1. Here are five essay topics that a professor might assign:

   ▶ A Very Angry Moment
   ▶ Employment Opportunities in My Field of Study
   ▶ A Brief History of [choose your favorite sport or hobby]
   ▶ Capital Punishment: Right or Wrong?
   ▶ The Person Who Has Most Influenced My Life

   Which of these topics are chronological in nature? Create a working outline for one of them.

2. Choose any one of the topics in Exercise 1 and create a topic map for it.

3. Choose any one of the topics in Exercise 1 and create a thesis statement for it.

   _____

   _____

4. Here are five thesis statements. Not all are satisfactory. Identify the unsatisfactory ones and rewrite them.

   ▶ Last summer my family spent our vacation at Disney World.

   _____

   ▶ Many people's objections to President Obama's policies were motivated by racism, their discomfort at seeing an African-American in the White House.

   _____

   _____

   ▶ Working as a "front of the house" receptionist in a restaurant is similar in some ways to being a member of the wait staff, but in many other ways it's very different.

   _____

   _____

   ▶ The famous short story "The Necklace" is about a woman who loses some borrowed jewelry.

   _____

   _____

▶   Abortion is nothing more than legalized murder.

_____

_____

5.   Here is an introductory paragraph from a student essay. Although well-written, it's incomplete because it has no thesis statement. Provide one.

A recent study published in the journal *Pediatrics* has shown that excessive exposure to television is even more harmful to young children than previously acknowledged. According to this study, the average child eight months to eight years old spends eighty minutes per day actively watching t.v., and is exposed to nearly four additional hours of background television noise. The study claims that this causes decreased attention spans, lower cognitive skills, and reduced parent-child interaction.

_____

_____

_____

CHAPTER 5

Drafting

LEARNING OBJECTIVES

When you complete this chapter, you will be able to

▶ Create a concise but meaningful essay title
▶ Craft an effective introduction that gets the reader's attention, identifies the topic, and states the thesis
▶ Write unified, coherent, well-developed body paragraphs that successfully demonstrate the validity of the thesis
▶ Write an effective conclusion that gracefully closes the discussion

fizkes/Shutterstock.com

CREATING A MEANINGFUL TITLE

Imagine how difficult it would be to find your favorite breakfast cereal in the supermarket if there were no product names on the boxes—just shelf after shelf of identical packages, with no way to tell hot cereal from cold, sweetened from unsweetened, or even Wheaties from Cheerios. How about your local multiplex movie theater? What if there were no film titles above the various doors? How would you know which viewing room to enter after buying your ticket? For that matter, how could you decide which stories to read in your hometown newspaper—whether hard copy or electronic—if there were no headlines? Clearly, all these situations would be quite unsatisfactory, and all for the same reason. The cereal boxes, the rooms, and the stories all need "labels" to indicate what's inside. The same is true of an essay. It must have a title that signals what it's about, thereby orienting the reader by providing a sense of what to expect.

Unfortunately, however, not all titles are created equal. Many are unhelpful because they're vague or incomplete. A title such as "Capital Punishment," for example, provides no clue as to where the discussion may be heading. Is the writer for or against the death sentence, or somewhere in-between? Certainly, "Capital Punishment: Legalized Murder" (or, conversely, "Capital Punishment: An Eye for an Eye") would be much better. Note that both of these revisions achieve their purpose by using a colon to create a two-part title in which the second half expands upon the first. This is a very useful strategy.

Let's consider once again the "Million Dollars" essay discussed in Chapter 4. The student knew that the paper would explore possible uses of a large monetary windfall. But the first several titles that suggested themselves during the pre-writing stage of composition were unsatisfactory. The first was "A Cool Million."

From *College English: The Basics, 2nd Edition* by George J. Searles. © 2017 by George J. Searles. Reprinted by permission of Kendall Hunt Publishing Company.

Next was "A Dollar and a Dream." The student realized that although both of these working titles were catchy, neither really conveyed fully what the essay was about. The first could be misinterpreted in a number of ways, perhaps even as relating to American author Nathanael West's highly-regarded 1934 novel of that name. The second could suggest that the essay was about the New York State Lottery, which uses that phrase as a slogan. So the student decided to play it straight, settling on "A Million Dollars." But that revision also left something to be desired, again because it could be interpreted in a great many ways. Eventually she decided to simply compress the content of her introduction, settling on, "What I'd Do With A Million Dollars: Wise Choices." This final revision is far better than the earlier versions, because it's clear and straightforward, allowing no opportunity for misinterpretation.

The same principle applies when you're writing about literature. A title such as "Romeo and Juliet" serves no purpose except to reveal which work you're discussing. It gives no indication of what the essay might have to say about Shakespeare's great tragedy. Indeed, a vague title like that is almost always an indication that the writer doesn't really know where the essay is headed. It usually accompanies a paper that lacks a real thesis statement and is nothing more than plot summary, a re-telling of the story, with little or no analysis or interpretation. This guarantees a low grade. So that's another feature of the title: to orient not only the reader but the writer as well. If you're having trouble coming up with a good title, you probably don't really know what you're trying to accomplish in the paper and should return to the pre-writing stage.

CRAFTING AN EFFECTIVE INTRODUCTION

The first thing to understand about the introduction to an essay is that it's simply a beginning and nothing more. You should not start the actual discussion of your topic until the *second* paragraph. The introductory paragraph is like first gear. You use it to pull away from the curb, not to drive down the street. Its purpose is only to get the reader's attention, identify the topic, and state the thesis. Granted, your title should already have suggested some of the essay's concerns, but the introduction—usually with its thesis statement at or near the end—firmly establishes the essay's direction.

A typical paragraph is approximately five or six sentences long, not just one, and the introduction is no exception. As stated above, it should identify the topic and state the thesis, but it must first get the reader's attention. This is important, because the opening sentence or two create the influential "first impression" the reader receives. Typically, the introduction opens broadly and becomes increasingly specific, funneling down until the writer reaches the thesis statement. Most good introductions follow that "general to specific" pattern. How, then, might the writer come up with four or five sentences that will lead effectively into the thesis statement? Here are three proven strategies that can help you get that job done.

Describe a situation

There's something in human nature that loves a story, especially if it involves conflict. The enduring appeal of fairy tales, myths and legends, soap operas, and sentimental country-western song lyrics proves the point. Even jokes—which nearly always involve conflict—are a kind of story! You can capitalize on this aspect of your reader's psychology by opening with a brief anecdote that somehow relates to your subject. An essay exploring the dangers of tobacco, for example, might begin like this:

> My friend Carol was a smart, beautiful young woman with a bright future, but she had one
> bad habit. She'd been smoking a pack of cigarettes every day since ninth grade. When I

attended our class reunion ten years after graduation, I was looking forward to seeing her again, but she wasn't there. Then I learned the sad truth. Carol had died of lung cancer shortly after her twenty-fifth birthday! But this didn't have to happen. If she'd kicked the habit she'd probably still be alive today.

Present an interesting fact or statistic

This will help you get the reader's attention by demonstrating that you're familiar with your topic. The annual edition of the *World Almanac and Book of Facts* is a rich source of statistical information on diverse topics, but there are many others as well. Any qualified librarian can direct you to government documents, corporate reports, and other useful resources. Even though statistics can be deceptive, people like what they perceive as the hard reality of such data and therefore find numbers quite persuasive. Although many Internet sites are untrustworthy, the web is another good source of statistics if used selectively. One useful website is *Statistical Resources on the Web* at www.lib.umich.edu/govdocs/stats.html. Another is the U.S. Department of Labor's Bureau of Labor Statistics at www.bls.gov/home.html. But there's one important point to remember if you want to retain credibility when citing a statistic. You must somehow acknowledge the source, usually on a Works Cited page at the end. Alternatively, you can identify a source in the body of the paper. Here's how an essay intended to demonstrate the need for stricter gun control legislation might open using this strategy:

> According to the Congressional Record, there are more than 35,000 handgun-related murders in the United States every year. In Japan, on the other hand, there are fewer than twenty. Of course, there are many reasons for this striking contrast. For one thing, Japan is an ancient, essentially monolithic culture in which most people share the same fundamental assumptions and beliefs, a fact that tends to discourage overt interpersonal conflict. As a result, violent crime in general is far less common in Japan. But the biggest reason for the difference is that in Japan the private ownership of firearms is strictly regulated. Clearly, it's time for the United States to re-think our self-destructive love affair with guns.

Use a quotation

Get a "Big Name"—Shakespeare, Martin Luther King, Jr., the Bible—to speak for you. Find an appropriate saying that will launch your own remarks with flair. Many useful books of quotations exist, but *Bartlett's Familiar Quotations* is surely the best known, and for good reason. Bartlett's includes nearly one hundred quotes on the subject of money alone, for example. It's available in any library or good bookstore and on the web, along with *Simpson's Contemporary Quotations* and the *Columbia World of Quotations*. As with statistics, you should always identify the source. And try to choose sources that your intended reader will be familiar with and fairly trustful of. Opening an academic essay with lyrics from an obscure Megadeath song, for example, probably won't win you any extra credit. Here's the kind of introduction that might, if you were writing an essay about climate change:

> As former vice-president Al Gore tells us in his best-selling 2006 book *An Inconvenient Truth,* "Not only does human-caused global warming exist, but it is also growing more and more dangerous, and at a pace that has now made it a planetary emergency." Yet there remain a great many skeptics who reject Gore's claims and those of the world's scientists, nearly all of whom agree that global warming constitutes a real, immediate, and potentially far-reaching threat. For whatever reason, these nay-sayers refuse to accept the obvious. Clearly, it's imperative that the United States take a leading role in the developed world's efforts to prevent environmental catastrophe.

As mentioned in Chapter 4 and illustrated above, the thesis statement most commonly appears at or near the end of the introduction. There are, however, exceptions to this loose rule. Some writers prefer to actually open with the thesis, or embed it somewhere within the introduction. This can sometimes be very effective. Notice, for example, that moving the thesis statement in the above introduction about global warming in no way damages the paragraph's integrity.

Opening Thesis

Clearly, it's imperative that the United States take a leading role in the developed world's efforts to prevent environmental catastrophe. As former vice-president Al Gore tells us in his best-selling 2006 book *An Inconvenient Truth,* "Not only does human-caused global warming exist, but it is also growing more and more dangerous, and at a pace that has now made it a planetary emergency." Yet there remain a great many skeptics who reject Gore's claims and those of the world's scientists, nearly all of whom agree that global warming constitutes a real, immediate, and potentially far-reaching threat. For whatever reason, these nay-sayers refuse to accept the obvious.

Embedded Thesis

As former vice-president Al Gore tells us in his best-selling 2006 book *An Inconvenient Truth,* "Not only does human-caused global warming exist, but it is also growing more and more dangerous, and at a pace that has now made it a planetary emergency." Clearly, it's imperative that the United States take a leading role in the developed world's efforts to prevent environmental catastrophe. Yet there remain a great many skeptics who reject Gore's claims and those of the world's scientists, nearly all of whom agree that global warming constitutes a real, immediate, and potentially far-reaching threat. For whatever reason, these nay-sayers refuse to accept the obvious.

When embedding the thesis, it's necessary to place it in the best possible location. Consider again the global warming example. If the thesis had been positioned as the third sentence in the paragraph, it would have been misplaced, disrupting the flow by creating an interruption between the two sentences about climate change deniers. So the placement of an embedded thesis requires careful deliberation. For this reason, most student writers find it easier to simply adopt the conventional practice of placing the thesis statement at the end of the introduction.

BODY PARAGRAPHS

Technically, an essay has no set length. The great nineteenth century American poet/philosopher Ralph Waldo Emerson wrote essays that are dozens of pages long. After the introduction, the writer provides several "body paragraphs" that demonstrate the validity of the thesis statement provided at the outset. An essay—like nearly every other kind of writing—is broken down into paragraphs, rather than simply pushing ahead in one long, relentless surge of text. This is because readers comprehend better when information is segmented into separate sections. We read in much the same way we normally eat: one bite at a time, chewing and swallowing before moving on to the next mouthful.

Indeed, the word "paragraph" has an interesting history that reinforces this basic concept. Hundreds of years ago, before the printing press had been invented or paragraphing as we know it had been developed, the medieval monks were responsible for creating handwritten manuscripts of sacred texts. They understood that readers prefer to digest information a little at a time. So they'd place a small drawing (a flower or a crucifix, for example) in the margin of the page as a signal to the reader when a new idea was beginning. These illustrations were called paragraphs, from the Latin *para* ("alongside of") and the Greek *gra'fo* ("writing"). Eventually these time-consuming drawings were replaced by the more efficient practice of simply beginning each new idea with indentation—some empty space. Thus was born what we now (somewhat inaccurately) call the paragraph.

Topic Sentences and Support Sentences

A good body paragraph should include a topic sentence identifying the paragraph's main idea, reinforced by a series of support sentences. Although the topic sentence sometimes appears elsewhere, it's usually the first sentence in the paragraph. For example, consider how the first (topic) sentence in the above paragraph sets the stage for what follows, a brief history. Notice also that the above paragraph is seven sentences long. That's fairly typical, although a paragraph can run a bit longer, especially if some of the sentences are very short.

Unity and Coherence

Because a good paragraph achieves unity by dealing only with the one main idea identified in its topic sentence, all the support sentences must relate directly to that idea. In addition, each of those support sentences should be sufficiently well-developed. This is done by providing factual data of a concrete, specific nature. For example, it's better to say *four* rather than *a few*, or *red, yellow, and orange* rather than *colorful*. Just as crucially, the paragraph must be coherently organized, so the support sentences must appear in the most logical sequence. Here is a body paragraph from the final version of the million dollar essay. Notice how it reflects the principles explained above. It focuses on one thing and one only, identified in the topic sentence. The support sentences that follow contain much specific detail and they appear in a logical, orderly sequence.

> Next would be my charge cards. When I got my Master Card in high school I spent more than $500 on a fancy wristwatch for a boy I was dating. Then there were other unwise spending sprees, so now the card is at its limit of $5,000. My Visa Card is also a disaster. I ran that one up after I could no longer use the Master Card. Last year I went to Florida with my girlfriends on spring break. They had no money so I covered a lot of our expenses, incurring more debt of nearly $2,000.

Just as the sentences within a paragraph should appear in the best possible order, so should the body paragraphs themselves. And the relationships among the main ideas of each can be clarified by the use of transition words and phrases. Transitions can serve as links between sentences, but can also be used at the beginning of a paragraph (as in the above paragraph, which opens with the transition "Next") to create a bridge between what's just been said and what lies ahead. This is highly important to consider when you reach the rewriting stage of composition.

What's been said so far applies to the body paragraphs of an essay, but these principles would hold equally true even in a one-paragraph assignment. Consider this example, a journal entry in which a student discusses the proverb, "Look Before You Leap":

> Like all well-known proverbs, "Look before you leap" expresses an obvious truth: that you shouldn't make quick decisions without full knowledge of the possible results. A good "real life" example would be what happened to my friend Pedro. With his last $3000 he bought a used car without bothering to have a mechanic check it first. Unfortunately, the car stopped running after a week, had to be towed, and has been parked in his driveway ever since. Obviously, he should have looked before he leaped.

As you can see, the topic sentence identifies the subject under consideration, the proverb in question. The support sentences explain the proverb's meaning and go on to describe an actual situation that illustrates the proverb's truth. The paragraph then concludes with a sentence that brings the reader back to the start by restating the proverb in slightly different wording. And adverbial transitions ("unfortunately" and "obviously") are used to facilitate the flow from idea to idea. This brings us to another consideration: the way in which the structure of a paragraph relates to the structure of the whole essay.

It would not be too much of an exaggeration to say that a paragraph can be seen as a mini-essay. Just as an essay begins with an introduction in which the thesis statement appears, a paragraph opens similarly, with a topic statement. And just as an essay develops its thesis through a series of body paragraphs, a paragraph develops its topic through a series of support sentences. Just as paragraphs sometimes open with helpful transitions, the sentences within paragraphs sometimes do as well. And just as an essay ends with a concluding paragraph, a paragraph ends with a concluding sentence. This makes sense because all writing—regardless of length—is attempting to do the same thing: Communicate with the reader. And this beginning/middle/end structure is usually what works best.

CONCLUSIONS

An essay's conclusion is just as important as its introduction. While the introduction constitutes the "first impression" the writer makes on the reader, the conclusion is what that reader comes away with. So if the essay ends poorly, what's gone before is undercut, diminished. Don't let that happen. Instead, end strong.

Always sum up in your last paragraph, which should begin with a re-phrasing of your thesis statement. In effect, the conclusion should resemble a *reversed* version of your introduction (although not word-for-word). Like an airplane rolling smoothly to a stop on the runway after reaching its destination rather than simply crashing there, the essay should close gracefully. This is easier to accomplish if you have used any of the introductory strategies explained earlier. You can simply revisit the scenario, statistic/fact, or quotation you opened with, thereby achieving a satisfying sense of closure by bringing the essay full-circle.

At several points now this book has mentioned the reader's psychology, a factor that any good writer bears always in mind. Conclusions are another example. People do not like to be driven out of town and stranded there. They much prefer to be chauffeured back home at the end of the day. In a sense, a good conclusion does that, by returning the reader to familiar turf. Accordingly, you should never introduce new ideas in your conclusion. Stick only to what's already been covered.

Let's look again at the revised introduction and conclusion of the "Million Dollar" essay. Notice how much they have in common. Several ideas introduced at the start are revisited at the end. (These have been underlined here for the sake of emphasis.)

Introduction

Most people have probably fantasized about what they'd do if they suddenly inherited a million dollars or <u>won it in a lottery</u>. Have you ever imagined yourself <u>being that lucky</u>? I know I have, many times. It will probably never happen, but I know what I'd do if it did. I'd make the absolute most of my <u>windfall, spending it wisely.</u>

Conclusion

So that's how I'd handle <u>my good luck</u>. Other people might spend their <u>windfall</u> differently, throwing wild parties or globe-trotting to the Caribbean, but not me. I'd prefer to react to my good fortune more cautiously, getting out of debt, making a few wise investments, taking a short trip to New York, buying a nice but not extravagant house and a new car, and helping out my loved ones and my church. Now that I've written my essay, I think I'll visit my neighborhood convenience store and <u>buy a lottery ticket</u>!

EXERCISES

1. Here are a half-dozen essay titles. Some are effective, but others are not. How might the ineffective ones be improved?

    ▶ The Lincoln and Kennedy Assassinations

    _____

    ▶ ISIS

    _____

    ▶ The Five Main Causes of the French & Indian War

    _____

    ▶ The Differences Between Neurosis and Psychosis

    _____

    ▶ Asperger's Syndrome and Attention Deficit Disorder

    _____

    ▶ My Proudest Moment

    _____

2. Select one of the *effective* essay titles in Exercise 1 and write an introduction paragraph based upon it. Make sure there's a firm thesis statement.

3. Here are five thought-provoking quotations. Choose three and write a good introductory paragraph based on each. Be sure that each paragraph ends with a firm thesis statement that echoes the quotation's wisdom (or lack of it), but in your own words.

    ▶ When you find you're on the side of the majority, it's time to reform. (Mark Twain)
    ▶ Poverty is the parent of revolution and crime. (Aristotle)
    ▶ There is only one religion, though there are a hundred versions of it. (George Bernard Shaw)
    ▶ Half the people you know are below average. (George Carlin)
    ▶ All human errors stem from impatience. (Franz Kafka)

4. Using your college library's most recent edition of *The Statistical Abstract of the United States*, find five interesting statistics that might be useful in the introduction (or body) of an essay about income inequality.

5. Using the "Look Before You Leap" paragraph on page 45 as a model, write similar paragraphs based on three of these other well-known proverbs. In each case, explain the proverb's meaning, and then describe an actual situation that illustrates the proverb's truth.

   ▶ A chain is only as strong as its weakest link.
   ▶ The early bird catches the worm.
   ▶ People who live in glass houses shouldn't throw stones.
   ▶ You can't judge a book by its cover.
   ▶ A leopard doesn't change its spots.

CHAPTER 6

Rewriting

LEARNING OBJECTIVES

When you complete this chapter, you will be able to

► Edit your writing to detect and correct problems with content, organization, style, and tone

► Proofread your writing to detect and correct typos and mechanical errors in spelling, punctuation, and grammar

► Develop peer reviewing skills that will enable you to assist classmates and benefit from their feedback in return

i_am_zews/Shutterstock.com

EDITING

Reportedly, the famous American author Ernest Hemingway spent ten days revising the last three paragraphs of his 1940 novel *For Whom the Bell Tolls*. You *must* rewrite (and more than once) to achieve satisfactory results. This is because nobody produces good writing on the first try. The former United States Poet Laureate Billy Collins has said that we fine-tune using both a big screwdriver and a little screwdriver. The big one is for editing, fixing problems with regard to content, organization, style, and tone. Once these larger issues have been addressed, it's time to take out the little screwdriver and use it while proofreading to correct typos and "mechanical" errors, careless slip-ups in spelling, punctuation, and grammar.

Most writers do at least a little editing and fine-tuning even while drafting. They commit an obvious error and they fix it right away. Or perhaps they realize that a particular sentence is awkwardly constructed, so they revise it before moving on. But it's unwise to get bogged down making numerous corrections while attempting to create a first draft, because the interruptions necessitated by revising can derail your train of thought. Although some minor tweaking is inevitable along the way, in general it's better to concentrate first on completing the initial draft and postpone most polishing until later.

The editing stage of the writing process involves correcting problems with content, organization, style, and tone. Editing for content is quite difficult, however, because when writing you already know what you mean. If you didn't, you wouldn't be able to write at all. But what may be obvious to you as the writer may not be self-evident to the reader. So you must momentarily step outside yourself while editing and pretend to be that reader—someone who does *not* already know what the writing is all about. Granted, this reader-impersonation is not easy and may be only partially successful. Still, it's likely to reveal at least some points that need clarification or further development. What may have seemed logical or sufficient at the drafting stage might now strike you as much less so. You might want to add something here and there or take something out. You might find the title you chose during the drafting process no longer works. The same might be true of the introduction paragraph. This is the time you can make those changes with confidence, as you should now know the scope and the focus of the paper.

Very importantly, how about organization? Is everything where it belongs? Consider: CTA does not spell CAT. Although this may seem almost comically obvious, it can remind us of a basic principle about writing: Just as there's one and only one best location for every letter in a word, organization is crucial at every level—not only within words, but within sentences, paragraphs, and longer pieces of writing. So you must always ask yourself,

- ▶ Are the individual words in each sentence precisely the right ones and is each exactly where it belongs?
- ▶ Are the sentences in each paragraph presented in the best possible order?
- ▶ Are the paragraphs arranged in the best sequence?

In addition, look for ways to tighten your style. Try to adhere to the following principles, which are discussed in Appendix A:

- ▶ create active sentences with subjects and verbs side by side
- ▶ position modifiers near what they modify
- ▶ use transitions effectively
- ▶ handle numbers correctly
- ▶ use familiar vocabulary—nothing fancy
- ▶ write short sentences
- ▶ edit for concision and economy

While it's important to cultivate a style that avoids wordiness by expressing ideas as simply and directly as possible, it's equally necessary to ensure that your tone is appropriate to your purpose and your reader. Revisit Chapter 3, which discusses this while focusing on the need for reader-centered, positive wording that's sensitive to connotation as well as gender bias and other kinds of offensive expression.

PROOFREADING

This last stage of the rewriting process is the least creative, but it's extremely important. Your writing may be thoughtful, well-developed, well-organized, and fully appropriate with regard to style and tone. But if it's marred by keyboarding miscues and careless blunders in spelling, punctuation, and grammar, your credibility will be severely compromised. Therefore, you must take the necessary time to check for surface errors of this nature. Of course, most word-processing software includes spell-checkers and other such devices, and Microsoft Word even highlights questionable constructions. Take full advantage of these features. But don't rely on them absolutely. There's no substitute for your own careful attention to detail, especially since electronic resources are not foolproof. Spell-checkers, for example, typically provide several possible alternatives when they detect a mistake. But it's risky to simply select the first word on the list. Frequently, it's not the right choice. Always consult your dictionary before replacing your misspelled word with the one at the top of the list. In some cases, the meaning of that first word is far removed from what you intended. This can cause misunderstanding and, in some cases, unintentionally comical effects.

Here are some strategies for effective proofreading:

- ▶ Don't rush. Force yourself to go slowly by using the cursor, examining one word at a time.
- ▶ Proofread three times, checking for one thing each time: spelling first, then punctuation, then grammar. Review the guidelines in Appendix B to refresh your memory about these matters.

- ▶ After proofing electronically, print out your work and proof it once again to discover anything that might have escaped your notice on the screen.
- ▶ Read your work aloud, taking notice of where you stumble. Usually those are weak spots, instances of awkward or unnatural expression that need to be revised.

PEER REVIEWING

We've all heard the old saying "Two heads are better than one," and in most contexts this proverb is certainly true. Therefore, it makes sense to get help from someone else when attempting to edit or proofread. Many teachers of college-level English devise in-class exercises that require peer collaboration on editing and proofreading. Sometimes the procedure involves two students trading papers and providing written comments on each other's work. Another approach is to provide the whole class with copies of several students' papers and have everyone discuss them all. In both kinds of situation, writers usually receive a great deal of helpful feedback. But even if your instructor does not employ such practices, it makes sense to involve yourself in this kind of activity on your own because it nearly always results in better writing.

But peer reviewing can be tricky. If a math student writes 2 + 2 = 5 and someone else rejects that equation as incorrect, it would be incorrect no matter who wrote it, so the rejection cannot be taken personally. Writing, however, is quite different, because it *is* personal—very much so. For this reason, most of us tend to be somewhat defensive about it. We don't like anyone to tinker with our prose. We take it as an affront. In reality, however, this instinctively self-protective reaction is actually self-defeating, because nothing is more helpful to a writer than constructive, well-intentioned criticism. But effective peer-reviewing can occur only if the reviewer employs the right tone. If the criticism is perceived as arrogant or hostile, nothing will be achieved. So the reviewer should be careful to avoid giving that impression.

This does not mean, though, that the reviewer should praise inferior work or refrain from pointing out shortcomings. Such reluctance to identify weaknesses does the writer no good. But the reviewer should exercise tact and sensitivity, mentioning strengths before focusing on areas needing improvement. And when weaknesses are mentioned they should be described gently, in a considerate way, while still providing specifics. For example, if the writer failed to include enough detail about some feature of the topic, it would be unhelpful to respond with remarks like, "I don't know what you're talking about. You're not giving me anywhere near enough information to understand what you're trying to say." A far better response would be something like, "This topic is such an interesting one that I'd like to hear about it in greater depth. Maybe more details would give me a better understanding of your perspective."

But what if the topic is really *not* interesting to you? In a case like that it's helpful to remember what the great American novelist Henry James once said, that we should grant writers their givens and evaluate them only on the basis of how well they perform within that context. Additionally, it's important not to let your personal feelings toward the writer color your responses to the work. It's tempting to be overly generous toward someone you like and overly critical towards someone you find irritating. But these tendencies must be resisted, because they invalidate the whole endeavor. In any case, you should focus on large issues first—content, organization, style, tone—before taking out your "little screwdriver." And resist the urge to actually rewrite. Simply provide thoughtful suggestions that will help the writer do that. In the process, you'll begin to develop editing skills that will enable you to improve your own work as well.

What follows are three versions of a student essay. In its original form, the paper has its strengths. For starters, it's well-developed and well-organized. And it's lively. But it also exhibits a great many weaknesses. Marred by typos, misspellings, and other mechanical errors, it's rather wordy and rambling. Even more damagingly, however, the student introduces unnecessary subject matter, lapses into offensive language, and often chooses other vocabulary that's too informal for academic writing. Additionally, both the title and the conclusion are insufficient. The second version of the paper has been rewritten to correct the major weaknesses already identified, but not the mechanical miscues. Notice how careful proofreading of the second version has identified those mistakes, which are corrected in the final version. Although that final version is not *perfect* (no essay ever is!), it's far better than the original, thanks to re-writing.

Maybe the original version strikes you as more "real," more engaging. You may relate well to the student's everyday wording and you may be amused by the references to her various misadventures. Further, you may feel that she's been admirably honest and sharing in mentioning her family problems. If so, that's understandable, but only up to a point. As explained in Part 1, we must always remember purpose, audience, and tone. Although this would be classified as an example of self-expressive writing, its main purpose should be to inform and persuade, not entertain—unless the assignment called for a humorous approach. So the student's unwise spending in the past, her excesses at State U., her problems with her parents, and her unexplained hostility toward her brother contribute nothing toward moving the essay forward. In fact, they distract. Sometimes we feel obliged to "put everything in" simply because it's the truth, but that's not necessarily a constructive impulse. A good writer includes only what's relevant.

Further, the student's audience here is her professor, who will almost certainly expect the somewhat higher level of formality achieved in the final version. Although we should try to keep our writing accessible by avoiding an *overly* elevated style, it's nevertheless true that academic writing does operate on a higher plane than routine conversation. While your writing should echo your voice, it should be your "best" voice: the one you might use in a job interview, for example, rather than the one used while hanging out in the student lounge with close friends.

"A Million Dollars"

Lots of people—pretty much everybody, in fact—has [*have*] probably fantasized about what they'd do if they suddenly inherited a million dollars or won it in a lottery or something like that. Have you ever imagined yourself being that lucky? I know I have, lots of times. It will probably never happen, but I know what I'd do if it did. I'd make the absolute most of my windfall.

Before rushing out and squandering it all, I'd take care of business first. I have a lot of debt, so I'd take care of that. My student loans would be first. Before coming to County Community [*C*] College [*C*] I spent a semester at State U., where I partied my but off and flunked out [*slang*]. So I basically wasted $8,000 in student loans. Since then I've racked up [*slang*] another coupla grand [*spelling, slang*] attending here. So that's about $10,000 I'm in the hole for [*slang*]. I'd pay that off first. Then there's my charge cards. Don't ask. When I got my first Master Card [*C*] back in high school I blew a bundle [*slang*] on a fancy watch for this retard [*offensive term*] kid I was dating. We broke up after less than a year, but I was down more than 5 bens [*slang*]. Then there were all these other stupid spendinmg [*typo*] sprees, so now the card's maxed out to the tune of five G's [*slang*]. My Visa, too, is a disaster. I ran that one up after I could no longer use the Master Card [*M*][*C*]. Last year I went to Florida with my girlfriends on spring break, they [*run-on*] had no money so I paid for a lot of stuff. More debt, three thou [*fragment*]. After I paid all that off, I'll [*I'd*] invest in some stocks. G.E., Google, [*spell out*] and Apple would be good bets. Of course, they could wind up being worthless, but I'm [*I'd be*] willing to gamble because they will [*would*] probably continue to gain value, giving me interest income from dividends in the future ~~after I've burned through my cool million~~.

After I cleaned up my financial mess, it would now be time to have some fun. Like all [*many*] girls, I LOVE [*no caps*] to shop. Now I'd finally be able to buy all new clothes and exsesserrys [*spelling*] without having to look at the price tags. But I wouldn't do my shopping around here, because all the stores here suck [*slang*]. ~~Me and~~ My [*M*] sister Jasmine, and I [*and I*] would take a weeklong trip to New York City and shop til we dropped. We'd buy shoes, designer jeens [*spelling*], tops, a coupla [*spelling*] new coats, purses, jewerly [*spelling*], u name it. And while we was their [*spelling*] we'd ~~do the whole tourist thing and~~ visit all the tourist attractions: Empire State Building, Stature of Loberty [*spelling*], Ground [*G*] Zero [*Z*], the Metropolitan Museum, and [*and*] Central Park ~~and ect~~.

My next big purchase would be my dream car—a red Mazda Miata. I've wanted one ever since I first saw it when visiting my aunt ~~in~~ *[on]* Cape Cod. There was one parked outside the restaurant where we ate one night and I said right then, "I've gotta have it!" My dream car would have a six-speed transmission and Pirelli racing tires. After getting my dream car I'd need someplace to live, because living with my parents really sucks *[slang]*, especially now because they've been hassling me big time *[slang]* ever since I flunked out of State. They act as if community college is some kind of disgrace. So I'd hire a contractor to build me a small place up in the mountains, ~~on~~ on a coupla *[spelling]* acres of land, with central air, *[conditioning,]* a fully equipped game room with bar, and a swimming pool.

I was complaining about my parents before, but really their *[spelling]* pretty cool, considering everything. So I wouldn't forget everything they done *[they've]* for me over the years, so I wouldn't forget *[avoid repetitious wording]* them. I'd give them a hundred thousand outright, maybe *[run-on]* that would make it a little easier for them to retire. They have always worked their buts off *[slang]* to support me and my sister, so they deserve it. I ain't giving nothing *[grammer]* to my brother, though. He sucks *[slang]*. Next would be my sister Jasmine. She's THE BEST! *[no caps]* There's Never been a cooler girl, she's *[run-on]* like my best friend so she'd get $25 thou *[slang]* in addition to our New York trip Next *[run-on]* would be my church. I'm not real *[very]* religious but my whole family's been involved in a lot of church activities, so I'd give the church ten grand *[slang]* to fix up the social room and the black top in the parking lot, it's *[run-on]* in really rough shape.

So that's it. That's how I'd burn threw *[spelling]* my cool million!

There are several problems here.

First, the tone is much too informal and conversational. Avoid slang and overly casual expression.

Second, there are too many "mechanical" errors in spelling, punctuation, and grammar. Try to be more careful about those matters.

Third, your conclusion is much too "thin" and abrupt. Try to end more gracefully.

Please revise, paying attention to the corrections provided.

What I'd Do With A Million Dollars

Most people have
~~Lots of people—pretty much everybody, in fact—has~~ probably fantasized about what they'd do if they suddenly inherited a million dollars or won it in a lottery ~~or something like that~~. Have you ever imagined yourself being that lucky? I know I have, ~~lots of~~ *many* times. It will probably never happen, but I know what I'd do if it did. I'd make the absolute most of my windfall.

~~Before rushing out and squandering it all,~~ I'd take care of business first. I have a lot of debt, so I'd take care of that. My student loans would be first. Before ~~coming to~~ *attending* County Community *Avoid repetitious wording* College I spent a semester at State U., where I neglected my studies and failed out, ~~So I~~ basically ~~wasted~~ *wasting* $8,000 ~~in student loans~~. Since then I've borrowed another $2,000 ~~to attend~~ *for tuition* here. So that's *start new paragraph* about $10,000 I owe. ~~I'd pay that off first.~~ *said this already* ~~Then there's~~ *Next would be* my charge cards. When I got my ~~first~~ Master Card back in high school I spent more than $500 on a fancy watch for a boy I was dating. ~~We broke up after less than a year, but I was down more than $500.~~ Then there were ~~all these~~ other stupid spending sprees, so now the card is at its limit of $5,000. My Visa, *card,* too, is a disaster. I ran that one up after I could no longer use the Master Card. Last year I went to Florida with my girlfriends on *run-on* *covered* *our expenses, incurring more debt of* spring break, *~~,~~ they* had no money so I ~~paid for~~ a lot of ~~stuff, amounting to~~ nearly $2,000. After I *$10,000* paid all that off, I'd invest in ~~some~~ stocks. General Electric, Google, and Apple would be good bets. Of course, they could wind up being worthless, but I'd be willing to gamble because they would probably continue to gain value, giving me ~~interest~~ income from dividends in the future.

After I cleaned up my financial mess, it would ~~now~~ be time to have some fun. Like many girls, I love to shop. Now I'd finally be able to buy all new clothes and *spelling* ~~exsesserrys~~ without having to look at the price tags. But I wouldn't do my shopping around here, because ~~all~~ the stores here are boring. ~~Me and~~ my sister ~~Jasmine~~ *and I* would take a weeklong shopping trip to New York City. We'd *spelling* *spelling* *were spelling* buy shoes, designer ~~jeens~~, tops, coats, purses, and ~~jewerly~~. And while we ~~was~~ ~~their~~ we'd visit all the *spelling* tourist attractions: the Empire State Building, the ~~Stature~~ of Liberty, Ground Zero, the Metropolitan Museum, and Central Park.

My next big purchase would be my dream car—a red Mazda Miata. I've wanted one ever since I first saw it when visiting my aunt on Cape Cod. There was one parked outside the restaurant where we ate one night and I said right then, "I've gotta have it!" My ~~dream car~~ would have a [*Avoid repetitious wording*]

six-speed transmission and Pirelli racing tires. After getting my ~~dream car~~ [*Miata*] I'd need someplace to

live, because living with my parents is unpleasant, especially now because they've been critcizing

me ever since I flunked out of State. They act as if community college is some kind of disgrace. So

I'd hire a contractor to build me a small place [*house*] up in the mountains, on a coupla [*spelling*] of acres of land,

with central air, [*conditioning,*] a fully equipped game room with bar, and a swimming pool.

I was complaining about my parents before, but really their [*spelling*] pretty cool, considering

everything. So I wouldn't forget ~~everything they~~ [*all they've*] done for me over the years, ~~so I wouldn't forget~~ [*said this already*]

~~them.~~ I'd give them ~~a hundred thousand~~ [*$100,000*] outright, [*run-on*] maybe that would make it a little easier for them

to retire. They have always worked hard to support me and my sister, so they deserve it. Next would

be my sister, Jasmine. She's the best! There's Never been a cooler girl, she's [*run-on*] like [*really*] my best friend so

she'd get $25,000 in addition to our New York trip, next [*run-on*] would be my church. I'm not very religious

but my whole family's been involved in a lot of church activities, so I'd ~~give the church~~ [*donate*] $10,000 to

fix up [*renovate*] the social room and ~~the black top in~~ [*repave*] the parking lot, it's [*run-on*] in really rough shape.

So that's how I'd handle my good luck. Other people might spend there [*spelling*] windfall differently,

throwing wild partys [*spelling*] or globe-trotting to the Caribbean, but not me. I'd prefer to react to my good

fortune more cautiously, getting out of debt, making a few wise investments, taking a short trip to

New York, buying a nice but not extravagent [*spelling*] house and a new car, and helping out my loved one's [*spelling*]

and my church. Now that I've written my essay, I think I'll visit my neighborhood convience [*spelling*] store

and by [*spelling*] a lottery ticket!

Better! Your conclusion, especially, is much improved.

Notice, though, how I've provided additional revisions to show you how to tighten the style, using fewer words to express the same ideas. In addition, I've pointed out the remaining misspellings, crossed out unnecessary content, and made a few other suggestions.

What I'd Do With A Million Dollars: Wise Choices

Most people have probably fantasized about what they'd do if they suddenly inherited a million dollars or won it in a lottery. Have you ever imagined yourself being that lucky? I know I have, many times. It will probably never happen, but I know what I'd do if it did. I'd make the absolute most of my windfall, spending it wisely.

First I'd take care of my debts, starting with my student loans. Before attending County Community College I misspent a semester at State University, where I neglected my studies and failed out, basically wasting $8,000. Since then I've borrowed another $2,000 for tuition here. So that's about $10,000 I owe.

Next would be my charge cards. When I got my Master Card in high school I spent more than $500 on a fancy wristwatch for a boy I was dating. Then there were other unwise spending sprees, so now the card is at its limit of $5,000. My Visa Card is also a disaster. I ran that one up after I could no longer use the Master Card. Last year I went to Florida with my girlfriends on spring break. They had no money so I covered a lot of our expenses, incurring more debt of nearly $2,000.

After I got out of debt, I'd invest $100,000 in stocks. The stock market is unpredictable, but General Electric, Google, and Apple would be relatively safe bets. Of course, they could wind up being worthless, but I'm willing to gamble because they will probably continue to gain value, giving me income from dividends in the future.

After I cleaned up my finances, it would now be time to have some fun. Like many girls, I love to shop. Now I'd be able to buy new clothes and accessories without having to look at the price tags. But I wouldn't do my shopping locally, because the stores here are boring. My sister and I would take a weeklong shopping trip to New York City. We'd buy shoes, designer jeans, tops, coats, purses, and jewelry. And while we were there we'd visit all the tourist attractions: the Empire State Building, the Statue of Liberty, Ground Zero, the Metropolitan Museum, and Central Park.

My next purchase would be my dream car—a red Mazda Miata. I've wanted one ever since I first saw it when visiting my aunt on Cape Cod. There was one parked outside the restaurant where we ate one night and I said right then, "I've gotta have it!" My dream car would have a six-speed transmission and Pirelli racing tires. After getting my Miata I'd need someplace to live, because living with my parents is unpleasant, because they've been criticizing me ever since I flunked out of State. They act as if community college is some kind of disgrace. So I'd hire a contractor to build me a small house up in the mountains, on a couple of acres of land, with central air conditioning, a game room, and a swimming pool.

I was complaining about my parents earlier, but really they're pretty cool, considering everything. So I wouldn't forget all they've done for me over the years. I'd give them $100,000. Maybe that would make it a little easier for them to retire. They have always worked hard, so they deserve it. Next would be my sister. There's never been a cooler girl. She's really my best friend, so she'd get $25,000 in addition to our New York trip. Next would be my church. I'm not very religious but my whole family's been involved in many church activities, so I'd donate $10,000 to renovate the social room and repave the parking lot.

So that's how I'd handle my good luck. Other people might spend their windfall differently, throwing wild parties or globe-trotting to the Caribbean, but not me. I'd prefer to react to my good fortune more cautiously, getting out of debt, making a few wise investments, taking a short trip to New York, buying a nice but not extravagant house and a new car, and helping out my loved ones and my church. Now that I've written my essay, I think I'll visit my neighborhood convenience store and buy a lottery ticket!

NOW you've got it!

You've achieved a more appropriate tone, corrected the mechanical errors, provided necessary paragraph-breaks, and created a satisfying conclusion that relates back to the Introduction.

Well done!

EXERCISES

1. The following paragraph (from a "My Angriest Moment" essay) needs a lot of rewriting. Fix it up, focusing on mechanics (spelling, punctuation, grammar) and tone.

   As soon as that iceball hit my drivers side window something inside me just sort of snapped. I was like, "Whoa! No way I'm gonna let that go without kicking some but. Without even thinking about it I threw a u-turn right in front of oncoming traffic and speeded down the street, everybody was honking and slaming on there breaks but I didn't give a crap. And when I saw this scumbag kid running I knew he was the one that thrown the iceball. I got a little bit passed him and pulled over and jumped out of the car and grabed him by the cote.

2. Closely examine two versions of a paper you've written recently. Create a chart that reflects the kinds of revisions you made to the original when creating the final version: changes in content, tone, organization, and mechanics. Subdivide the mechanics section into typos, spelling, punctuation, and grammar. The chart can then be used as a helpful guide when rewriting in the future, as it will highlight the areas in which you tend to make the most mistakes.

3. Look again at the "Million Dollar" essay. Which of its middle paragraphs is the least well-developed? Why? If you were the writer, how would you improve it?

4. Before submitting your next essay assignment, exchange papers with someone else in the class and provide helpful feedback to each other.

PART 3

The Essay as Argument

As already discussed, a well-structured essay opens with a meaningful, clearly stated thesis. Since by definition a thesis is an assertion—something to be defended and proven—it's not an overstatement to say that in a sense all essays are argumentative and persuasive in nature. As the American author Joan Didion once said, writing is "the act of saying *I*, of imposing yourself on other people, of saying *listen to me, see it my way, change your mind*."

But the whole idea of arguing to persuade is a complex proposition. If your listener or reader already agrees with you, there's no need to argue. You'd be "preaching to the choir." If your audience is neutral or undecided about the issue, it's possible they're not especially interested in it. And if they're in disagreement with you, you'll probably have a hard time changing their minds no matter how convincingly you make your case. Our harshly polarized political climate illustrates this.

Nevertheless, the ability to present your position clearly and coherently is a valuable skill, if only to clarify your own thinking or perhaps nudge resistant readers toward a somewhat broader perspective. Further, a well-argued essay can convince receptive readers to adopt a particular stance or solution in response to a given situation or problem.

Of course, there are many ways to flesh out an argument. Part 3 will acquaint you with some of the essential features of argumentative writing and will also discuss seven basic modes of development commonly used in structuring college-level essays.

From *College English: The Basics, 2nd Edition* by George J. Searles. © 2017 by George J. Searles. Reprinted by permission of Kendall Hunt Publishing Company.

CHAPTER 7

Essential Features of Argument and Persuasion

LEARNING OBJECTIVES

When you complete this chapter, you will be able to

- ► Compose a persuasive essay that uses valid evidence to successfully defend a relevant thesis
- ► Acknowledge and refute opposing viewpoints
- ► Employ both inductive and deductive reasoning
- ► Avoid logical fallacies

Andrey_Popov/Shutterstock.com

EVIDENCE-BASED THESIS

Legitimately persuasive writing must be based on valid evidence. According to Aristotle, this is argumentation based on *logos*—that is, verifiable facts. An objective, third-person approach is the most effective narrative perspective for logos-based argument, especially when dealing with a resistive audience. For example, it's better to say, "Women should be able to assume combat roles in the military" rather than "*In my opinion, I think* women should be able to assume combat roles in the military," because every person's statements are obviously that individual's opinion or belief, so it goes without saying.

But Aristotle also identified two other modes of argument: those based on *ethos* and *pathos*. Ethos-based evidence relies on establishing the speaker or writer's credibility, sincerity, and good intentions, and is therefore best-suited to undecided audiences. Not surprisingly, ethos-based argumentation often does employ first-person rather than third-person narration. Pathos-based argumentation appeals to the reader's personal values and feelings, and is very effective when dealing with an already receptive audience. However, this style of argumentation runs the risk of veering into the "appeal to emotion" fallacy. More about that later.

Regardless of the narrative perspective employed, the introductory paragraph of a persuasive essay should identify the issue at hand and then provide a firm, unambiguous thesis statement that clearly identifies your position. The thesis can be phrased positively ("X is good") or negatively ("X is not good"), but the reader should have no doubt about the direction of the argument. As explained in Chapter 4, however, you should avoid phrasing the thesis statement too absolutely. Allow for exceptions. For example, instead of saying "X is *always* good (or not good)," say *often* or *usually*. In truth, most situations are not subject to "black and white" treatment. There's nearly always at least some grey involved. Accordingly, terms like *rarely* (instead of *never*), *ordinarily* (instead of *always*), and others reflect this complexity and therefore make your thesis statement more credible because less inflexible.

In addition, the thesis statement should not only establish your position on the issue, but should also provide the basic reason for that position. For example, consider the difference between this thesis statement and its more persuasive revision:

Thesis:	Cremation of the dead is usually more practical than traditional burial.
Revised Thesis:	Cremation of the dead is usually more practical than traditional burial, because sprawling cemeteries are a waste of needed space, especially in densely developed urban areas.

ACKNOWLEDGING AND REFUTING OPPOSING VIEWPOINTS

Because any controversial issue is by definition debatable, an excellent strategy is to acknowledge at least some of the opposition's most credible arguments and then refute them, perhaps by applying an *ethos*-based strategy, reminding your audience of your expertise. Again, this makes your own assertions appear more reasonable and considered—and therefore more persuasive. Indeed, you can even structure the entire essay this way, opening each body paragraph with an opposing argument and then showing why it's mistaken. But it's crucial to ensure that your side has the last word at every point along the way. (This is mentioned again in the Comparison/Contrast section of Chapter 8.)

The proofs you use to refute the opposition and bolster your own thesis can be in the form of facts, statistics, expert testimony (that is, quotes from qualified authorities on the subject), anecdotes, and the like. Importantly, your evidence must be relevant, representative, and current. Many writers and public speakers like to invoke *pathos* at the end of their remarks, driving the main point home by appealing to the audience's hopes, fears, and desires. For the sake of credibility in written arguments, though, the sources of all your information must be fully documented, within the text and on an MLA- or APA-style list of sources, as in the model essay at the end of this chapter.

INDUCTIVE AND DEDUCTIVE REASONING

Clearly, all meaningful argumentation must be grounded in logical reasoning. There are essentially two kinds: *inductive* and *deductive*.

Inductive reasoning proceeds from the specific to the general. As such, it's probability-based. For example, let's say that you eat an apple on ten different occasions and become ill every time. Each instance of illness is a specific case, but taken together those ten cases lead to a safe assumption—that you're probably allergic to apples. Deductive reasoning, however, operates the other way around, proceeding from the general to the specific. For example, if you know that all the members of a particular campus club have a tattoo of a platypus on their left biceps, and you meet a student who's a member of that club, you can reasonably assume there's a platypus tattoo on his left biceps.

This kind of reasoning can be expressed in the form of a *syllogism*, which operates as follows:

Major Premise:	All new BMWs are expensive. (True.)
Minor Premise:	Her new car is a BMW. (True.)
Conclusion:	Her new car was expensive. (No-brainer; conclusion is clearly true.)

Of course, for the conclusion to be reliable, both premises must be true, as in the above example. Here's a syllogism in which the major premise is false, because too sweeping in its assertion.

Major Premise:	All Republicans oppose gun control. (Untrue: Sweeping Generalization.)
Minor Premise:	Senator Longwind is a Republican. (True.)
Conclusion:	Senator Longwind opposes gun control. (Not necessarily true.)

However, a syllogism's conclusion can be unreliable even if both premises are *true*, as in this example:

Major Premise:	Saxophones are loud. (True.)
Minor Premise:	This musical instrument is loud. (True.)
Conclusion:	This musical instrument is a saxophone. (Not necessarily true.)

Clearly, the reason why this syllogism is faulty is that the instrument mentioned in the minor premise does not necessarily belong to the category (saxophones) identified in the major premise.

Obviously, syllogisms are tricky, requiring careful thinking in order to arrive at meaningful conclusions. But that's why they're valuable to anyone attempting to construct a well-reasoned, genuinely persuasive argument.

LOGICAL FALLACIES

Argumentation using pathos-based strategies can be highly persuasive, because our emotions often color our responses. The influential psychologist Abraham Maslow (1908–1970) formulated an extensive list of our physical and emotional needs. Here's a fairly comprehensive inventory of emotional needs, based partly on Maslow's theories:

- ► The need to feel safe from harm or embarrassment
- ► The need to feel financially secure
- ► The need for meaningful accomplishments
- ► The need for recognition, affection, and approval
- ► The need to fit in with others and have friends
- ► The need to stand apart and be an individual
- ► The need to advise and nurture
- ► The need *for* advice and nurturing
- ► The need for fun, adventure, and escape
- ► The need for romance and sexual satisfaction

To recognize how appeals to emotion can function to persuade, we need look no farther than the world of advertising. In ad after ad, the implied message is that the purchase of a particular product or service will result in the fulfillment of one or more of these basic emotional desires. However, there is nothing logical about this. The product or service that the ad is promoting will not *necessarily* provide the promised emotional reward. It may or it may not, because many variables are always at work. Therefore, the appeal to emotion is perhaps the most common example of *logical fallacy*—that is, flawed reasoning.

There are many different kinds of fallacies in addition to the appeal to emotion. Here are ten of the most common:

Ad Hominem: From the Latin phrase meaning "to the person," an attack on the individual rather than a response to the actual issue. Example: "Of course you're opposed to capital punishment—you're always wrong about everything."

Appeal to Questionable Authority: Basing an argument on the opinion of someone who's not necessarily well-informed about the subject. Example: "There's no such thing as global warming. My barber was just saying so yesterday."

Bandwagon Appeal: Everybody's doing it, so you should (jump on the bandwagon) too. Example: "Everybody else in the neighborhood is voting for Joe Schmo, so you should also."

Begging the Question: A thesis that's phrased as if the point in contention were already proven. Example: "All those murderous people who work at Planned Parenthood should be fired and made to get real jobs."

False Dilemma: The "either/or" fallacy. Example: "If you don't major in business in college, you'll be a failure later on."

Generalizing from the Particular: Sometimes called "hasty generalization," using one case to support a sweeping claim. Example: "Women don't know anything about sports. My sister's a perfect example."

Invalid Analogy: Comparing two things that are not actually parallel. Example: "When there's a Democrat in the White House, it's like when Hitler was in charge in Germany."

Post Hoc, Ergo Propter Hoc: From the Latin phrase meaning "after this, therefore because of this," an assumption that one thing caused another just because it happened first. Example: "My sister always drank a lot of coffee, so she got cancer."

Red Herring: Introducing an irrelevant assertion to distract attention from the real issue. Example: "There's no need to worry about corporate tax evasion as long as the labor unions keep ruining the country."

Slippery Slope: The argument that one event will automatically lead to a whole subsequent chain of undesired results. Example: "If County Community College bans smoking on campus, nobody will enroll, faculty and staff will quit, and the college will have to close."

Clearly, effective persuasion must avoid fallacies—statements that violate basic principles of logic. If your essay is guilty of any such flaws, your argument is immediately discredited.

Flamingo Images/Shutterstock.com

MODEL ARGUMENTATIVE ESSAY

Physician-Assisted Death: A Basic Right

Let's say your elderly, widowed mother has been diagnosed with terminal cancer. She has only six months to live. Moreover, she's in terrible pain. She has repeatedly said she wants to die as soon as possible and be reunited with your father in the afterlife. The whole family supports her wishes. She asks her doctor to prescribe a lethal dose of medicine so she can die with dignity when she feels fully ready. But unless you live in Oregon, Washington, or Montana, this can't happen (Braddock). Everywhere else, physician-assisted death (PAD) is illegal. This makes no sense. Mentally competent persons with terminal illness should certainly be able to end their own life if they want to.

Opponents of PAD claim that a doctor who complies with such a request violates the Hippocratic oath which says, in part, "First, do no harm." But this argument depends on how we define "harm." To enable a suffering patient to escape a prolonged period of pointless suffering and inexorable physical and psychological deterioration is actually an act of mercy. The true harm is in preventing that escape. Because of our laws, therefore, doctors in all but three states are actually *required* to do harm, oath or no oath. (Nitschke)

A related objection is that PAD denies the sanctity of human life. But there's nothing more important in life than a person's freedom and autonomy. Indeed, countless wars have been fought to ensure such liberty. Conversely, there's absolutely nothing sacred or noble about simply wasting away, becoming a mere shell of one's true self, all the while enduring pain, indignity, and the loss of independence (Messerli). Besides, the emphasis on sanctity is essentially a product of religious traditions, and since our laws require separation of church and state, such essentially faith-based preoccupations should have no influence on legislation.

Then there's the claim that if PAD is legalized, it will lead to widespread abuses. Selfish relatives and cost-conscious health insurance providers will somehow coerce patients into ending their lives unnecessarily, the argument goes, and PAD will occur disproportionately among the poor, uneducated, and otherwise marginalized members of society. But this is an example of the "slippery slope" fallacy (Frey). Thanks to strictly enforced procedural rules, there is no evidence demonstrating that any such over-use has occurred in the three states (and several European countries) where the practice is permitted. (Ganzini)

Admittedly, any debate involving death is weighty by nature. People argue all the time about such practices as abortion and capital punishment. But PAD is different, because it can occur only if the person involved chooses it; it's not up to anyone else. As Derek Humphrey, president of ERGO, an Oregon-based advocacy group, says on his Web site, "every competent adult has the incontestable right to humankind's ultimate civil and personal liberty—the right to die in a manner and at a time of their own choosing." ("Liberty")

Works Cited

Braddock, Clarence H. "Physician Aid-in-Dying." *Ethics in Medicine: University of Washington School of Medicine.* www.washington.edu/bioethx. Accessed 13 April 2017.

Frey, R.G. "Slippery Slope to Legalized Murder." *Euthanasia.* www.pro.con.org. Accessed 13 April 2017.

Ganzini, Linda. "Social Groups at Risk of Abuse." *Euthanasia.* www.pro.con.org. Accessed 13 April 2017.

Humphry, Derek. "Liberty and Death: A manifesto concerning an individual's right to choose to die." *ERGO: Euthanasia Research and Guidance Organization.* Accessed 13 April 2017.

Messerli, Joe. "Should an incurably-ill patient be able to commit physician-assisted suicide?" *In a Nutshell.* www.balancedpolitics.org. Accessed 13 April 2017.

Nitschke, Philip. "Hippocratic Oath and Prohibition of Killing." *Euthanasia.* www.pro.con.org. Accessed 13 April 2017.

EXERCISES

1. Here are ten examples of persuasive writing. Identify which of Aristotle's three modes (*logos, ethos, pathos*) would be operating in each situation.

   ▶ Fund-raising letter to local residents, soliciting money for the town's Cub Scout troop.

   _____

   ▶ Mayoral candidate's campaign speech emphasizing her experience and other credentials.

   _____

   ▶ Letter to the editor, urging that a traffic light be installed at a particularly dangerous intersection.

   _____

   ▶ Magazine article outlining the scientific community's collective stance on the dangers of climate change.

   _____

   ▶ Job application letter highlighting the applicant's qualifications and potential value to the employer.

   _____

   ▶ Social worker's report citing specific reasons why a particular child should be placed in protective custody.

   _____

   ▶ A landscaping services company's advertisement emphasizing the company's highly qualified personnel and many years in business.

   _____

   ▶ A public service announcement reminding senior citizens to get flu shots.

   _____

   ▶ An advertisement detailing the capabilities of a new model of surveillance drone.

   _____

▶ A feasibility study exploring the advantages and disadvantages of closing a major downtown street and creating a pedestrian mall.

_____

2. Two of these syllogisms are valid examples of deductive logic, but three are invalid. Identify which are which, and provide reasons for your decisions.

Major Premise: Heavy metal bands all use drugs.
Minor Premise: Josh plays bass in a heavy metal band.
Conclusion: Josh uses drugs.

Valid or Invalid? _____

_____

Major Premise: Aaron always does poorly in math courses.
Minor Premise: MA 201-Trigonometry is a math course.
Conclusion: Aaron will do poorly in MA201.

Valid or Invalid? _____

_____

Major Premise: Many basketball players are tall.
Minor Premise: LaTonya is tall.
Conclusion: LaTonya is a basketball player.

Valid or Invalid? _____

_____

Major Premise: Steam locomotives are large.
Minor Premise: This locomotive is large.
Conclusion: This is a steam locomotive.

Valid or Invalid? _____

_____

Major Premise: Our team rarely loses a home game.
Minor Premise: This weekend's game is at home.
Conclusion: Our team will probably win this weekend's game.

Valid or Invalid? _____

_____

3. Envision a beer advertisement depicting a group of attractive, well-dressed young men and women partying at a fancy nightclub and drinking the advertised brand. Identify at least three basic human needs targeted by such an ad.

_____

_____

4. Identify the logical fallacy at work in each of the following statements:

   ► Everybody is voting for Carlos in the Student Government election, so you should vote for him too.

   _____

   ► If the United States government doesn't put a stop to immigration, pretty soon there won't be any native-born Americans here.

   _____

   ► You're a liberal, so nothing you say can be trusted.

   _____

   ► My baseball coach says there's no such thing as evolution, so that's good enough for me.

   _____

   ► Don't ever buy a Ford Mustang. My cousin had one and it was a total lemon.

   _____

   ► Drug addiction is just simple immorality, like cheating on a test.

   _____

   ► All those thieves on welfare should be required to pay back all that money they've stolen from us honest, hard-working citizens.

   _____

   ► To get ahead today you have to either know somebody or break the rules.

   _____

   ► I'm not going to listen to country-western music anymore. Every time I spend more than a couple of hours at a bar where there's country-western music I always have a headache the next day.

   _____

▶ Don't worry about getting cancer from smoking. Everybody has to die from something sooner or later.

_____

5. Choose one of the following topics and write a well-argued, fully-developed persuasive essay of 500–750 words.

▶ Assault Rifles Should/Should Not Be Banned
▶ Big-Time College Athletes Should/Should Not Be Classified as Professionals
▶ Student Evaluations of Teaching Should/Should Not Be the Main Way Professors are Evaluated for Promotion and Tenure
▶ Marijuana Should/Should Not Be Legalized for Recreational Use
▶ Mixed Martial Arts Competition Should/Should Not Be Banned

CHAPTER 8

Modes of Development

LEARNING OBJECTIVES

When you complete this chapter, you will be able to
    Compose persuasive essays using each of the
following modes of development:

- ► Narration
- ► Definition
- ► Description
- ► Exemplification
- ► Comparison and Contrast
- ► Process Analysis
- ► Cause and Effect

As mentioned earlier, an argumentative essay must make its case as persuasively as possible, presenting convincing evidence in support of its thesis. But there are many ways—modes of development—in which this can be accomplished. In *narration*, for example, the writer defends the thesis by providing an account of an event or experience that demonstrates the validity of the thesis. Similarly, an essay employing *exemplification* as its principal mode of development would provide several cases—or one fully developed instance —to illustrate the point at issue.

In any event, the mode of development chosen should be the one best-suited to the thesis. For instance, an essay attempting to prove that a particular situation is the result of several factors would obviously be best served by the *cause and effect* approach. Likewise, an essay asserting that a particular procedure is important and easy to learn would almost certainly adopt the *process analysis* mode. Indeed, it would not be an exaggeration to say that in argumentative writing the thesis itself, as much as the writer, chooses the mode of development.

Narration

On the most basic level, a narration is simply a chronological account of a series of events, whether factual or fictional. By that definition, there are many kinds of narration-based writing: newspaper stories, accident reports, and novels, to name just a few. In college English courses, however, the most typical form of narration-based assignment is the autobiographical essay, an account of a personal experience. It can also be an account of an envisioned *future* experience, as in the "Million Dollar" essay in Part 2. Most college writing instruction begins with this kind of essay because it's the easiest, requiring few resources other than the writer's already-established knowledge of the events. But a narrative essay should not be merely a meandering exercise in self-expression for its own sake. Like any essay, a narration should make a meaningful, impactful point that will interest and maybe even enlighten the reader.

CONFLICT

To create an effective narrative essay, you must choose relevant subject matter that will enable you to get and hold the reader's attention. For this reason, a narrative involving conflict is always a good choice because there's usually something instructive about how that conflict was—or was not—resolved. Indeed, the outcome of the conflict should illustrate the validity of your thesis. In literature (nearly all fiction and drama, along with much poetry), authors routinely portray conflict because without it there is essentially no story. Conflict is explored in somewhat greater depth in Chapter 10. More briefly stated, however, there are several basic kinds of conflict, categorized as follows:

- ▶ **Individual vs. Self**: Sometimes called "inner conflict," this always involves a person trying to choose between competing impulses. At its simplest it's a "good vs. evil" situation, but sometimes the conflict is more complicated.
- ▶ **Individual vs. Individual**: Essentially the "good guy vs. bad guy" scenario, but the variations are virtually unlimited: In short, one person against another—or, collectively, "us vs. them."
- ▶ **Individual vs. Society**: The person in conflict with the group, refusing to accept the norms of a repressive or otherwise mistaken community.
- ▶ **Individual vs. Nature**: The person in conflict with the great natural forces: forest fire, tornado, flood, blizzard, earthquake, and the like.
- ▶ **Individual vs. Fate**: Sometimes called "Individual vs. God (or the gods)," this conflict nearly always operates to the individual's disadvantage, as might be expected. By definition, fate has the upper hand.

POINT OF VIEW

There are two main ways to handle point of view in a piece of narrative writing, as shown below:

First-Person: I did this, I did that.

Third-Person: He/She/It/They did this, He/She/It/They did that.

Some English teachers instruct students never to use first-person, because in most kinds of writing the more objective third-person approach is preferable. Autobiographical narration, however, is the exception. Indeed, it's essentially impossible to write about your own experience *without* saying "I." When writing autobiography you are a participant in the action—indeed, the main participant—rather than merely an observer reporting it.

Since autobiographical narration is based on the writer's experience, the tone should be natural and conversational—the voice you might use when actually telling the story to a friend. Even at its most casual, however, writing is always a bit more formal than speech, especially in the academic context. Therefore, you should minimize the use of slang and should certainly avoid any terms that may give offense: no profanities, for example, and absolutely no slurs of any kind. Notice how the original version of the "Million Dollar" essay in Part 2 was "cleaned up" to achieve a more acceptable tone in the final version.

ORGANIZATION AND DEVELOPMENT

In autobiographical narrative, chronological organization usually works best. For this reason, it's wise to create a step-by-step outline of the sequence of events before writing the essay. This will help you refresh your memory of what happened and present the details in the most accurate order. A chronological outline for the model essay at the end of this section might look like this:

> Failed math
> Was in bad frame of mind
> Found toy gun
> Aimed gun at old man
> Man drew own gun
> Man identified self as detective
> Detective scolded me
> Learned lesson

Notice, however, that the introduction to that essay sort of plunges right into the climax ("I pulled a gun on a police officer") *before* recounting the events that led up to that moment. Although this is clearly a violation of chronological order, it's highly effective because it grabs the reader's full attention. Anyone seeing that sentence will almost certainly want to know the whole story. Another twist is the *flashback*, by which the narrator interrupts the unfolding story to mention an earlier event that has now taken on new importance because of its ability to shed light on more-recent developments.

VERB TENSE

Whether adhering to a strictly chronological approach or not, you must use verb tense consistently throughout the story. Some writers prefer present tense because it conveys a greater sense of immediacy, as in this example based on the sample essay:

> Present: I should be in a good mood, but I'm not.

> Past: I should've been in a good mood, but I wasn't.

But the present-tense approach is not advisable, because it's quite difficult to sustain without accidentally lapsing into the more accustomed past-tense style of narrating. Stick to past tense, and never shift back and forth between past and present, as in this example:

> (Past)
> So when my friend Tom and I <u>were</u> aimlessly walking…

> (Present)
> the stage <u>is</u> set for trouble.

This is a very common error, and is extremely disruptive to the narrative flow. Make every effort to avoid it.

In addition, you should use chronology-based transition words and phrases a bit more than you might in actual conversation. Here are some useful ones that enable the reader to more easily follow the unfolding narrative.

after	last
as	later
at last	meanwhile
before	next
during	soon
eventually	suddenly
finally	then
first, second, third	while

SENSORY DETAIL

A good narrative provides enough specific details to enable the reader to "experience" the events. Especially helpful are details that relate to the senses: not only sight but also hearing, smell, taste, and touch. Notice, for example, the many descriptive words that appear in the sample essay: The night was *dark*, the handgun was *small*, the trash bag was a *big plastic* one, the *old* man was wearing a *suit and tie,* and so on. But you should resist the urge to tell every single thing about the experience simply because it happened. Instead, choose details selectively, including those that will help the reader follow, understand, and relate to the story. Discard the irrelevant. For example, in the revision of the "Million Dollar" essay in Part 2, the student's mention of her unexplained hostility toward her brother has been deleted because it's not pertinent to the discussion.

DIALOGUE

One effective way of moving a narrative forward is to have the characters in the story talk to each other, just as people do in real life. The technical term for such conversation is *dialogue*. It's important to use dialogue correctly, observing certain rules.

FrameStockFootages/Shutterstock.com

▶   To prevent confusion, always indicate who is speaking, like this:

> "How are you today?" he said.
> "Not so good," she said.
> "Why? What's the matter?" he said.

▶   Although "said" is the most common verb in such situations, it can become annoyingly repetitious if over-used. Note how this revision corrects that:

> "How are you today?" he asked.
> "Not so good," she replied.
> "Why? What's the matter?" he inquired.

▶ Remember that in real life people nearly always use contractions. Therefore, your dialogue should as well. For example, in the above exchange, "What's" is used rather than "What is."

▶ Providing "he said/she said" phrases is called *attribution*. Here are a dozen useful attribution verbs:

coaxed	muttered
demanded	responded
exclaimed	sobbed
explained	shouted
inquired	stammered
insisted	urged

Indeed, virtually any verb having to do with speaking can be used for attribution. But it's crucial to use the most appropriate attribution verb in each situation, because these words convey a lot about the characters and their interactions. To say "whispered," for example, when there's no reason for the person to be whispering would make no sense.

▶ Use quotation marks correctly, placing them only around the speaker's exact words, rather than around summary statements of what was said.

WRONG: He asked her, "how she was today."
RIGHT: He asked her, "How are you today?"

Notice that—as in the above examples—attribution sometimes appears before the quote, rather than after. It can also interrupt the quote, as in this example:

"Actually," she replied, "not so good."

CONCLUSION

A good autobiographical narrative should have an instructive message or lesson of some sort and that moral should emerge clearly. Although this point is sometimes stated—or at least implied—in the thesis statement in the introduction, it usually appears most forcefully in the conclusion, where the writer sums up. After the reader finishes, there should be no doubt about the writer's feelings toward the experience described. And if the narrative has been skillfully crafted, the reader should now share those sentiments. Ideally, the reader should have learned something about life or at least been reminded of a truth already known.

Like the "Million Dollar" paper in Part 2, the essay that follows is an example of first-person autobiographical narrative. It has an attention-getting introduction, is well developed with relevant details, makes effective use of dialogue, employs an engagingly colloquial style, and summarizes persuasively in the conclusion.

CHECKLIST: NARRATIVE ESSAY

A good narration-based essay

- ► Has a meaningful title that clearly identifies the topic

- ► Opens with an interesting, attention-getting introduction that establishes the significance of the topic, and provides a firm thesis statement

- ► Recounts something that has happened (often something involving conflict)

- ► Is organized into three or four body paragraphs, covering the topic in a coherent, step-by-step way, focusing on one main idea at a time, usually in chronological order

- ► Provides enough concrete, specific detail to enable the reader to envision the events of the narrative

- ► Employs dialogue to advance the story

- ► Closes with a smooth, meaningful conclusion that gracefully resolves the discussion by somehow relating back to the introduction

- ► Uses clear, simple, straightforward language—nothing fancy

- ► Maintains an appropriate tone, neither too formal nor too conversational

- ► Contains no inappropriate material

- ► Contains no typos or mechanical errors in spelling, capitalization, punctuation, or grammar

- ► Satisfies the length requirements of the assignment

MODEL NARRATIVE ESSAY

Yes Doctor

In the middle of the surgery the doctor tells me "I need to do a cholangiogram, this patient has choledocholithiasis." I turn to the nurse and tell her "I need the supplies I set aside for the cholangiogram please." To me this is one of the simplest most common words I use in my job, but to a person with no medical background it probably sounds like gibberish. I can't help but remember that I too was once medically illiterate.

I remember sitting in surgical tech school feeling overwhelmed and intimidated. I scanned through my new textbooks and the words that I read had no meaning to me. I thought to myself, how am I going to learn all this in five months? As school went on, I realized it was all memorization. I found studying difficult because the words were hard to pronounce, so I used flash cards. I thought, who comes up with these words. I realized it is just a fancier way to say what you mean. Take the word cholecystectomy, -ectomy meaning the removal of . . . , and choledocho refers to the gallbladder and its bile duct. Put these words together and you get the removal of gallbladder, which includes the duct that comes attached to it.

Five months in the classroom pass, and now I find myself in the operating room with a live patient on the operating bed, as opposed to the dummy we practiced on in our mock surgery runs we had. I could hear the monitors beeping in the background and the nurse and the doctors conversing in a language that is fluent only to them. I'm scrubbing my hands and arms using aseptic technique, my brain racing in many directions: Maybe I haven't learned enough or all I need to know. What if the doctor asks me something and I have no idea what he's asking me for? What if my ignorance causes some harm to the patient? What if I get fired before I get hired? Oh my God, what am I going to do!

So I put on my surgical attire, then gowned and gloved the doctor. We start the surgery, the room is dark and cold and the only light is the one coming from the television screens because we use special cameras and scopes to perform the surgical procedure. The doctor then asks me if I have the catheter to do a cholangiogram. A cholangio what? So I quickly started to think back to what I learned in the classroom. I broke down the word cholangiogram. Chol meaning gallbladder angiogram referring to the picture of in this case the bile ducts. So at this point I think the doctor wants to take a picture of cystic and the bile ducts. So I responded, "Yes doctor." At that point I hand him the catheter while sighing with relief. I knew what he was talking about. We did the x-ray and all goes well. I caused no harm to the patient. The surgery was a total success. I understood this foreign language that this group of people spoke. I was now a part of this group that helps people feel better.

I am now seven years in to my career. I have gone on to become a Certified Surgical Technologist and a Certified Surgical First Assistant. This language that was once a barrier has now become fluent to me. Do I dare to be confident and say I am trilingual? I choose not to but I realize that the career I have chosen is a never ending classroom. There is always something new I can and will always learn. I am no longer medically illiterate, but I will always be a student.

From *First-Year Writing Guide, Thirteenth Edition* By Trent M. Kays, Gen. Ed., Elizabeth Cuddy, Lauren Delacruz, Joyce M. Jarrett, Craig Wynne, Assoc. Eds. Copyright © 2018 by Hampton University. Reprinted by permission.

Definition

FrameStockFootages/Shutterstock.com

One of the obvious reasons why speakers of a shared language are able to communicate is that words have specific, agreed-upon meanings. Sometimes, however, a word might be known to the speaker or writer but not to the listener or reader. Additionally, many words have more than one meaning. These complications can result in miscommunication and sometimes even angry disagreement. Therefore, it's often necessary to define our terms in order to prevent misunderstanding. But there are several kinds of definition, ranging from very simple to more developed.

KINDS OF DEFINITION

When we attempt to define, our topic is always predetermined by the situation at hand, and our reasons for addressing it—in short, our purpose and our audience. As in virtually all writing situations, these considerations will in turn dictate our approach. There are several kinds of definition, each serving a different kind of objective.

Synonym Definition

The most basic form of definition is the *synonym*, a word whose meaning is essentially the same as that of another word—the one being defined. This concept is well-known to anyone who enjoys crossword puzzles or has ever used a thesaurus—essentially a dictionary consisting entirely of synonyms. When using this type of definition, however, it's very important to choose a synonym that will be readily understood. If the synonym and the word or phrase being defined are equally unfamiliar, the definition is useless. For example, to define *coterminous* as *contiguous* would probably accomplish nothing because both words would be unknown to most readers.

Sentence Definition

At the next level is the *formal* or *sentence* definition, which follows a standard format: the term being defined, its class, and the features or characteristics that differentiate it from other members of that class. Conveniently, two such definitions appear above:

Term	Class	Differentiating Characteristics
synonym	word	whose meaning is…the same as…another
thesaurus	dictionary	consisting entirely of synonyms

Stipulative Definition

There is also the *stipulative* definition, which is necessary when a particular word or phrase is subject to multiple interpretations and the speaker or writer wishes to establish which of them applies in the given instance. For example, the term "well-qualified" means different things to different people, so a Human Resources director using that term should define it, perhaps like this: "We are seeking a well-qualified applicant, someone with a college degree and at least three years of experience."

As always, audience analysis is crucial. Someone writing about military service, for example, would have to clearly define any acronyms or terms unique to that environment unless the intended reader(s) also had experience in the armed forces. When uncertain about such matters, it's always best to err on the side of caution. Avoid jargon (specialized or technical language of a particular profession or group) unless you are sure it will be understood, and provide brief parenthetical definitions of any terms that might be unfamiliar. Notice, for example, how the term "jargon" has been clarified here.

Extended Definition

Most challenging is the *extended* definition, an in-depth, essay-length treatment of the term, expression, or concept under consideration. Because on its own it's rather "thin" and uninteresting, extended definition is nearly always used in conjunction with other rhetorical strategies such as description, exemplification, cause and effect, and so on. For instance, the model essay at the end of this section discusses schizophrenia by employing not only definition but also descriptions and examples of specific behaviors throughout. In addition, the essay uses cause and effect, specifying how those actions result in various undesirable outcomes. Thanks to these features, the essay is successful in making its point that schizophrenia is a multifaceted diagnosis, important to pin down precisely.

When employing such approaches to help develop an extended definition, it's best to rank-order and present the examples and other details in "important/more important/most important" sequence. As explained in Chapter 4, this ascending order is always best because it positions the most interesting or convincing material near the end, thereby giving the essay greater forward momentum.

DEFINITION AND PERSUASION

Although the primary purpose of definition is to inform and clarify, extended definition nearly always functions in support of a thesis. As mentioned earlier, the writer might be applying spin, casting the subject in a new light, perhaps to encourage the reader to re-think it. Clearly, the most useful purpose of definition is to persuade.

Let's consider the legal term "plea bargaining," which Barron's *Law Dictionary* defines objectively as "the process whereby the accused and the prosecutor negotiate a mutually satisfactory disposition of the case." But plea bargaining has its opponents, many of whom might define it rather differently in order to discredit it.

For example, Albert Alschuler, Professor Emeritus of Law at Northwestern University and longtime critic of plea bargaining, has provided this definition: "A perfectly designed system to produce convictions of the innocent." Indeed, Alschuler's version served as the basis of a well-argued condemnation of the practice during a 2004 PBS *Frontline* interview. But his definition, while perhaps accurate, is obviously not objective. Still, absolute objectivity is difficult if not impossible to achieve. Even the above dictionary definition could be challenged on the basis that the word "satisfactory" is open to interpretation.

RESEARCH-BASED DEFINITION

In many cases a definition can be derived from observed evidence. An essay about zydeco, for example, might define it simply as "lively, upbeat, accordion-based folk music." Other situations, however, may require a higher level of technical detail. This is extremely difficult—indeed, impossible—unless the writer possesses the necessary knowledge. If not, research must come into play. For example, the *Merriam-Webster* online dictionary defines *zydeco* as "popular music of southern Louisiana that combines tunes of French origin with elements of Caribbean music and the blues and that features guitar, washboard, and accordion." In such cases you must somehow acknowledge the sources of your information, preferably by using a standard system of documentation. In English classes, the Modern Language Association (MLA) style is required. The following model essay, for example, includes parenthetical citations within the text and a correctly formatted Works Cited page crediting the paper's sources.

CHECKLIST: DEFINITION ESSAY

A good definition-based essay

- ▶ Has a meaningful title that clearly identifies the topic

- ▶ Opens with an interesting, attention-getting introduction that establishes the significance of the term, expression, or concept that will be defined, and provides a firm thesis statement

- ▶ Is organized into three or four body paragraphs, covering the topic in a coherent, step-by-step way, focusing on one main idea at a time, in logical sequence

- ▶ Provides enough concrete, specific detail to fully develop the ideas, using examples, descriptions, and other modes of development to clarify the definition

- ▶ Closes with a smooth, meaningful conclusion that gracefully resolves the discussion by somehow relating back to the introduction

- ▶ Uses clear, simple, straightforward language—nothing fancy

- ▶ Maintains an appropriate tone, neither too formal nor too conversational

- ▶ Contains no inappropriate material

- ▶ Contains no typos or mechanical errors in spelling, capitalization, punctuation, or grammar

- ▶ Satisfies the length requirements of the assignment

MODEL DEFINITION ESSAY

Schizophrenia: What Is It?

In the field of abnormal psychology, there are many identifiable conditions that have by now been studied and clearly labeled. Of these, schizophrenia is among the most well-known. Basically, schizophrenia can be defined as a chronic form of psychosis that causes the misinterpretation of reality, resulting in behavioral irregularities. But it's not simply one disorder. Rather, there are a number of variations, all related but distinct (Miller 3). As explained on the Mayo Clinic's Web page on the subject, there are three major kinds of schizophrenia: paranoid, catatonic, and disorganized. For purposes of treatment, it's important to understand the differences among these. (Schizophrenia)

Catatonic schizophrenia is a psychosis that causes the sufferer's conduct to veer from one end of the behavioral spectrum to the other. The person may experience episodes of total immobility, entering a nearly catatonic state in which all ability to communicate or even move is suspended. But the person may also become extremely hyperactive, excitedly pacing, twitching, or flailing around for no apparent reason, grimacing or gesturing inappropriately, or repeatedly mimicking other people's words or movements (Rosa). Clearly, catatonic schizophrenia is extremely disruptive to normal functioning.

Paranoid schizophrenia is a psychosis that causes the sufferer to lose touch with actuality and develop delusional beliefs. Such persons sometimes "hear things" and nearly always imagine that someone is "out to get them." They manage to function reasonably well in everyday situations, but their far-fetched ideas create a range of problems. For example, the paranoid schizophrenic might suffer from anxiety and anger, and may become violent if the delusions are dismissed or ridiculed by others. At the very least, the person's comments typically cause others to disassociate, and the person's consequent emotional isolation and generalized unhappiness and can even lead to suicide. ("Paranoid")

Also known as hebephrenic schizophrenia, disorganized schizophrenia is yet another chronic form of psychosis. The worst kind of schizophrenia, it causes the sufferer to exhibit behaviors that greatly interfere with normal living, because the person's thoughts, words, and actions often follow no logical pattern. As a result, the person may be quite unable to function independently, having no ability to perform necessary activities such as bathing, cooking, getting dressed, and the like. In addition, the person might babble, laugh inappropriately, or even become combative. (Carey)

Clearly, schizophrenia in all its forms is a major problem. Fortunately, however, it is relatively manageable today, thanks to a various medications that can be prescribed. But drugs are only one component of treatment. The patient's treatment plan may also include psychotherapy, psychosocial therapy, electroconvulsive therapy, and—in crisis situations—hospitalization, as well as additional features such as family therapy and vocational training. Treatment teams may also include psychologists, social workers, psychiatric nurses, and a case manager who coordinates the effort ("Schizophrenia"). For any of this to be effective, however, there must first be an accurate diagnosis of what kind of schizophrenia is present.

Works Cited

Carey, Benedict. "Schizophrenia—Disorganized Type." *New York Times*. www.health.nytimes.com. Accessed 10 Feb. 2017.

Miller, Rachel, editor. *Diagnosis: Schizophrenia*. Columbia UP, 2002.

"Paranoid Schizophrenia." *CNN Health*. www.cnn.com/health. Accessed 10 Feb. 2016.

Rosa, Matthew H., M.D. "What is Catatonic Schizophrenia? What Causes Catatonic Schizophrenia?" *Medical News Today*. www.medicalnewstoday.com. Accessed 10 Feb. 2017.

"Schizophrenia: Treatments and Drugs." *Mayo Clinic*. www.mayoclinic.com. Accessed 10 Feb. 2017.

Description

The purpose of description is to provide the reader with a vivid mental picture of the subject: the person, place, or thing described. This is done by including specific details that capture the subject's physical characteristics. Writing instructors often assign an essay whose whole purpose is to describe. However, effective description will energize any essay, allowing the subject—and the writer's attitude toward it—to emerge more clearly. Accordingly, good description not only enables the reader to experience what's being described, but also creates an overall impression of it. Hence, description is a highly effective means of persuasion.

Monkey Business Images/Shutterstock.com

POINT OF VIEW

A description-based essay can employ either first-person or third-person point of view. The choice is determined by the essay's topic and purpose. For example, the writer of the model essay at the end of this section is describing her own room, and is attempting to demonstrate that, as her thesis says, "this room…suits my purposes perfectly." Therefore, she uses first-person point of view. To do otherwise would make little sense in this context.

But in other instances, third-person point of view might be the better choice. For example, this description of upright pianos is entirely objective, with no personal dimension:

> Upright pianos are sometimes called vertical pianos because, although their keyboards look the same as those of grand pianos, their inner workings are perpendicular to the floor. Less expensive than grand pianos and only a few feet wide (as opposed to the five-to-nine feet of grand pianos), they take up much less space and can be found in homes, schools, and bars. Their only real weakness is that their sound quality is not as impressive as that of grand pianos. There are basically three kinds of uprights: the spinet, the console, and the studio. These vary primarily in size; the spinet is about three feet high, the console is a few inches higher, and the studio ranges from about forty-five to fifty inches. There's also the upright player piano, very popular during the early twentieth century but not often seen today. It's really just a gimmick, and requires no actual musicianship. The music is produced automatically by a kind of music box mechanism inside.

Even the seemingly judgmental comments about player pianos are based on verifiable facts with which no musician would disagree. Therefore, third-person point of view is consistently maintained—and fully appropriate—in this paragraph.

ORGANIZATION AND DEVELOPMENT

Good description is well organized, providing details in logical sequence. If the purpose is to describe a personal experience, as in the sample narrative essay that appears earlier in this chapter, *chronological* order is nearly always the best approach, facilitated by the use of transitions. But if the purpose is to describe a place or thing, *spatial* order is usually the appropriate choice. Correct spatial order is partly determined by the writer's vantage point—that is, whether the writer is observing and reporting from a fixed position or is describing while on the move. It's usually better to write descriptions from a fixed vantage point, because this approach makes the organization easier to control. The writer can describe the subject by sequencing the details in a systematic way—from top to bottom, perhaps, or from left to right. Such description often uses special transition words such as the following:

above	in
alongside	inside
behind	near
below	on
between	outside
beyond	under

Notice, for example, how the model descriptive essay at the end of this section uses a fixed vantage point (from the doorway of the room) and uses spatial transitions (*inside, beneath, between,* and others) to describe the room and its furnishings in an orderly way.

SENSORY DETAIL

Our perceptions of physical reality are provided by our five senses: sight, hearing, smell, taste, and touch. Like narration, effective description relies on these. Indeed, it would be impossible to describe anything without stating what it looked like, sounded like, and so forth. While sensory impact is crucial to good descriptive writing, selectivity and specificity are just as important. Rather than burdening the reader with *unnecessary* description, the essay should focus on what's relevant—those key details that will best enable the reader to fully experience the subject. And those details should be expressed concretely rather than in general terms. Simile and metaphor can be quite useful in this context. For example, the phrase "an acrid, skunk-like stench" gives the reader far more information than simply "a bad smell." Here are other examples of bland, unhelpful description followed by revisions enlivened by key sensory details:

SIGHT: He was big

    Revision: He was well over 6′1″ and weighed more than 250 pounds.

SOUND: The machine was making a loud noise.

    Revision: The machine was producing a high-pitched, screeching whine like the noise caused by a loose fan belt.

TASTE: The dessert tasted good.

    Revision: The dessert had a sweet, peachy flavor.

TOUCH: The shirt felt nice.

    Revision: The shirt had a smooth, silky texture.

SUBJECTIVE AND OBJECTIVE DESCRIPTION

When describing a person or a concept, neither chronological nor spatial organization really applies. In those situations, writers sequence the details according to relative importance (usually moving from least to most significant) or from general details to more-specific ones. Of course, this kind of sequencing depends on the writer's judgment about those distinctions. This brings us to the differences between *subjective description* and *objective description*.

Imagine that you have been asked to write two paragraphs: first, a straightforward description of a barn; second, a description of how that same barn might appear to you if you knew that a murder had been committed there. Such an assignment would be certain to produce two very contrasting treatments of the subject. The first paragraph would be observation-based, mentioning the barn's size, color, and other readily noticeable features. Factual and dispassionate, it would probably not differ too greatly from someone else's description of the barn. In short, it would be an example of *objective description*. But the second paragraph would be colored by your awareness of the crime. The barn would not have changed, but you would be seeing it differently now. Hence the resulting description would probably be quite dissimilar from the earlier version. Influenced by personal feelings, it would be an example of *subjective description*.

USING DESCRIPTION TO PERSUADE

Because subjective description is governed by the writer's own attitudes toward the subject, subjective description primarily seeks to influence—unlike objective description, which primarily seeks to inform. But this is more complicated than it seems; most description is a blend of the two. Notice, for instance, that in the model narrative essay, the writer says that his toy pistol "looked very, very real." This is a subjective judgment, but he supports it by providing the objective detail that it was "made of dull black plastic." And when he describes the detective as "a slightly intoxicated old man wearing a suit and tie," the first part of that description is subjective (and perhaps inaccurate) while the mention of the man's clothing is objective. Clearly, subjective and objective description can function in support of each other. But, like a narrative essay or a definition essay, a descriptive essay should not be merely an exercise for its own sake. Rather, it should serve a larger purpose—to convey the dominant impression or controlling idea identified in its introduction. Description usually functions in the service of an essay's thesis.

In the sample descriptive essay at the end of this section, for example, the student plainly states in her introduction that she considers her room ideal for her current circumstances: "this room…suits my purposes perfectly." She then uses an abundance of objective description to reinforce that subjective thesis. The many details that follow in the body paragraphs all serve to support her claim. Notice that the organization of the essay is quite disciplined. She begins by establishing the physical characteristics of the room: its size and shape, the locations and features of windows and doors, and its technical components (heat, lighting, electrical outlets). From there she goes on to describe the décor and furnishings, and finally she describes the personal belongings that make the room recognizably her own. Whether you're writing description or anything else, always strive for that level of orderliness.

CHECKLIST: DESCRIPTIVE ESSAY

A good description-based essay

- ▶ Has a meaningful title that clearly identifies the topic

- ▶ Opens with an interesting, attention-getting introduction that establishes the significance of the person, place, or thing that will be described, and provides a firm thesis statement

- ▶ Is organized into three or four body paragraphs, covering the subject in a coherent, step-by-step way, focusing on one main idea at a time, in logical sequence

- ▶ Provides enough concrete, sensory detail to convey a vivid mental image of the subject

- ▶ Achieves balance between subjective and objective description

- ▶ Closes with a smooth, satisfying conclusion that gracefully resolves the discussion by somehow relating back to the introduction

- ▶ Uses clear, simple, straightforward language—nothing fancy

- ▶ Maintains an appropriate tone, neither too formal nor too conversational

- ▶ Contains no inappropriate material

- ▶ Contains no typos or mechanical errors in spelling, capitalization, punctuation, or grammar

- ▶ Satisfies the length requirements of the assignment

MODEL DESCRIPTIVE ESSAY

My Room: A Home Away From Home

When I enrolled at County Community College, I had to find suitable living arrangements somewhere nearby. Luckily, I was able to rent a comfortable furnished room in a relatively crime-free neighborhood within walking distance of campus, in a house owned by Mrs. Greene, an elderly widow. This has turned out to be an excellent arrangement. I have kitchen privileges, my own bathroom, and very reasonable rent. In return, I'm supposed to keep my room and bathroom clean, help with household chores like mowing the lawn, shoveling snow, and dragging the garbage can out to the curb every week. That's fine with me, because Mrs. Greene needs the assistance and I need this room, which suits my purposes perfectly.

Located just inside the back door of the house and right next to my bathroom, the room is fairly small, no more than fifteen feet square, but it has a ten-foot ceiling that makes it feel bigger. In addition to my door, which is equipped with a lock, there are three windows that make the room bright and airy, two on the wall that's to your right when you enter and one on the wall directly in front of you. All three windows are covered by adjustable white venetian blinds and there's a heat vent beneath each of them. There's an oval ceiling light and several convenient electrical outlets built into the baseboards. Strangely, there's no closet, but there are three coat-hooks on the back of the door and that's all I really need because I don't have a lot of clothing. The room is painted beige, with white woodwork.

As I said, the room is furnished, and it has light brown wall-to-wall carpeting. My bed, covered with a red blanket, is against the left-hand (windowless) wall. The window in the wall straight ahead of you is surrounded on all sides by built-in, floor-to-ceiling bookcases painted white. There's a comfortable tan corduroy easy chair in the right corner, with a floor lamp behind it. Between the two windows in the right-hand wall is a brown, six-drawer bureau. There's a large wooden desk and matching chair positioned on the last wall, to the right of the door as you enter.

There's plenty of room for my belongings. In fact, I use some of the bookshelves for storing shoes, sweaters, and other clothing, along with my textbooks and other school supplies. Also on the shelves are six trophies I've won in local running races, and my three favorite stuffed animals. I have a few decorations on the walls: my high school diploma, a framed photo of my parents and brother, and a framed poster of the late Grete Waitz, a famous marathoner who has always been an inspiration to me. Hanging from a hook is my old field hockey stick. Although I no longer play that sport, seeing the stick brings back many great high school memories. I have to admit that the desk is pretty cluttered, holding not only a lamp, an alarm clock, and my computer, but piles of books, magazines, and school-related papers, along with a stapler and a college mug containing pens, pencils, a small ruler, a letter opener, and a pair of scissors.

Nobody could ever accuse me of living the lifestyle of the rich and famous, but for now this room is all I need. It's safe, affordable, adequately furnished, conveniently located, and large enough for my needs, and I'm lucky to have found it. Moreover, Mrs. Greene and I have become good friends, so I expect to be here until I graduate.

Exemplification

Sometimes called *illustration*, this essay development strategy supports and clarifies the thesis statement by providing specific examples that move the essay forward, beyond mere generalization. In short, the thesis statement tells the reader what the essay is about, but the examples *show*, taking the discussion from the abstract to the concrete and preventing pointless repetition. Examples can reinforce an easily understood thesis (e.g., "a longer school day will not actually improve student performance"), but can

also be used to illustrate difficult or unfamiliar concepts (e.g., "economy of scale"). In either case, examples must always be accurate, relevant, and interesting. Among the most common kinds are statistics, pertinent facts, anecdotal evidence, and expert opinion.

Of course, examples should be lively and engaging, to ensure that the reader will remain interested in the discussion. Therefore, highly technical examples should be avoided, unless the intended reader can be assumed to possess the knowledge or training necessary to understand such references. This is true whether exemplification is the essay's governing approach or not. If the topic of any essay requires specialized examples, they must be clarified in layperson's terms. Notice, for instance, how the model definition-based essay that appears earlier in this chapter accommodates the uninitiated reader. The three categories of schizophrenia—catatonic, paranoid, and hebephrenic—are illustrated by plainly-worded examples of specific behaviors typical of each.

POINT OF VIEW

Like most kinds of writing, exemplification-based essays ordinarily employ third-person point of view. There's usually nothing to be gained by using the subjective first-person approach when presenting factual information. The one exception to this would be an essay in which exemplification were used to discuss the writer's personal experiences in support of the thesis. An example might be an essay in which the writer challenges the concept of gender stereotypes and provides three or four examples of personal friends who transcend those broad assumptions. Of course, most essays of any kind seek to argue a point and provide support for the writer's personal opinions, as in the model essay at the end of this section. Notice how that essay employs a blend of first- and third-person narration to achieve its purposes.

ORGANIZATION AND DEVELOPMENT

Unless your approach to the topic requires a chronological handling, examples should be presented in ascending order of importance, with the most compelling examples appearing last. But an exemplification-based essay can be organized in several other ways as well:

▶ It can build on one specific example that's mentioned within the thesis statement. The body paragraphs of the essay would then provide sub-examples—examples of the example, so to speak. Such a thesis statement might look something like this: "Although good food is fundamental to a restaurant's success, other factors are also crucial; the wait staff, for example, can make or break an establishment." The essay would then go on to provide examples of good and bad service.

▶ A more common strategy, however, is to proceed from a broader thesis statement and then provide varied illustrations of that generalization. An essay seeking to defend the thesis that athletic stardom does not necessarily make someone a worthy role model could be supported by a series of one-paragraph discussions of individual athletes' bad behavior. This is the approach used in the model essay at the end of this section.

RESEARCH-BASED EXEMPLIFICATION

Any thesis statement is essentially an expression of the writer's opinion. To defend your thesis—especially if it's controversial—it's sometimes advisable to go beyond personal experience and provide authoritative examples more likely to convince the reader. Therefore, it may be necessary to conduct research, drawing upon statistics, case studies, expert opinion, and the like. Although an exemplification essay need not become a full-blown research project, there's nothing wrong with using quotation, paraphrase, or other supporting details from reputable sources to reinforce your position. As always when using outside sources, documentation is required.

To serve their purpose, examples must be typical and *representative*, rather than unusual or outlying. A quote from a scientist who's a global warming denier, for instance, would be unpersuasive because the scientific community is nearly unanimous in recognizing the dangers of climate change. But an NRA spokesperson's condemnation of gun control legislation would be a valid example, because that large and influential organization strongly opposes such restrictions. For that matter, such a statement could even operate in reverse, serving as a *negative* example in an essay attempting to discredit the NRA's position. Genuinely representative examples can be used with equal effectiveness to bolster opposing viewpoints on the same issue. Of course, the way in which examples are used—positively or negatively—will depend on the essay's thesis.

CHECKLIST: EXEMPLIFICATION ESSAY

A good example-based essay

- ► Has a meaningful title that clearly identifies the topic

- ► Opens with an interesting, attention-getting introduction that again identifies the topic, establishes its significance, and provides a firm thesis statement

- ► Is organized into three or four body paragraphs, covering the topic in a coherent, step-by-step way, focusing on one main idea at a time, progressing from the abstract to the concrete

- ► Provides enough typical, representative examples to fully support the thesis

- ► Organizes support in ascending order of importance

- ► Closes with a smooth, satisfying conclusion that gracefully resolves the discussion by somehow relating back to the introduction

- ► Uses clear, simple, straightforward language—nothing fancy

- ► Maintains an appropriate tone, neither too formal nor too conversational

- ► Contains no inappropriate material

- ► Contains no typos or mechanical errors in spelling, capitalization, punctuation, or grammar

- ► Satisfies the length requirements of the assignment

MODEL EXEMPLIFICATION ESSAY

Conversationalists from Hell

The basic theme of French philosopher Jean Paul Sartre's famous 1944 play "No Exit" can be summed up rather concisely: Hell is other people. Fortunately, most of us would be reluctant to adopt such a dreary perspective. Indeed, it's a given that our most meaningful experiences in life derive from our relationships with others. Sometimes, however, I'm tempted to suspect that Sartre was actually onto something—especially when I encounter certain particularly irritating habits among people with whom I must interact.

For example, there are certain individuals who simply do not understand the concept of the "rhetorical question." You must never say "Hi! How are you?" when encountering these folks, because you'll be required to stand there for at least a half an hour, nodding with feigned commiseration while being regaled with a seemingly endless catalog of complaints, grievances, and generalized whining. This is especially tiresome if the tale of woe involves medical difficulties. Social norms require such bellyaching to be received sympathetically, even when we suspect that the malady is being exaggerated, or—worse—if we've heard it all before. If only they'd they just lie and say, "Fine, thanks. And you?"

In a similar vein, there are those intensely annoying characters who feel obliged to "one-up" whomever they're conversing with, especially at the workplace lunch table or break room. If you happen to mention that your cousin just won a Mercedes Benz in a raffle, there's always the co-worker who will counter with an anecdote about *his* cousin, who just won a full-sized, working replica of the Starship Enterprise. You know it's absolute nonsense, in part because you've seen this act before (repeatedly!). And it's insulting because the implication is that you're gullible enough to swallow such malarkey. But again, social norms prevent you from calling him out. That would be giving him too much importance. Besides, what if—just this once—he's telling the truth? So you're exasperated once again.

Perhaps my pet peeve, however, involves people who have no sense of phone etiquette. There are few experiences more deeply aggravating than to engage in conversation with one of these knuckleheads, and realize that you're involved in unwitting competition with their mobile device. They're talking to you, yes, but all the while glancing down at incoming text messages, giving you—at best—half their attention. This maddening gaffe is so widespread that it was the subject of a December 2015 Doonesbury cartoon, in which the title character actually walks away from his wife, who continues to text, not even realizing he's gone. A comic strip, but all too real.

What all three of these examples have in common is a basic lack of consideration. It might also be seen as simple arrogance, the underlying belief that other people's needs must take a back seat to our own. When that kind of dynamic is at work, it's tempting to embrace Sartre's pessimistic message. Luckily, however, the behaviors discussed here are still exceptions rather than norms, so we need not despair—tempting though it can sometimes seem when confronted with boorish conduct.

Comparison and Contrast

In everyday life we often compare and contrast in order to make routine decisions. At lunch, for example, we might be torn between the healthful salad and the "heart attack special." The same is true of large, life-altering choices; when selecting a college, a job, or even a mate, we must evaluate the available options. Of course, the lunchtime scenario involves a quick, "on the fly" (perhaps even subconscious) decision, while these other examples would require true deliberation. Indeed, in the latter context it's advisable to actually write down a list of the similarities and differences of the two or more competing alternatives in order to identify their relative advantages and disadvantages—in other words, to conduct a

cost/benefit analysis. It would be unwise not to, because it's important to organize our thoughts. Certainly this is equally true when attempting to compose a comparison/contrast essay in response to an assignment.

This kind of essay explores similarities and/or differences between two related subjects in order to shed light on both, and—often—to demonstrate that one is preferable to the other. Another common purpose is to show that two subjects that seem very different are actually similar, or vice-versa. Accordingly, the introduction must identify the two subjects, indicate that they will be compared and/or contrasted, and provide a firm thesis statement that reflects the essay's larger purpose and intentions. Ideally, the essay will go beyond the obvious, pointing out similarities and/or differences that are not immediately apparent. And, to be convincing, the essay should focus on at least three shared characteristics of the two subjects.

POINT OF VIEW

A biology test might require you to compare and contrast DNA and RNA; an art exam might require you to discuss contrasting features of early and late Renaissance painting; a history exam might ask you to discuss how the contrasting approaches of Malcolm X and Martin Luther King served their common objectives. In each case, the subjects under consideration are related to each other in some meaningful way, belonging to the same class or category. If they weren't, the whole exercise would be pointless or even absurd. It's possible to compare a peach and a pear, because both are foods—specifically, fruit. But it would be silly to compare a peach and a pork chop; although both are foods, they belong to entirely different categories of food, rendering comparison meaningless. The subjects must share a fundamental basis of similarity, upon which a treatment of their differences can be built. Otherwise, it becomes impossible to devise a worthwhile thesis—a controlling idea that gives the essay its direction.

The thesis in a comparison/contrast essay should not simply state the obvious fact that the two subjects are alike and/or different. It must go a step further, establishing why these parallel features are meaningful. Here's an example of a weak (because self-evident) thesis, coupled with a revised version that identifies the real point:

Weak Thesis: Los Angeles and San Francisco are the two most important cities in California, but they are very different.

Revision: The differences between Los Angeles and San Francisco clearly reflect the contrasting histories of California's two most important cities.

Notice, however, that in comparison/contrast essays—as in most kinds of writing—the purpose is to defend a position, make a point. Therefore, the objective third-person point of view is again preferable to subjective first-person narration.

ORGANIZATION AND DEVELOPMENT

If you're experiencing difficulty formulating a thesis, you might not have devoted enough time to pre-writing. For example, creating lists of the similarities and differences between the two subjects will enable you to determine the three or four most *significant* ways in which they're alike or different, and this can lead you to your real point. One interesting strategy is to play *devil's advocate* (presenting a viewpoint that contradicts the consensus). If the subjects are basically alike, you may want to focus on the most important way in which they differ. Conversely, if they are clearly dissimilar, you may want to find the most relevant point of similarity. Here are examples of both kinds of thesis.

> The laptop computer and the iPad are essentially alike, performing many of the same functions. But the latter has at least one distinct advantage; its much smaller size makes it lighter and therefore more conveniently portable.

> Although Ezra Pound and T. S. Eliot were very different poets, they did share one characteristic in addition to their considerable fame: a deplorable strain of anti-Semitism that must negatively affect our estimate of both.

Sometimes your list-making will reveal that there are actually more similarities than you'd originally supposed, or more differences. Such a discovery can be troubling, because now you're fighting an uphill battle. The solution? Simply adjust your thesis, reversing it in response to this new evidence. This kind of situation is another illustration of the fact that writing helps us clarify our own thinking.

SUBJECT-BASED STRUCTURE VS. CHARACTERISTIC-BASED STRUCTURE

A comparison/contrast essay can be structured in either of two ways. The discussion can begin by dealing with the first subject and its characteristics and then move on to deal with the second subject and its parallel characteristics. This approach is a bit unwieldy, however, because it results in an essay with two fairly lengthy "middle" paragraphs rather than the customary three or four. In effect, it becomes two mini-essays spliced together. Additionally, it requires the reader to hold in memory everything that's been said about the first subject while reading about the second.

On the other hand, this can actually work to your advantage if you're deliberately trying to discredit the first subject in order to promote the second. Nevertheless, a more typical approach is to discuss one *characteristic* at a time. The following chart, which represents a hypothetical essay discussing two baseball teams, illustrates the two differing approaches.

Approach # 1 (Subject-Based)
Introduction
Team A—fielding, hitting, pitching
Team B—fielding, hitting, pitching
Conclusion

Approach # 2 (Characteristic-Based)
Introduction
Fielding—Team A & Team B
Hitting—Team A & Team B
Pitching—Team A & Team B
Conclusion

When using Approach #2, it's appropriate to deal with both similarities and differences when discussing each characteristic. The paragraph about pitching, for example, might develop like this:

Both teams have deep pitching staffs, with both right-handed and left-handed hurlers, and both teams have two effective relief pitchers. In addition, both pitching staffs are relatively young, averaging about twenty-five years of age. But statistics reveal that during the past three seasons Team B's lefties have a far lower earned-run average than Team A's, and Team B's relief pitchers have recorded more saves. In addition, Team B's pitching coach is far more respected than Team A's; in fact, he's considered one of the best in the game. Clearly, Team B has the advantage when it comes to pitching.

As shown on the previous page, the essay should deal with the same three or four characteristics for each subject. Importantly, these characteristics must be relevant and meaningful. It would be pointless, for example, to discuss the similarities and/or differences between the two teams' uniforms, because these would in no way influence the teams' performance. In addition, the characteristics of the two subjects should be covered in the same sequence, moving from simplest to most complex. This ensures that the discussion will be balanced in its treatment of the two subjects, thereby avoiding the appearance of bias.

TRANSITIONS

As mentioned throughout this book, transitions are very helpful. Chronologically oriented transitions appear in narrative writing and spatial transitions in descriptive writing. Since comparison/contrast is by its very nature directly concerned with similarities and differences, this kind of essay benefits greatly from the use of transitions that relate accordingly. Words and expressions like *and, similarly,* and *likewise* (to reinforce similarity) and *but, conversely, on the contrary,* and *on the other hand* (to reinforce difference) and others go a long way toward conveying the points being made. Notice how transitions (underlined) function in this paragraph.

The lead guitar and the bass guitar are similar in some respects. Both are electrified string instruments fundamental to jazz, rock, and other kinds of popular music. <u>On the other hand</u>, they are quite different in a number of ways. The lead guitar has a fretted neck, while the bass guitar's neck is sometimes fretless. With its six strings, the lead guitar can produce a broad range of notes. <u>Conversely</u>, the bass guitar's four heavier strings produce only lowernotes, as the instrument's name reflects. The dominant lead guitar appears to stand apart, independent. <u>But</u> this is an illusion. The unobtrusive bass plays an equally important role, interacting with the drums to provide a supportive foundation on which the lead very much depends.

SIMILE, METAPHOR, ANALOGY

When using comparison/contrast, whether as an end in itself or in the service of some other strategy, *similes* and *metaphors* are quite helpful in clarifying the subject matter. Basically, simile involves a comparison using the words "like" or "as." Metaphor, on the other hand, does not use those words, and simply equates the two things being compared, often by using some form of the verb "to be" (is, are, was, were, will be).

mark reinstein/Shutterstock.com

Simile: "Float like a butterfly, sting like a bee" (Muhammad Ali)

Metaphor: "All the world's a stage" (Shakespeare)

Analogy is yet another creative form of comparison. Basically an extended simile or metaphor, it typically compares one thing to another in order to illustrate or dramatize the latter of the two, enabling the reader to better envision it. The names of many tools and similar devices are essentially analogies; think *claw* hammer, *C* clamp, and *T* square. In the sports world, analogies abound. In football we have the *blitz* and the *Hail Mary*, in baseball the *stolen* base and the *double-header*, in basketball the *travelling* violation and the *stutter-step*. In the same way, we employ analogy when we speak of an *avalanche* of data, a *tsunami* of bad news, a *landslide* election victory, or a legal decision that *opens the floodgates*. But analogies can be far more developed than these compact terms. Here's an example.

> The student who becomes entrapped in a poorly-taught online course faces the same predicament as Kafka's hapless, groping protagonists in his novels *The Castle* and *The Trial*. Despite their best efforts, those characters cannot determine what's expected of them, and wholesale confusion results. In much the same way, the frustrated student lacks clear directions or regular, constructive feedback from the instructor, and must operate on instinct, relying largely on guesswork when attempting to satisfy course requirements.

USING COMPARISON AND CONTRAST TO PERSUADE

Since your purpose in a comparison/contrast essay is usually to persuade the reader that one subject is superior to another, it makes sense to give "your" subject the advantage of having the last word by always discussing it second. This was mentioned in Chapter 7 and illustrated by the baseball example provided earlier in this chapter. Team B has a clear advantage because in both approaches its characteristics can function in refutation or contradiction of Team A's. Coupled with third-person point of view, this is a very effective strategy.

CHECKLIST: COMPARISON/CONTRAST ESSAY

A good comparison/contrast-based essay

- ▶ Has a meaningful title that clearly identifies the topic

- ▶ Opens with an interesting, attention-getting introduction that again identifies the topic, clearly reveals whether the essay will focus on similarities or differences, and provides a firm thesis statement

- ▶ Is organized into three or four body paragraphs, covering the topic in a coherent, step-by-step way, focusing on one main idea at a time, in logical sequence

- ▶ Employs either a subject-based or characteristic-based approach

- ▶ Provides enough concrete, specific detail to fully develop the ideas (perhaps using simile, metaphor, or analogy)

- ▶ Closes with a smooth, satisfying conclusion that gracefully resolves the discussion by somehow relating back to the introduction

- ▶ Uses clear, simple, straightforward language—nothing fancy

- ▶ Maintains an appropriate tone, neither too formal nor too conversational

- ▶ Contains no inappropriate material

- ▶ Contains no typos or mechanical errors in spelling, capitalization, punctuation, or grammar

- ▶ Satisfies the length requirements of the assignment

MODEL COMPARISON/CONTRAST ESSAY

Rover and Kitty: The Odd Couple

Of all the household pets, dogs and cats are certainly the most common. And although many people own at least one of each, it's typical to prefer one species over the other. This is understandable because—despite their obvious similarities—dogs and cats are very different animals. Dogs, for example, say "Bow Wow," while cats say "Meow Meow." But the contrasts go far beyond their vocabularies.

For starters, dogs are territorial and protective. If a stranger (or even the letter carrier) comes to your door, the dog will immediately announce himself, barking and maybe even snarling, as if to say, "This is OUR house! Keep your hands where I can see them and don't try any funny business." The cat, on the other hand, will probably ignore the person's arrival, or perhaps scurry away and fall asleep under the sofa. There are advantages and disadvantages to both behaviors. While most dogs will protect you from intruders, their frequent barking and howling can annoy the neighbors and become a real nuisance. Worse, dogs have been known to attack for little reason. Ever notice how many are muzzled? Conversely, the cat is no help in a crisis, but her quiet, understated demeanor makes her less likely to become an aggravation, and she's surely not a danger to anyone. She'll never get you sued.

Dogs crave attention, and need a lot of tender, loving care. Among other things, this involves training, to moderate their naturally rambunctious and destructive tendencies. They must be taught manners and self-control. This can take a lot of time and effort, and requires a great deal of patience. Unfortunately, many dog owners neglect this responsibility and wind up with a canine felon on their hands. And—for obvious reasons—even well-trained, perfectly behaved pups still need to be walked, sometimes very early in the morning…in all weather. Training the cat? Forget about it. She'll sharpen her nails on the upholstery no matter what you do to discourage her. But she's aloof and independent, requiring nothing much more than a couple of square meals a day and a clean litter box. She comes and goes as she pleases, and as long as she doesn't get run over by a car, that's that.

As for companionship, the differences are again apparent. The dog gives constant feedback, panting excitedly, jumping about, and enthusiastically agreeing to practically any kind of game. He'll shake hands, roll over, play dead. He'll chase a stick, he'll swim with you, and he loves to go out for a run. True, most kittens also like to goof around, but the adult cat withholds affection. She'll rub against your leg, sit in your lap, and purr contentedly when petted—but only when she's in the mood. In short, she calls the shots. It's her ball, her gym, her game.

Bottom line? Pet ownership is like most things in life. There are trade-offs. The dopey dog is high maintenance, but he'll reward you more generously. The clever cat doesn't ask for much at all, but she owns you, rather than the other way around. Maybe that's the cat's appeal. We love our dogs, but we continue to accommodate and pamper our cats because on some level we suspect they may actually be smarter than we are.

Process Analysis

There are two kinds of process analysis: informational and instructive. Informational process analysis clarifies how something happens. An example would be an explanation of how rust forms or how soil erosion occurs. Clearly, the purpose of such writing is not to enable the reader to perform the process, but simply to understand it. Instructive process analysis, on the other hand, does explain how to perform a particular procedure. An example would be an essay about how to apply the Heimlich maneuver or negotiate the purchase of a new car. In college writing classes, process analysis assignments are usually instructive in nature. Accordingly, this section focuses primarily on that kind of process analysis.

$$f(x) = \sum_{i=0}^{\infty} \frac{f^{(i)}(0)}{i!} x^i$$

Africa Rising/Shutterstock.com

PROCESS ANALYSIS IN RELATION TO OTHER MODES

Clearly, process analysis is related to other kinds of essay development. It resembles narrative, for example, because it's chronological. It often involves definition and/or description because—depending on the procedure being explained—certain terms and objects might have to be identified. And process is always related to cause and effect because the whole purpose of following those steps is to ensure a desired outcome. Perhaps most importantly, process analysis can certainly function to persuade, as in an anti-hazing essay deploring what a fraternity pledge must endure when subjected to demeaning and dangerous initiation rituals. Similarly, an instructive process analysis essay outlining healthy pre-natal practices can serve to encourage responsible behavior by expectant mothers. Clearly, process analysis can be a highly effective tool of persuasion.

POINT OF VIEW

Like any other essay, a process analysis paper should open with an effective introduction that provides a thesis—a firm statement not only of what the reader will learn how to do, but also why it's worthwhile to know. Consider these examples:

> **Thesis:** When using Microsoft Word to create a document, it's important to know how to move text from one location to another.

> **Revised Thesis:** When using Microsoft Word to create a document, it's important to know how to move text from one location to another, because the ability to "cut and paste" will enable you to avoid unnecessary re-typing.

Notice, however, that this revised thesis uses the word "you," as if the writer were actually addressing the reader in conversation. This is the most effective narrative approach to employ in process analysis. But it's not first-person point of view, because the emphasis should be on the reader rather than the writer. Therefore, the word "I" should not appear. Like most kinds of writing, then, process analysis uses third-person point of view, but with the kind of reader-centered perspective discussed in Chapter 3.

ORGANIZATION AND DEVELOPMENT

In addition to providing necessary context and establishing the thesis, the introduction (or perhaps the first body paragraph) should identify any required tools or other equipment. The body paragraphs of the essay should then walk the reader through the procedure, following a logical, step-by-step chronology and providing all pertinent details, presented in the form of simple, active commands, like this: "Push the red button, then push the blue button." But if two actions must be performed simultaneously, they should be combined. For example, instead of saying, "Push the blue lever forward. Before releasing the blue lever, push the red button," say this: "While holding the blue lever forward, push the red button."

And, for the sake of both convenience and safety, it's important to alert the reader to anything that might go wrong, and provide "troubleshooting" suggestions about how to prevent or solve such problems, as in the following paragraph about operating a gasoline-powered snow thrower.

> If the machine begins to vibrate excessively, there may be loose parts or a damaged auger. Stop the engine immediately, disconnect the spark plug wire, and tighten all nuts and bolts. Reconnect the spark plug wire and restart the engine. If the vibration continues, have the machine serviced by a qualified technician.

Although logical organization is a fundamental requirement of all writing, it's especially crucial in process analysis because the steps involved in most procedures must be performed in order, with no deviation. Perhaps more than any other kind of essay, therefore, process analysis requires extensive pre-writing exercises, to guarantee that nothing is left out or mis-sequenced. A good way to test the sequencing of your process analysis is to observe while someone unfamiliar with the procedure attempts to perform it while reading your essay. But for this test to be valid, you must resist the temptation to provide assistance if the person hesitates or expresses uncertainty. This will enable you to detect problems and revise accordingly. Another effective test is to ask someone who *is* familiar with the procedure to critique your essay. Even better, subject your essay to both forms of evaluation.

TRANSITIONS

In process analysis, transition words and phrases are especially helpful in clarifying the relationships among the steps in the procedure. Terms like "first," "next," "then," and "finally" are quite helpful to the reader. What's not helpful, however, is the adoption of what might be called "recipe style," in which short words like "a" and "the" are left out.

The omission of such words creates a choppy, disjointed effect that actually interferes with the reader's comprehension. Notice the differences between these two explanations of how to control the temperature of a two-burner electric hot plate.

> **Original:** Use control knobs to adjust temperature of heating coils. Turn knobs clockwise to raise temperature, counter-clockwise to lower temperature.

> **Revision:** Use the control knobs to adjust the temperature of the heating coils. Turn the knobs clockwise to raise the temperature, counter-clockwise to lower the temperature.

We sometimes talk about people's ability to envision things in their "mind's eye," but it's equally important to consider the "mind's ear" because readers mentally "hear" as they process text. For this reason, the more conventional phrasing of the above revision is preferable to the original.

CHECKLIST: PROCESS ANALYSIS ESSAY

A good process analysis-based essay

- ▶ Has a meaningful title that clearly identifies the topic

- ▶ Opens with an interesting, attention-getting introduction that again identifies the topic, establishes why the procedure is important to master, and provides a firm thesis statement

- ▶ Identifies all necessary equipment, tools, and materials

- ▶ Is organized into three or four body paragraphs, covering the topic in a coherent, step-by-step way, focusing on one main idea at a time, in chronological sequence

- ▶ Provides enough concrete, specific detail to fully explain the procedure

- ▶ Closes with a smooth, satisfying conclusion that gracefully resolves the discussion by somehow relating back to the introduction

- ▶ Uses clear, simple, straightforward language—nothing fancy

- ▶ Maintains an appropriate tone, neither too formal nor too conversational

- ▶ Contains no inappropriate material

- ▶ Contains no typos or mechanical errors in spelling, capitalization, punctuation, or grammar

- ▶ Satisfies the length requirements of the assignment

MODEL PROCESS ANALYSIS ESSAY

How to Change a Flat Tire

Nearly every motorist experiences a flat tire sooner or later. Therefore, you should be prepared for such a situation. To change a tire you'll need the following items, which should be carried in your trunk at all times: at least six flares, a properly-inflated spare tire, a lug wrench, a wide wooden board, and a jack. Changing a flat is fairly simple, but the correct procedure must be followed to prevent injury or vehicle damage.

As soon as you realize you're developing a flat, drive the car onto the road shoulder. Park as far from the road as you can, and on as flat and level a surface as possible. Activate the warning flashers, put the transmission in park, set the emergency brake, and turn off the engine. If your car has a standard transmission, put it in reverse. Open the trunk and set up the flares behind and in front of the car as a signal to other drivers.

Remove the spare and other equipment from the trunk. If your lug nuts are visible, you're ready to proceed. But if they're hidden by a hub cap, use the jack handle to pry it off. Using the lug wrench, fully loosen—but do not remove—the nuts by turning them counter-clockwise. If they're reverse-threaded and must therefore be turned clockwise, there will be an "L" on each lug bolt. Removal of the lug nuts is the only difficult part of the task, because it requires some physical strength. A very long-handled lug wrench is helpful, because it provides greater leverage. A common practice is to use your foot to push down on the wrench handle.

Since there are several kinds of jacks, consult your owner's manual for proper assembly and use, and then position the jack. If the ground is soft, put the wooden board under the jack base to stabilize it. Jack up the car until the flat is just clear of the ground, and remove the jack handle. The handle should always be removed when you're not using it, because this prevents you from accidentally knocking into it and dislodging the jack—a dangerous error. Remove the lug nuts by hand and put them into your pocket or into the hubcap for safekeeping. Remove the flat. Roll the spare into position and put it on the wheel by aligning the holes in the rim with the lug bolts on the wheel. You may have to jack the vehicle up a bit more to accomplish this, as the properly inflated spare will be fatter than the flat and will therefore require more ground clearance. Holding the spare firmly against the wheel with one hand, use your other hand to manually replace the lug nuts as tightly as possible. Do *not* use the wrench.

Lower the car back down. Now you may use the wrench to fully tighten the nuts. To ensure even distribution of stress, tighten the nuts a little at a time, moving from one to another repeatedly in a diagonal pattern. Finally, put the flat, jack, and other tools back into the trunk. Don't bother to replace the hubcap until you get home, but when you do, make sure that the tire valve is correctly positioned, protruding through the hole in the hubcap. You may need to tap the hubcap into place with a rubber mallet.

If correct procedure is followed, most people are able to change a flat tire successfully. Knowing the procedure is no help, however, unless all the necessary tools are in your trunk, along with a properly-inflated spare tire. For this reason, it's important to check the air pressure of the spare from time to time, thereby enabling yourself to use it if necessary.

Cause and Effect

Sometimes called "causal analysis," cause and effect writing attempts to explore the relationship between events and their origins. It can focus on the reasons (causes) for a particular outcome, on the end results themselves (effects), or on both. This can get complicated: one cause can have multiple effects and vice-versa; multiple causes can produce multiple effects; and sometimes a chain of causation exists, in which a cause leads to an effect that becomes the cause of another effect, and so on. In college writing classes, however, the most common kind of assignment involves identifying the several main causes of one effect or the several main effects of one cause. Therefore, this chapter focuses mainly on those approaches.

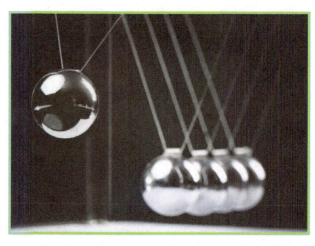

ilkercelik/Shutterstock.com

Like most writing, causal analysis is essentially informative. But it can also be an effective strategy for arguing a point, either by explaining how one or more causes bring about one or more (desirable or undesirable) effects, or by focusing on one or more effects resulting from one or more causes. In other words, the "cause" focus answers the question "Why?" and the "effect" focus answers the question "What?" In this regard, it's useful to understand that causal analysis can be approached in the context of past, present, or future, as in these examples:

Cause	Effect
Why **did** X happen?	What **was** the effect of X?
Why **does** X happen?	What **is** the effect of X?
Why **will** X happen?	What **will be** the effect of X?

In other words, causal analysis can be used to explain events occurring in the past, the present, and the future. Clearly, then, it has broad applications.

POINT OF VIEW

Like most kinds of writing, cause and effect essays ordinarily employ third-person point of view. As already mentioned, there's usually nothing to be gained by using the subjective first-person approach when presenting factual information. The one exception to this would be an essay in which cause and effect were used to discuss the writer's personal experiences in support of the thesis. An example might be an essay in which the writer outlines the negative consequences of substance abuse and draws upon personal experience to illustrate those outcomes. Of course, most essays of any kind seek to argue a point and provide support for the writer's personal opinions, as in the model essay at the end of this section. Nevertheless, unless the examples are of a personal nature, as in the substance abuse essay, a third-person approach is still the better choice because it creates the impression of objectivity and is therefore more persuasive.

ORGANIZATION AND DEVELOPMENT

Like any essay, a cause and effect paper must have a clear thesis statement that establishes the approach to the topic, like this: "Although some overweight people blame their condition on heredity, it seems more likely that our nationwide obesity epidemic is actually the result of two main causes: poor eating habits and lack of exercise."

Notice, however, that this thesis statement carefully avoids overstating its case. The wordings "some people" and "seems more likely" are wise choices, because causation is extremely complex, quite difficult to prove absolutely. For the sake of credibility, therefore, a somewhat tentative thesis statement is always appropriate in causal analysis.

Once the causes are identified, they must be presented in the most effective order. If the causes occur in chronological sequence, then the essay could be arranged that way. But this is not always the case. When arranging non-chronological causes, it's best to begin with the simplest causes and move on to the more complex ones. And, since the points being made in a cause and effect essay are by their nature interrelated, it's helpful to use transitions—words and expressions like "accordingly," "therefore," "as a result," and "consequently"—a bit more often than usual to help the reader make the connections.

KINDS OF CAUSES

There are three main kinds of causes.

- ▶ Necessary Cause: Something that must happen in order for a given outcome to occur.

  A PIN number is necessary in order to conduct an ATM transaction.

- ▶ Sufficient Cause: Something that could cause a given outcome.

  Head injuries often result in death.

- ▶ Precipitating Cause: The final, "triggering" cause in a series of causes in which the first cause results in an effect that then becomes the cause of the following effect, and so on, until the final effect.

  The driver became distracted while texting, veered into oncoming traffic, over-corrected, lost control of his car, swerved off the road, struck a utility pole, and totaled the vehicle.

In the above example, the precipitating cause could also be called the *main* or *direct* or *immediate* cause, while the driver's earlier errors could be called the *contributing* or *indirect* or *remote* causes. These are all common terms in discussions of cause and effect. When writing a causal analysis essay, however, it's unwise to overload the discussion with remote causes because it will not be possible to include them all in three or four body paragraphs without the essay becoming simply a boring catalog or list, rather than an interesting, in-depth discussion.

CAUSATION VS. COINCIDENCE

When writing a causal analysis essay you must avoid the *post hoc ergo propter hoc* fallacy mentioned in Chapter 7. As explained there, this is a Latin phrase meaning "after this, therefore because of this." But X does not necessarily cause Y simply because X happens first. Although there is a chronological sequence of events, there may or may not be a causal relationship. Consider this example:

> Tyler had a heated argument with his brother this morning. Therefore, he failed his math exam this afternoon.

While it's safe to say that the argument probably didn't *improve* Tyler's powers of concentration (or his knowledge of math), there is no proof that it caused him to flunk the test. The fact that the argument and the exam happened on the same day is mere coincidence. There were probably a great many other, more influential reasons for Tyler's failure. Most of us are able to recognize and avoid the *post hoc* fallacy when considering everyday situations such as Tyler's, but it's a bit more difficult when writing about complex subject matter. So it's important to remember that without valid evidence, there is no justification for assuming causation.

RESEARCH-BASED CAUSAL ANALYSIS

As in any information-based essay, a causal analysis paper's claims must be valid assertions, reinforced by evidence. This often requires research in order to gather proof—statistics, quotes, verifiable facts. Although a causal analysis essay need not become a full-blown research project, there's nothing wrong with using quotation, paraphrase, or other supporting details from reputable sources to bolster your discussion. As always when using outside sources, you must somehow acknowledge those authorities, either by using formal MLA documentation or simply by providing acknowledgement in the body of the paper, as in the sample essay at the end of this chapter, in which a professor's remarks are quoted to support the writer's assertions.

CHECKLIST: CAUSE & EFFECT ESSAY

A good cause and effect-based essay

- ▶ Has a meaningful title that clearly identifies the topic

- ▶ Opens with an interesting, attention-getting introduction that again identifies the topic, establishes its significance, and provides a firm thesis statement

- ▶ Is organized into three or four body paragraphs, covering the topic in a coherent, step-by-step way, focusing on one main idea at a time, in logical sequence

- ▶ Focuses on *either* causes or effects

- ▶ Provides enough concrete, specific detail to fully develop the ideas

- ▶ Avoids the *post hoc ergo hoc* fallacy

- ▶ Closes with a smooth, satisfying conclusion that gracefully resolves the discussion by somehow relating back to the introduction

- ▶ Uses clear, simple, straightforward language—nothing fancy

- ▶ Maintains an appropriate tone, neither too formal nor too conversational

- ▶ Contains no inappropriate material

- ▶ Contains no typos or mechanical errors in spelling, capitalization, punctuation, or grammar

- ▶ Satisfies the length requirements of the assignment

MODEL CAUSE & EFFECT ESSAY

The Keys to Academic Success in College

When you hear that a friend of yours made the college honor roll by earning straight As last semester, you're probably impressed and maybe a little envious too. But there's really no need for jealousy, because you could probably perform just as well yourself. Academic excellence is within the reach of any student who understands what's required: attending regularly, paying attention and participating in class, studying enough, and completing assignments, tests, and exams satisfactorily.

Obviously, regular attendance is fundamental. Students who are frequently late or absent miss important lecture material and in-class activities. In addition, they are often unaware of assignments and other requirements mentioned by the instructor, and wind up handing in late or incorrect work, thereby receiving low grades. As Professor George Searles of Mohawk Valley Community College explains, "When I compute the final averages at the end of the semester, there's always a direct correlation between attendance and grades. Students who show up at least 90% of the time nearly always do well, while those with an attendance mark of 70% or lower often get a D or an F. To hit the ball, you have to swing the bat. But first you've got to show up at the ballpark."

But it's not enough to simply sit there in class every day. To extend Professor Searles's metaphor, batters who fail to keep their eye on the ball don't get many hits. So paying close attention in class is very, very important. In addition to listening carefully to the instructor's lectures and feedback from classmates, it's necessary to take good notes that will facilitate home study and review. A good rule of thumb is that for every hour spent in class you should spend an hour outside of class revisiting the material.

Equally crucial is the need to be fully aware of the rules governing assignments. If in doubt, ask—either in class or afterwards. Most instructors don't mind providing clarification, especially if an assignment is complex or potentially confusing. And nearly all instructors welcome constructive in-class participation in the form of relevant questions and comments in response to the material. The student who sits up front, conveys a positive, engaged attitude, and expresses interest in the subject matter always does better than someone who retreats to the back of the room, tunes out, and spends the class period texting.

Simple enough, then: Attend regularly, pay attention, and hit the books with willingness and enthusiasm. These are the keys. They'll unlock the door to academic success for you, as they've done for your friend. And once that door is open, you can go right through it to achieve your goal: a college transcript you can be proud of.

EXERCISES

1. Choose one of the following topics and write a well-organized, fully-developed **narrative** essay of 500–750 words.

   ► A Very Embarrassing Moment
   ► A Very Angry Moment
   ► A Very Satisfying Accomplishment
   ► My Best Summer
   ► What I Expect My Life To Be Like in Ten Years

2. Choose one of the following topics and write a well-organized, fully-developed **definition** essay of 500–750 words.

   ► Existentialism
   ► Feminism
   ► Title IX
   ► Socialism
   ► Political Correctness

3. Choose one of the following topics and write a well-organized, fully-developed **description** essay of 500–750 words.

   ► My Most Interesting Relative
   ► My English Professor's Office
   ► The Street Where I Live
   ► My Favorite Bar/Restaurant/Nightclub
   ► My Ideal Boyfriend/Girlfriend (or Husband/Wife)

4. Choose one of the following topics and write a well-organized, fully-developed **exemplification** essay of 500–750 words.

   ► Mindless Reality Shows
   ► Sexual Harassment in the Workplace
   ► Advantages (or Disadvantages) of Dormitory Living
   ► Benefits of Participating in Extracurricular Activities
   ► Muscle Cars

5. Choose one of the following topics and write a well-organized, fully-developed **comparison/contrast** essay of 500–750 words.

   ► Two Generations' Clothing Styles
   ► Train Travel vs. Air Travel
   ► Basketball vs. Golf
   ► City Life vs. Country Life
   ► Poetry vs. Fiction

6. Choose one of the following topics and write a well-organized, fully-developed **process analysis** essay of 500–750 words.

    ▶ How To Prepare a Western Omelet
    ▶ How To Program a Digital Wristwatch
    ▶ How To Create a Playlist on an MP3 Player
    ▶ How To Create a Facebook Page
    ▶ How To Sell on eBay

7. Choose one of the following topics and write a well-organized, fully-developed **cause and effect** essay of 500–750 words.

    ▶ The Health Hazards of Cigarette Smoking
    ▶ The Effects of Online News Sites On Print Media
    ▶ The Causes of Prejudice Against Immigrants
    ▶ The Effects of Global Warming
    ▶ The Causes of Political Apathy

PART 4

Specialized Essays

Regardless of its purpose and its intended audience, and irrespective of which strategy has governed its development, every essay reflects the basic features of the essay genre. Nevertheless, there are certain specialized situations in which the writer of an essay must adapt to atypical circumstances. Foremost among these are assignments requiring the composition of an *essay examination* or a *literary criticism essay*. Both of these situations pose unique challenges, as discussed in the following chapters.

From *College English: The Basics, 2nd Edition* by George J. Searles. © 2017 by George J. Searles. Reprinted by permission of Kendall Hunt Publishing Company.

CHAPTER 9

Essay Examinations

LEARNING OBJECTIVES

When you complete this chapter, you will be able to

fizkes/Shutterstock.com

- ► Recognize key words in an essay exam to understand the question and provide the kind of answer the directions require
- ► Complete take-home exams successfully by performing the three-step process of pre-writing, writing, and rewriting, and providing any necessary documentation
- ► Complete in-class exams successfully by practicing efficient time-management

In practically every college course, regardless of subject area, students are expected to demonstrate their knowledge of the material by completing quizzes and tests. If only short answers are required, the most typical formats are multiple-choice and fill-in-the-blanks. For in-depth responses, however, the essay examination is the norm. In many respects, writing an essay exam is essentially the same as writing any other essay. Your audience, for example, is still your professor. Accordingly, your tone should remain rather formal. But there are some significant differences, particularly if the exam is an in-class assignment rather than a take-home. When you complete this chapter you'll be ready to successfully complete both kinds of essay exams.

UNDERSTANDING THE QUESTION

Whether you're writing in-class or at home, the single most important factor in writing any essay exam is that you must *answer the question*. A common error is to overlook part of the question or to provide a different kind of answer from what the directions require. To prevent this, you should read the question (and the directions!) several times to ensure that you fully understand them. Be alert for specific commands that signal the type of answer that's expected. Here's a list of ten such terms:

- ► *Analyze*: Break a subject down into its parts to reveal its meaning, nature, or significance.
- ► *Compare/Contrast*: Show similarities and/or differences between two or more things.
- ► *Define*: Provide a clear statement of the literal meaning of a word, expression, or concept.
- ► *Describe*: Use specific details to create a visual image in the mind's eye.
- ► *Discuss*: Talk in a general but meaningful and enlightening way about a specific subject.

- ▸ *Evaluate*: Make an informed, evidence-supported judgment about the merits (and/or demerits) of something.
- ▸ *Explain*: Expound on a subject to make it understandable and/or defensible.
- ▸ *Identify*: Establish the identity or essential nature of something.
- ▸ *Summarize*: Create a concise restatement of something.
- ▸ *Trace*: Show the development of a process through its sequential stages.

Each of these verbs requires a different—and very specific—approach, and you must respond accordingly. For example, if you simply summarize when the question asks you to discuss, you shouldn't expect a high grade. Indeed, you might very well fail. On the other hand, if you discuss when the question asks you to summarize, you're guilty of overkill, which most professors find irritating. Try to gear your answer, and the way you frame it, to the approach required by the wording of the question. If you're not sure what's expected, raise your hand and ask. And don't be shy about that. There are probably other students who share your uncertainty and they'll also benefit from any clarification the professor might provide in response to your inquiry.

TAKE-HOME EXAMS

The most basic thing to remember about take-home exams is that they're no different from any other kind of essay. To produce a good exam you must follow the usual three-step procedure: pre-writing, writing, rewriting. And essay exams follow the usual essay format: title, introduction (including a firm thesis statement), body paragraphs, and conclusion. And they are developed using the same approaches explained in Part 3. But *which* approach you use will be determined by the wording of the question.

A key feature of take-home exams is that you can research your topic, drawing upon your textbooks and other resources. But you must be certain you're providing full documentation, using MLA, APA, or whatever other style the professor requires, to avoid committing plagiarism.

IN-CLASS EXAMS

No matter what the question and the required approach, an in-class exam poses certain challenges beyond those of a take-home. For starters, there's a time limit. Obviously, this restricts your ability to pre-write and rewrite. As explained in Part 2, however, writing is a process and those two steps remain crucial. It would be a big mistake to simply plunge into your essay without some planning, or to hand it in without fine-tuning it a bit at the end of the allotted time. But you have to accomplish these steps a lot faster than you would if writing at home. In a one-hour class period, for example, you might allow approximately ten minutes for pre-writing, forty minutes for writing, and ten minutes for rewriting. In a longer class period, you could pre-write and rewrite a little more. But even then you'd have to hurry, holding your pre-writing and rewriting to no more than fifteen minutes each.

As a result, an in-class essay cannot be as polished as a homework assignment, and no reasonable professor expects it to be. Unless the exam is written for an English class, your professor will probably be far more interested in the *content* of your essay than in your spelling, punctuation, and grammar. In other words, your grade will depend mostly on how well and how fully you respond to the question. That's not to say, however, that you can completely ignore the mechanical aspects. Your writing should always be as professional and error-free as you can make it. One very helpful strategy is to firmly memorize the correct spelling of any names or specialized terms relating to what you've studied during the semester. And if any such words actually appear in the question itself, make *absolutely* certain that you get them right. Most professors are reasonably tolerant of the occasional miscue, but careless—and therefore inexcusable—misspellings will probably lower your grade.

At the rewriting step in the process, therefore, you should revise not only for content and organization but also for obvious errors. If handwriting rather than working on a computer, don't be afraid to cross out or erase. You can provide margin notes or arrows indicating the repositioning of words, sentences, or whole paragraphs. Sloppy and strong is better than neat and weak. Make sure, though, that all revisions and changes are easy to read and understand. If the exam is so messy that it's hard to follow, the grade will almost certainly suffer.

Another difference between an in-class essay exam and one written at home is that the introduction of the in-class piece need not be as fully developed. Given the time constraints of the in-class situation, it makes more sense to focus your energies on the body paragraphs because that's really where you must showcase your understanding of the subject matter. Indeed, the introductory paragraph of an in-class essay exam is sometimes little more than a rewording of the question. Here's an example from an introductory psychology course:

> **QUESTION:** In a well-organized, fully-developed essay, explain the differences between neurosis and psychosis, and provide examples of behaviors that might be considered typical of each.

> **INTRODUCTION:** There is a firm distinction between neurosis and psychosis, and certain behaviors that are typical of each condition illustrate the differences between the two.

Similarly, the conclusion of an in-class essay can also be rather brief, as little as two or three sentences summarizing what's been said. The same is true of take-home exams in subjects other than English. The one exception to all this would be an English composition exam designed to test your knowledge of essay structure. In that situation, you'd need a fully developed introduction and conclusion in addition to your several body paragraphs.

CHECKLIST: ESSAY EXAMINATION

A good essay exam

- ▶ Has a meaningful title that clearly identifies the topic

- ▶ Opens with an interesting, attention-getting introduction that again identifies the topic and provides a firm thesis statement

- ▶ *Answers the question* (rather than some other question) by responding appropriately to key verbs in the phrasing of the question

- ▶ Is organized into three or four body paragraphs, covering the topic in a coherent, step-by-step way, focusing on one main idea at a time, in logical sequence

- ▶ Provides enough concrete, specific detail to fully develop the ideas

- ▶ Closes with a smooth, satisfying conclusion that gracefully resolves the discussion by somehow relating back to the introduction

- ▶ Uses clear, simple, straightforward language—nothing fancy

- ▶ Maintains an appropriate tone, neither too formal nor too conversational

- ▶ Contains no inappropriate material

- ▶ Contains no typos or mechanical errors in spelling, capitalization, punctuation, or grammar

- ▶ Satisfies the length requirements of the assignment

EXERCISES

Here's an actual midterm essay exam from a first-year English composition course, along with three students' responses. Which of the three is the best essay in response to the exam? Why? What are the shortcomings of the other two?

Midterm Examination

In a well-organized essay, fully describe three visible articles of clothing that you are wearing right now. Your descriptions should be detailed enough so that someone reading your essay could pick you out of the crowd. In addition, explain how, where, and when you got each article and—if you know—how much it cost. Lastly, select one of the three articles and discuss in some depth what you think it suggests about your personality.

ESSAY EXAM #1

My Clothes

What am I wearing today? A baseball hat, a sweatshirt, a short skirt, knee-high socks, and my Uggs shoes. All of these things say alot about who I am.

The baseball hat has the Yankee's logo on the front. What it shows is that I'm a huge Yankees fan. My whole family loves the Yankees. We try to go to at least one game at Yankee Stadium every year. It's very expensive, but it's worth it. Until he retired, Derek Jeter was my favorite player. I still love the team, but the Yankees just aren't the same without him.

My sweatshirt says "Central High Basketball" on the front in red letters, with a picture of a basketball underneath. I got this shirt for free because I was on the team in high school. When I was a senior we had a pretty good year, winning most of our games and going to the regionals. In our last game I scored seventeen points, but we lost. The score was something like 50–35. We never really had a chance because those girls were really, really tall and they had this one girl who seemed to make every shot she tried.

My skirt is made of jeans material and, like I said, its short. But even though its pretty cold today I'm not to uncomfortable because I'm also wearing the knee-high socks and my Uggs, which are really warm and comfortable. I guess that shows that I like to be comfortable.

So that's what I have on today. To be honest, I didn't really think alot about what I was putting on this morning because I overslept and was rushing around, just grabing whatever was laying around. But I think I look pretty good anyway, and that's important to me too.

ESSAY EXAM #2

Three Articles of Clothing

Most people like to look good. I know I do. Part of looking good is figuring out how to dress in a way that suits your body type and personality. When I got dressed for school this morning I was keeping that in mind, just like I do everyday. I think the outfit I came up with today is a good one. Let me tell you about three of the things I'm wearing. My hoodie, my tights and my sneakers.

The hoodie is a slightly oversized pullover (no zipper down the front) and is pure white. It has no writting on it. I prefer not to wear clothes with slogans or anything like that, unless it's a designer logo. Actually this hoodie does have a very small black Nike "swoosh" on the left side of the front. I paid about twenty-five dollars for it on sale. I think it looks very clean and attractive.

My tights are just ordinary ballet-style tights, in black. I think I look good in tights because I'm slim, and the contrast between the baggy white hoodie and the sleek black tights is effective and attention-getting. I bought these tights last month at the Danskin outlet in the South Side mall.

On my feet I'm wearing basketball sneakers made by Converse—the kind that people call "Chucks." The sneakers are low-cut and black. I like the way the black color of the shoes echoes the color of the tights and even the Nike "swoosh" on my hoodie. I actually received these Chuck's as a birthday present from my sister, who knew I'd been wanting a new pair ever since my old ones wore out.

Really everything I'm wearing today reflects my personality. As I said in the introduction, I like to look good, and I think this outfit makes that happen. It's simple yet elegant and eye-catching, and the Chuck's add a little hint of something a little adventureous, which is always good if you want to look interesting.

ESSAY EXAM #3

Three Articles of Clothing I'm Wearing Today

Many countries have specific styles of dress or articles of clothing that are associated with those cultures. Consider hats, for example: The beret is thought of as essentially French, while the derby originated in England, and the sombrero is worn principally in Mexico. In the United States, many styles of clothing can be seen, because of the diversity of our population. In this essay I will describe and discuss three articles of clothing I'm wearing today, and will attempt to explain what one of them reflects about my personality.

At this moment I'm wearing my favorite sweater. It's a long-sleeved, crew neck, navy-blue pullover with an approximately one-inch red stripe that runs horizontally across my chest. It's a size large. My mother gave it to me last Christmas. I don't know where she bought it or how much she paid, but I think it was probably fairly expensive because it has a substantial feel to it and has held up very well for almost a year now, even though I wear it often.

On my feet I'm wearing Asics running shoes, model number GT-2110, size 10. They're basically white, trimmed in gray, navy blue, and reflective silver and gold. On the back of each shoe is a label that reads "GEL," with the letters arranged vertically. Just below, in horizontal letters, is the label "I•G•S." I'm not entirely sure what the labels actually mean, but I once read that "Asics" stands for "animus sanus in corpore sano" (Latin for "a sound mind in a sound body"). I bought these shoes at the Foot Locker store in the Cantortown Mall. They cost about eighty dollars—expensive but worth it, because I run a lot.

Lastly, I'm wearing basic Lee jeans, size 30/32. They have two pockets in the front (with a smaller "watch pocket" sort of inside the right pocket, but still visible just below the waist line) and two square, stitched-on pockets in the back. These jeans have a total of seven belt loops and the rectangular leather Lee logo patch that can also serve as a belt loop on the right in the back. I bought these jeans about two years ago at Bernstein's Army & Navy on Main Street, which has since gone out of business. If I remember correctly, they cost about thirty dollars.

I like all three of these items, but I think the one that says the most about me personally would be the Lee jeans. Practically everybody wears jeans, but mine are different, because they are both traditional and unconventional at the same time, just like me. They're traditional because they're cut normally, not oversized or decorated with zippers and snaps, and they're a fairly well-known brand. But they are not blue or black like most of the jeans you'll see people wearing. Mine are gray, a rather unusual color for jeans. So, as I said, the jeans—like me—are typical but quite atypical all at once.

You're probably wondering what exactly I mean when I claim to be, like my jeans, "traditional and unconventional at the same time...typical but quite atypical all at once." Well, the traditional and typical part is plain to see. For better or worse, nothing about my appearance—except maybe my gray jeans—or usual behavior would cause anyone to notice me. But there's another whole side to me that's not immediately obvious: a highly individualistic, even somewhat eccentric dimension. Want details? Sorry, but that's a subject for another whole essay altogether.

CHAPTER 10

Literary Criticism

LEARNING OBJECTIVES

When you complete this chapter, you will be able to

- ► Write a successful essay of literary criticism that correctly explicates the content of a literary work by applying a specific critical perspective
- ► Write a successful essay of literary criticism that correctly explicates the form of a literary work by applying the principles of formalist criticism
- ► Write a successful essay of literary criticism that incorporates the unique features of essays of literary criticism

WAYHOME studio/Shutterstock.com

Writing about literature is known as *literary criticism*. Ordinarily when we criticize, we're finding fault. In this context, however, criticism simply means interpretation, analysis, discussion—and, ultimately, evaluation. Granted, we may finally decide that the work under consideration is flawed in one way or another. However, the main purpose of literary criticism is not to point out weaknesses but to clarify the meaning of a work and/or the methods by which the author created it. In the college setting, this typically involves writing an essay.

A literary criticism essay is fundamentally no different from any other essay. As already explained, an essay should have a title, an introduction with a firm thesis statement, three or four body paragraphs, and a conclusion. And, as always, if you're quoting from outside sources or incorporating information gathered from research, the essay must also include full documentation. Literary criticism is different from other kinds of essay writing, however, because you must decide upon a *critical perspective* before you can begin.

The task of literary criticism is further complicated by the fact that in a given work, several critical perspectives may overlap. For example, many feminist works that portray discrimination against women are colored by the historical reality that such injustice has been a fundamental feature of many societies throughout recorded time. Accordingly, the Marxist perspective becomes relevant because of women's traditional dependence on men for financial support. Of course, these complexities are at work in so-called "real life" as well as in literature. Indeed, that's why literary criticism has value. To better understand literature is to better understand the human predicament.

CRITICAL PERSPECTIVES

There are a variety of critical perspectives—that is, angles from which to approach a work of literature. As mentioned, there is often some overlap among these perspectives, but each is rather different from the others. Here are some of the most common:

Biographical

In what ways have the author's own background and life experience influenced the work? To what extent is the work autobiographical? In what ways—if any—does our knowledge of the author's life help us interpret the work? Biographical criticism seeks to answer one or more of these questions.

Historical

Every work is written in a certain place at a certain time, and most works are set in a particular place and time. In what ways have the known attitudes and cultural assumptions of locations and eras influenced the author or the characters and events depicted?

Mythological

Sometimes called the *archetypal* approach, and drawing upon the famous psychologist Carl Jung's theory of the "collective unconscious," the mythological approach explores the ways, if any, that the work echoes ideas or themes central to the famous myths of the ancient world, thereby reaffirming timeless, universal truths. The Myth of Sisyphus, the Myth of Icarus, and the Myth of Oedipus come immediately to mind as examples of myths that many later writers have invoked—sampled, if you will—to give shape and meaning to their own works.

Marxist

What is the role of money and materialism in the work? How do those considerations influence the narrative voice and/or the characters? To what extent does the work reinforce or challenge the norms of capitalism as opposed to the contrasting principles of socialism?

Feminist

What is the role of gender in the work? In what ways are the characters and situations influenced, shaped, or limited by society's differing assumptions about and expectations of women and men?

Psychological

Based on the pioneering work of Freud, Jung, and Adler in the early twentieth century, this approach seeks to determine how the characters' inner workings (their subconscious fears, obsessions, compulsions, and the like) explain their behavior and the consequent events of the plot—and, similarly, how the *author* might have been influenced by psychological considerations.

Deconstructionist

In what ways does the work contradict itself, creating justification for interpretations not immediately obvious to the reader—perhaps not even intended by the author? And what does this suggest about the nature of literature in general, about writers' intentions and readers' expectations—indeed, about all interpretation of human experience, whether actual or fictional?

Formalist

The most traditional approach, formalism de-emphasizes biographical, historical, and other considerations and attempts to focus only on the work itself, its structural and aesthetic elements. Because the formalist approach can explore so many different features of a literary work, it warrants separate discussion.

FORMALIST CRITICISM

Here are some of the most common areas of concern in the formalist approach:

Title

Nearly all literary works have titles, which function much like the titles of essays. Their purpose is to orient the reader by somehow forecasting what lies ahead. In literature, however, titles are sometimes ironic, suggesting something directly opposite to what the work finally delivers. In any case, it's a mistake to ignore the titles of literary works; they always function meaningfully.

Narrative Perspective

There are basically two ways to tell a story: "I did this, I did that" or "He did this, he did that." The first is called first-person narration, in which a character in the story tells the story. The second is called authorial (or omniscient) narration, in which the author is not a participant in the action but simply reports it. Each approach has its advantages, and anyone who sits down to compose a fictional narrative must decide which to use. Some writers—the American novelist Jennifer Egan, for example—may use both within a given work.

The first-person approach makes the action seem somehow more "real" and immediate. But a first-person narrator's knowledge of events is necessarily somewhat limited because, just as in actuality, one person cannot know for sure what other people are thinking and usually does not know everything about the situation—background, for example. Hence the first-person narrator may well be an *unreliable* narrator, one whose version of reality cannot be trusted and may in fact lend itself to deconstructive interpretation. As an example, consider the unnamed narrator of Robert Browning's famous (and disturbing) poem "Porphyria's Lover" or, for that matter, Browning's unnamed duke in "My Last Duchess." An authorial narrator, on the other hand, knows all; that's what "omniscient" means—all-knowing. So an omniscient narrator can be trusted to "get it right." Unless the narrative is a memoir, though, it's always a mistake to assume that a first-person narrator is a stand-in for an author writing autobiography or fiction based on autobiography. In fiction, every narrator is an invention created by the author.

Setting

As mentioned in the above discussion of historically-oriented criticism, every actual event occurs in a particular place at a particular time. When an author writes a story, therefore, the fictitious events must be grounded in place and time in order to be convincing. Naturally, the author will try to choose wisely, selecting a setting appropriate to the narrative's purposes. It's no accident, for example, that the fictitious city of

Dempsey in Richard Price's novel *Clockers* (about urban drug dealers) was modeled on the Jersey City slums, which are among the northeast's grittiest.

Conflict

Without conflict—a clash of some sort, X vs. Y—there's no story. By identifying a work's central oppositions we come to a clearer sense of what the story's really all about. As briefly outlined in Chapter 8, there are several basic kinds of conflict:

▶ **Individual vs. Self**: Sometimes called "inner conflict," this always involves a person trying to choose between competing impulses. Usually it's a "good vs. evil" situation, but not always; the character may be trying to decide between the lesser of two evils, or between the greater of two goods. Many of Shakespeare's heroes struggle with such dilemmas.

▶ **Individual vs. Individual**: Essentially the "good guy vs. bad guy" scenario, but the variations are virtually unlimited: child vs. parent, wife vs. husband, worker vs. boss, and so on. In short, one person against another—or, collectively, "us vs. them."

▶ **Individual vs. Society**: The person in conflict with the group, a common theme in much science fiction. Usually the protagonist is an enlightened non-conformist refusing to accept the norms of a repressive or otherwise mistaken community. Often, the individual pays dearly for this oppositional stance, despite its validity. Think Romeo and Juliet, or Winston Smith in George Orwell's novel *1984*.

▶ **Individual vs. Nature**: The person in conflict with the great natural forces: fire, tornado, flood, blizzard, earthquake, and the like. Sometimes, however, nature is represented by the animal kingdom, as in the *Jaws* movies or Alfred Hitchcock's famous film *The Birds*.

▶ **Individual vs. Fate**: Sometimes called "Individual vs. God (or the gods)," this conflict nearly always operates to the individual's disadvantage, as might be expected. By definition, fate has the upper hand. Resistance may be noble but is usually futile. Oedipus, for example, does everything in his power to prevent the fulfillment of prophecy, but to no avail. Indeed, his actions ensure that the awful prophecy *will* be fulfilled.

Irony

Authors are particularly fond of this device, which basically involves reversal of expectation. The word derives from the *eiron*, a stock character in ancient Greek comedy who pretends to be unsophisticated but is actually wise. There are three kinds of irony in literature:

▶ **Verbal Irony**: Related to sarcasm, verbal irony involves deliberately using words or expressions whose meanings are the opposite of what is meant. Often it functions as a kind of "in joke" between writer and reader, as in Kate Chopin's "The Story of an Hour" (like much of Chopin's work, an exceptionally ironic story on many levels), in which the narrator says

> Her husband's friend Richards was there, too, *near her*. It was he who had been in the newspaper office when intelligence of the railroad disaster was received, with Brently Mallard's name leading the list of "killed." He had only taken the time to *assure* himself of its truth by a second telegram, *and had hastened to forestall any less careful, less tender friend in bearing the sad message.*

The wording that's been italicized here is clearly ironic because Richards is obviously attracted to Mrs. Mallard, and may well be experiencing mixed emotions—some of them self-serving—in response to the news that her husband appears to have been killed.

▶ **Dramatic Irony**: Like verbal irony, this involves a discrepancy between actuality and what is said. But the difference is that in this case the speaker is unaware of the discrepancy. Although most common in plays, it functions in fiction and poetry as well. To cite another example from "The Story of an Hour," we learn that the doctors believe Mrs. Mallard's fatal heart attack has been caused by "joy that kills" when actually she has died of heartbreak.

▶ **Situational Irony**: This occurs when the expected or desired outcome of a situation is thwarted or reversed—often with tragic consequences—for no valid reason. For example, Romeo kills himself because he thinks that Juliet is dead when in fact she is not.

Symbolism

This device involves details that the author has deliberately inserted into the work because they operate on more than one level. They are details that may indeed be present in "real life" but have been carefully selected for their particular significance. For example, in Shirley Jackson's famous short story "The Lottery" (in which the winner is killed) Old Man Warner brags that he has participated seventy-seven times. Obviously, Jackson could have used any large number but chose seventy-seven because of its connotations ("lucky sevens"). Colors are often used this way because certain colors connote certain ideas. Red, for example, can symbolize danger or sexuality, while blue is associated with sadness, and yellow can suggest either decay or cowardice. Names can also function symbolically. To cite "The Lottery" once more, the two men who officiate at the deadly event every June are Mr. *Summers* and Mr. *Graves*. And Old Man *Warner*, of course, is a warn-er who counsels the townspeople about the imagined dangers of ending the lottery. Indeed, most of the names in "The Lottery" are symbolic on some level.

UNIQUE FEATURES OF THE LITERARY CRITICISM ESSAY

Everything that's been said so far applies to writing about all three of the principal literary genres: poetry, fiction, and drama. Regardless of genre, any essay of literary criticism exhibits certain features unique to that kind of writing. Here they are:

▶ **Title**: If you're having trouble writing a good title, you probably haven't really decided what you're trying to say. For example, a title like "The Catcher in the Rye" tells the reader what work will be discussed but provides no clue as to where the discussion is headed. In all likelihood, the writer doesn't know, and needs to go back to the pre-writing stage and find out. Here's a much better title, one that clearly indicates what lies ahead and reflects thoughtful planning by the student writer: "Innocence vs. Experience in J.D. Salinger's *The Catcher in the Rye*." Always try for that level of specificity.

▶ **Introduction**: To open an essay of literary criticism, it's customary to begin with a few sentences of generalization about the author, work, or literary technique you'll be discussing. But, as in any essay, those first few sentences should lead logically and smoothly to a firm thesis statement at or very near the end of that opening paragraph. The essay's thesis statement and the title should echo each other. The title is a short version of the thesis statement, while the thesis statement is an expanded version of the title. In our hypothetical *Catcher in the Rye* essay, the thesis statement might be something like this: "This novel includes several key scenes in which pure, child-like innocence comes into conflict with more-worldly behaviors, thereby highlighting some of the book's main themes."

► **Plot Summary:** While *some* plot summary is appropriate in order to create context at the beginning of the essay, you must very quickly move past it and begin a discussion of more-substantial issues. A literary criticism essay must not simply re-tell the story. When you do refer to plot developments, though, be sure to phrase those references in present tense rather than in past tense. Why? Because, unlike events in "real life," the events in a literary work are not actual occurrences. Usually when we write about the past it's appropriate—indeed, necessary—to use past tense verbs, because those events are over and done with. But the fictitious events in a work of literature exist in a kind of eternal present there on the page. Consider: When Carrie burns down her high school gym in the Steven King novel (and movie) named after her, that gym is in flames whether we are reading the novel (or watching the movie) yesterday, today, or tomorrow. So—to repeat—use present tense, not past tense, when referring to plot developments and do not rely on plot summary alone. Go deeper.

► **Identifying Characters:** Most works of literature—fiction and drama especially—involve at least two or more characters whose interactions essentially constitute the story. To ensure that your discussion moves along smoothly and coherently, therefore, it's important that you somehow identify characters the first time you refer to them. A short, descriptive phrase will accomplish this. For example, the writer of the *Catcher in the Rye* essay would not simply say "Holden feels inferior in some ways to Stradlater" if Stradlater had not been mentioned before. Instead, the writer would identify the character, like this: "Holden feels inferior in some ways to Stradlater, his handsome, athletic roommate."

► **Relevance:** Stick to your thesis. Don't go off on unrelated tangents. Of course, asides and relevant parenthetical remarks can be enlightening, but make sure they do not derail the essay's train of thought. Similarly, resist the urge to "preach." Stay away from the "As everyone knows" or "Ever since the dawn of civilization" approach. And avoid "stage directions" such as "Now I shall attempt to show that…." Just say what you have to say, and if your presentation is coherent, it will be self-explanatory. Distracting phrases like "As you can plainly see" and "From the above it is clear that" actually weaken your essay because they serve no real purpose. Let your discussion speak for itself.

► **Conclusion:** As in any essay, you should pull things together at the end. This can be tricky if your essay has discussed more than one work of literature. The conclusion of such an essay must summarize not only what you've said about the last author or work mentioned, but should put into perspective all the works mentioned in the essay by clearly showing how your thesis interrelates among all of them.

The model essay at the end of this chapter uses the biographical approach to satisfactorily fulfill the requirements of literary criticism.

CHECKLIST: LITERARY CRITICISM ESSAY

A good literary criticism essay

- ▶ Has a meaningful title that names both the author(s) and works(s) under consideration and clearly indicates the slant of the discussion

- ▶ Opens with a clear, focused introduction that again names the author(s) and work(s) under consideration and plainly states the thesis

- ▶ *Says something*, rather than rambling aimlessly or relying on mere plot summary

- ▶ Is organized into three or four body paragraphs, covering the topic in a coherent, step-by-step way, focusing on one main idea at a time, in logical sequence

- ▶ Uses present tense for references to plot developments, and briefly identifies characters the first time they're mentioned

- ▶ Provides enough concrete, specific detail to fully develop the ideas; quotes and other supporting evidence from the literary work itself and/or secondary sources are properly incorporated into the essay

- ▶ Closes with a smooth, satisfying conclusion that gracefully resolves the discussion by somehow relating back to the introduction

- ▶ Uses clear, simple, straightforward language—nothing fancy

- ▶ Maintains an appropriate tone, neither too formal nor too conversational

- ▶ Contains no inappropriate material

- ▶ Contains no typos or mechanical errors in spelling, capitalization, punctuation, or grammar

- ▶ Satisfies the length requirements of the assignment

MODEL LITERARY CRITICISM ESSAY

Autobiographical Elements in Kate Chopin's "The Story of an Hour"

Speaking about the protagonist of his great novel *Madame Bovary*, the French writer Gustave Flaubert once said, "c'est moi" ("this person is me"). Kate Chopin, the American author who penned "The Story of an Hour," might well have said the same about her own protagonist, Louise Mallard. Although there are major differences between the fictional character and Chopin herself, there are many similarities as well—enough, in fact, for us to safely conclude that Chopin based Louise's situation at least partly upon events in her own life.

The plot is simple, though ironic. Louise learns that her husband, Brently, has been killed in a train accident. Rather than becoming upset, she experiences feelings of relief and joy, for she thinks she has been freed from the constraints of marriage. A few minutes later, though, her husband reappears, unharmed. Louise drops dead from shock—and, we can assume, from disappointment as well. Interestingly, Kate Chopin's father had been killed in a railway mishap when she was five years old and her own husband, Oscar, had died in 1882, twelve years before this story was published; like her mother, she never remarried (Toth, "What" 13). We cannot know whether Chopin's feelings toward her own marriage were similar to Louise's, but it's a safe bet that they were not totally dissimilar. The narrator, after all, speaks at one point of Louise's husband's "powerful will bending her in that blind persistence with which men and women believe they have the right to impose a private will upon a fellow-creature." (Chopin 158)

As we know, authors are at liberty to name their characters whatever they choose. It's probably not mere coincidence, then, that Mrs. Mallard is named "Louise," for Chopin was originally from St. Louis, before marrying and relocating to Louisiana. Although the French name "Mallard" is not unknown in the south, it's a slightly uncommon one, and seems like an odd choice, unless we consider that the mallard duck is one of the few species that mate for life. So the name "Louise Mallard" was most likely based on Chopin's personal geography, and also, perhaps, on her feelings about the lifelong nature of wedlock. Often in her work, female characters rebel against the traditional role of wife and mother, as in stories such as "The Storm" and "The Silk Stockings." Her novel *The Awakening* is yet another example; "its sympathetic treatment of adultery shocked reviewers and readers throughout America." (Charters 114)

Finally, there is Brently's friend, Richards. He appears only briefly, once at the beginning of the story and again at the end. It is quite clear that he is attracted to Louise, as evidenced by the fact that he is "near her" when she is told of Brently's supposed death, and by the fact that when Brently walks through the front door, Richards attempts to "screen him from the view of his wife. But…was too late" (Chopin 157, 158). It is as if Richards is almost celebrating Brently's demise, and then trying to deny his resurrection. While there is no hard evidence for such a suggestion, it is at least a possibility that Richards is based on Albert Sampité, with whom the widow is known to have had a scandalous relationship after her husband's death. (Toth, "My" 28)

Of course, there are also major differences between the details of Kate Chopin's life and those of Louise's. For one thing, Oscar Chopin actually died and Brently Mallard does not. And Chopin lived to be 54 years old, while Louise dies as a much younger woman. Further, Chopin was left with six children when her husband died, and there is no mention of children in the story (Toth, "What" 13). Therefore, while Louise is able to imagine that she is "free, free, free" and that "there would be no one to live for . . . she would live for herself" (Chopin 157, 158), the author had no such luxury. And finally, Louise has no apparent role to assume in widowhood, whereas Chopin used her newly single status to pursue her vocation as a writer, giving us an impressive body of work. Her output includes novels, essays, translations, poems, and more than a hundred stories, of which "The Story of an Hour," clearly influenced by her own experiences, is among the best-known. (Charters 114)

Works Cited

Charters, Ann and Samuel Charters. *Literature and Its Writers: A Compact Introduction to Fiction, Poetry, and Drama.* 4th ed., Bedford/St. Martin's, 2007.

Chopin, Kate. "The Story of an Hour." *The Longman Masters of Short Fiction.* Edited by Dana Gioia and R.S. Gwynn. Longman, 2002, pp. 157–58.

Toth, Emily. "My Part in Reviving Kate Chopin." *Awakenings: The Story of the Kate Chopin Reviva.* Edited by Bernard Koloski. Louisiana State UP, 2009, pp. 15–31.

---. "What we do and don't know about Kate Chopin's life." *The Cambridge Companion to Kate Chopin.* Edited by Janet Beer. Cambridge UP, 2008, pp. 13–26.

EXERCISES

Here are two essays of literary criticism dealing with Shirley Jackson's famous short story "The Lottery." Which essay is better? Why? What is the main weakness of the less successful essay?

LITERARY CRITICISM ESSAY # 1

The Lottery

The Lottery is a famous short story about a small town where once a year the people have a lottery. Usually when you think of a lottery you think of it as a good thing, a chance for someone to win something. But this lottery is different. The winner actually *loses* something—their life. Each man in the village must draw a piece of folded paper from the black box. Then after everyone has drawn, the papers are opened and they discover who has the paper with the black dot. At that point everyone in the man's family—the wife, the children, and the man himself—all have to draw again. Whoever gets the black dot this time is immediately stoned to death by everyone else in the village.

In the story Tessie Hutchinson is almost late for the lottery. As she says, she "clean forgot what day it was." But when she remembers, she comes running to the town square, so she's just in time. Mr. Summers and Mr. Graves are the two men in charge of the lottery. Mr. Summers runs the coal company and Mr. Graves is the town's postmaster. Mr. Summers is the one who actually calls out the family names in alphabetical order, so the men can come forward to take their turn.

Some of the people seem to be a little nervous about the lottery. For example, Mrs. Adams says, "some places have already quit lotteries." And Mrs. Delacroix says uneasily, "seems like there's no time at all between lotteries any more . . . . Seems like we got through with the last one only last week." Young Jack Watson has to be told, "Don't be nervous, Jack. Take your time, Son," when it's his turn to draw for his family. (Actually it's just he and his mother, as his father is apparently dead.) Other people, however, seem very supportive of the event. Old Man Warner, who has been in the lottery seventy-seven times, is the most enthusiastic of all. "There's always been a lottery," he points out, after reminding everyone that there "Used to be a saying about 'Lottery in June, corn be heavy soon.'" And Tessie Hutchinson herself seems fully supportive, even urging her husband forward when he hesitates after the Hutchinson family name is called. "Get up there, Bill," she tells him.

After everyone has drawn, it is revealed that Bill Hutchinson has the piece of paper with the black dot on it. Suddenly Tessie has a whole new outlook. "You didn't give him time enough to take any paper he wanted. I saw you. It wasn't fair," she complains. "I think we ought to start over." But nobody listens. The Hutchinsons—Bill, Tessie, and their three children—now all have to pick papers from the box. Whoever gets the black dot this time will be stoned to death by the other people. One by one they open their papers, everyone but Tessie. Bill and the three children each have blank papers, and it becomes obvious that Tessie must be the "winner." Bill must force the paper out of her hand and hold it up so everyone can see the black dot. Then Mr. Summers says, "All right, folks. Let's finish quickly," and Tessie is stoned to death. Her two best friends, Mrs. Delacroix and Mrs. Dunbar, seem especially eager to participate.

Mrs. Delacroix selected a stone so large she had to pick it up with both hands and turned to Mrs. Dunbar. "Come on," she said, "Hurry up." Mrs. Dunbar had small stones in both hands and she said, gasping for breath, "I can't run at all. You'll have to go ahead and I'll catch up with you."

Somebody even gives Tessie's young son Davy some pebbles so that even he can participate in the stoning. That was really sick!

In fact, the whole story is sick. This could never happen in real life. The F.B.I. or some other law enforcement agency would find out about the lottery and put a stop to it. Probably the organizers would be arrested and put in jail where they belong. I know that if I lived in that town, I would move away and not have to participate in this crazy, pointless ritual. I think The Lottery is one of the worst stories I have ever read.

LITERARY CRITICISM ESSAY #2

Symbolism in Shirley Jackson's "The Lottery"

Many writers of serious literature use symbols to help convey the meaning(s) of their work. A symbol is any detail that would perhaps occur in "real life" but which has been carefully selected by the author to achieve maximum significance. Colors, for example, can be symbolic: red traditionally symbolizes danger, yellow is sometimes associated with cowardliness, and green can stand for a variety of things, such as envy, hope, and inexperience. But any detail—not just color—can function symbolically. Shirley Jackson's short story "The Lottery," in which the "winner" is stoned to death, employs various kinds of symbolic details that help to propel the plot and reinforce the author's underlying messages.

Let's begin with numbers. This lottery is traditionally held on June 27, just a few days after the summer solstice (the longest day of the year). In some ancient cultures, many of which worshipped the sun, the summer solstice was a common time for human sacrifice. The belief was that such sacrifices would please the sun, thereby ensuring a good harvest. This connection is reinforced by Old Man Warner, who reminds his fellow villagers, "Used to be a saying about, 'Lottery in June, corn be heavy soon.'" And Warner's age, 77, is also highly significant. The author could just as easily have created a character who was 76 or 78 or any other advanced age, but 77 ("lucky sevens") reinforces the idea that he has repeatedly survived the lottery simply by chance or good luck.

Consider also that the two men who actually conduct the lottery both work at highly appropriate occupations. Mr. Summers operates a coal company. Coal is, of course, black—the color most often associated with death and mourning. Similarly, it's probably no coincidence that the black box resembles a coffin and that at one point it has been stored "underfoot" in the office of Mr. Graves. In his role as the town postmaster, he is responsible for delivering the mail. But in the context of the lottery, he helps to deliver a very specific message: notification of death. Obviously, Shirley Jackson could have provided these two men with any number of occupations, but she selected jobs that would create the appropriate symbolic associations in the reader's subconscious mind.

Significant too is the exchange between Mr. Summers and Tessie Hutchinson near the beginning of the story, when Tessie is nearly late for the gathering. "Thought we were going to have to get on without you, Tessie," Mr. Summers says; she replies, "wouldn't have me leave m'dishes in the sink, now, would you, Joe?" In light of the story's ending, in which Tessie "wins" the lottery and is stoned to death, these comments take on an obviously symbolic—and highly ironic—significance. In a comparable way, Old Man Warner's complaint that "It's not the way it used to be. People ain't the way they used to be" has symbolic meanings that are ironically opposite to what he intends. The whole point of the story is that everything *is* the way it used to be. The lottery does in fact continue, and the people remain generally unopposed to it. Apparently nobody ever really objects to it unless they—as in Tessie's case—are chosen as the "winner." That's the whole problem.

The most obvious symbols in the story are the characters' names. Not all the names function this way, but many—Summers, Graves, Warner, Hutchinson, and others—clearly do. As already mentioned, Mr. Summers and Mr. Graves conduct the annual lottery; as a result of this ritual, every summer there is another grave. Certainly this parallelism must be a deliberate one on the author's part. Likewise, *Old Man Warner* is the symbolic embodiment of tradition, the village's living link to the past; but he is also a warn-er, one who sternly lectures his neighbors about the presumed dangers of abandoning the old ways. It has been suggested that the name Hutchinson is intended to evoke images of the hutch, in which rabbits live. The idea is that this family is representative of the village in general, where people—like scared rabbits—huddle together in their mindless fear, and are therefore always at risk. The names of several minor characters also function in this symbolic way.

In conclusion, Shirley Jackson's "The Lottery" is an excellent and well-known example of how an author can invest a work of fiction with meaningful symbols that create an additional level of resonance. The main message of the story is that our traditions and beliefs are not necessarily correct, and need to be continuously questioned and perhaps revised. Jackson's skillful manipulation of significant details—dates, ages, occupations, comments, names, and other specifics—reinforces the events of the plot, providing a further literary dimension that helps to convey the story's meaning in a highly effective way.

PART 5

Workplace Writing

Nearly all first-year English courses focus mainly on the traditional 500–750 word essay (including essay exams and literary criticism essays). As mentioned in the introduction, however, various other kinds of writing are often covered as well, and that trend is increasing. Accordingly, the chapters in this section explore several types of workplace writing that may be assigned: e-mail, business letters, short reports, proposals, and employment application materials.

From *College English: The Basics, 2nd Edition* by George J. Searles. © 2017 by George J. Searles. Reprinted by permission of Kendall Hunt Publishing Company.

CHAPTER 11

E-Mail

LEARNING OBJECTIVES

When you complete this chapter, you will be able to

- ► Compose brief but purposeful e-mail messages
- ► Achieve the appropriate tone for your audience
- ► Observe the principles of e-mail etiquette and avoid common e-mail blunders

SFIO CRACHO/Shutterstock.com

By far the most common form of written communication in today's workplace is e-mail, and by now almost everyone is familiar with how to use it. Typically, you log onto the system by typing your name and a secure password that prevents unauthorized access. You can then read any new e-mail listed in the inbox. Depending on your preferences, those messages can be deleted, saved for future reference, printed, answered, or forwarded—or some combination of these options. To respond to a message, you choose the appropriate prompt and insert the reply. To create an entirely new e-mail, choose the appropriate prompt, causing a blank template to appear on the screen, ready to be completed. When you finish the message it can then be sent to as many other persons as you wish simply by typing their e-mail addresses into the TO line. Like replies, this new e-mail is also stored in your electronic SENT file and kept there for future reference.

Virtually all e-mail includes the following features in addition to the message itself:

- ► **DATE line**: This is provided automatically and usually includes the *time* of transmission as well.
- ► **TO line**: This enables the e-mail to be addressed.
- ► **FROM line**: Like the date line, this is provided automatically as soon as the writer logs into the system.
- ► **SUBJECT line**: This identifies the topic. Like the title of an essay or the headline on a newspaper story, but even more concisely, the subject line prepares the reader for what's ahead. A good subject line answers this question: "In no more than three words, what is this e-mail about?"

PURPOSE

Although e-mail's usual purpose is to inform, often its secondary purpose is to create an electronic "paper trail"—a written record of a request or other message previously conveyed in person, by phone, or through the grapevine. Accordingly, e-mail comes directly to the point, focusing sharply on what the reader needs to know. Depending on the subject, an e-mail can usually do that in three or four short paragraphs: a concise introduction, a body paragraph or two conveying the details, and perhaps a brief conclusion. But some e-mails are as short as one paragraph or even one sentence. As in all writing, length is determined by purpose and audience.

TONE

The sample e-mail that follows embodies all of the features listed above and provides an opportunity to consider further the principle of *tone* introduced in Chapter 3.

Date: May 7, 2018   9:00 A.M.

To: All Employees

From: Frank Scott

Subject: Ernest Fitzgerald

As you may already know, Ernest Fitzgerald of the Claims Department was admitted to Duval Memorial Hospital over the weekend and is scheduled for surgery tomorrow.

Although Ernie will not be receiving visitors or phone calls for a while, you may want to send him a Get Well card to cheer him up. He's in Room 9.

We'll keep you posted on Ernie's progress.

Frank Scott, Director
Human Resources

The personnel director has picked his words carefully to avoid sounding bossy. He says, "You *may want to* send him a get-well card" rather than "You *should*" even though that's what he really means. As this message demonstrates, a tactful writer can soften a recommendation, a request, or even a demand by phrasing it diplomatically.

In the college setting, sometimes students find it necessary to e-mail their professors. They may be seeking clarification of an assignment, explaining an absence, or attending to some other matter. And in the context of online study, such correspondence is of course routine. In any case, however, nearly all professors expect students to observe the norms of conventional spelling, punctuation, and grammar, and to maintain an appropriately respectful tone. Indeed, an overly conversational approach when writing to your professor violates the principles of upward communication explained in Chapter 3 and can cause resentment. If your e-mail opens with a salutation like "Hey, Sarah" (or even "Hey, Prof") it's definitely headed in the wrong direction.

E-MAIL ETIQUETTE

There are good reasons why e-mail has been so universally adopted since becoming available in the 1980s. On the most obvious level, it's incomparably faster than traditional correspondence. In the past, communicating by memo or letter involved at least five distinct steps:

1. Writing
2. Typing (usually by a secretary)

3. Proofreading and initialing by the writer
4. Photocopying for the writer's file
5. Routing to the intended reader(s)

Depending on office workload and clerical staffing levels, this process could become quite time-consuming. With e-mail, however, all five steps are compressed into one, permitting far speedier communication. Unfortunately, however, the very ease with which e-mail can be produced also creates some problems. In the past, a writer would not bother to write a memo or letter without good reason. Too much time and effort were involved to do otherwise. But now, much needless correspondence is generated. Yesterday's writers would wait until complete information on a given topic had been received, organized, and considered before acting on it or passing it along. But today it's not uncommon for several e-mails to be written on the same subject, doling out the information little by little, sometimes within a very short time-span. The resulting fragmentation wastes the energies of writer and reader alike and increases the possibility of confusion, often because of premature response. One way to minimize this danger is to inspect your entire menu of incoming messages, taking note of multiple messages from the same source or bearing the same subject line, before responding to any.

Similarly, e-mail about sensitive issues is often dashed off "in the heat of battle" without sufficient reflection. In the past, writers could choose to revise or discard a memo if, upon proofreading, it had come to seem a bit too harsh or otherwise inappropriate. But the built-in speed of e-mail eliminates any such opportunity for second thoughts. This can result in counter-productive venting if emotions are not kept under control. Do not hit "Send" until you've had time to cool down and reconsider.

Hasty composition also causes a great many keyboarding miscues, omissions, and other fundamental blunders. These must then be corrected in subsequent messages, creating an annoying flood of "e-mail about e-mail." Indeed, the absence of a secretarial filter has given rise to a great deal of embarrassingly bad writing in the workplace. You risk ridicule and loss of credibility unless you closely proofread every e-mail before sending it. Make sure the information is necessary, accurate, and complete. Fix typos, misspellings, faulty capitalization, sloppy punctuation, and basic grammatical errors. While this is always important, it's especially so when corresponding with readers outside your own workplace. Because you and your outside readers are usually not personally acquainted, a higher level of courteous formality is necessary. Additionally, subject matter is often more involved than that of in-house correspondence, so e-mail sent outside is commonly longer and more fully developed than messages for co-workers. Accordingly, outside e-mail nearly always includes a letter-style salutation and complimentary close.

Here are some additional points to consider about e-mail:

► Resist the temptation to forward chain letters, silly jokes, political rants, tasteless images, and the like. This not only wastes people's time but can get you into trouble.

► Never forward legitimate e-mails to other readers without the original writer's permission. The message may have been intended for you alone.

► Create new e-mail only when necessary, sending only to the person(s) needing it; resist the urge to mass-mail. Similarly, when responding to a mass-mailing do not "Reply All" unless there's a valid reason to do so. Reply only to the sender.

► When engaged in a lengthy back and forth exchange, the situation under discussion will evolve. Keep revising your subject line to reflect that.

► Because e-mail is only partially able to convey "tone of voice," avoid it in delicate situations—the denial of a request, for example. Instead, use voice mail or actual conversation.

CHECKLIST: E-MAIL

A good e-mail

- ▶ Includes certain features:

    DATE line (date and time appear automatically)

    TO line, which provides the name(s) of the intended reader(s)

    FROM line (writer's name appears automatically)

    SUBJECT line, which is a clear, accurate, but brief statement of what the e-mail is about; usually a word or short phrase is enough

- ▶ Is organized into paragraphs (one is often enough) covering the subject fully in an orderly way

- ▶ Contains no inappropriate material

- ▶ Uses clear, simple, straightforward language—nothing fancy

- ▶ Maintains an appropriate tone, neither too formal nor too conversational

- ▶ Contains no typos or mechanical errors in spelling, punctuation, or grammar

EXERCISES

1. You're the manager of the bookstore at County Community College. The semester is drawing to a close and, as always, students will soon be selling back their textbooks. But the store has decided not to buy back any books on the subject of hospitality management, because that program will be discontinued after the current majors graduate this spring. Students are aware that the program is being terminated, but you must send e-mail notification about the textbook situation.

2. Pressing personal business prevented you from attending your English class yesterday. Send your professor an e-mail apologizing for your absence and requesting to make up any missed work or assignments.

3. The management of the company at which you work has decided to create an employee newsletter that will feature articles about the company, along with general news about trends in the national market. In addition, there will be coverage of employees' personal news—births, marriages, and other noteworthy events and achievements. You have been appointed editor, and your supervisor has asked you to write an e-mail requesting your co-workers to submit any such information they would like included.

4. You are the President of the Liberal Arts Club at your college. With support and oversight from the administration, the club has decided to launch *Literama*, a literary magazine that will feature poetry, fiction, and creative non-fiction. The deadline for submissions—which must be in Microsoft Word—is six weeks from now. Send an e-mail to the student body, asking for submissions. Be sure to provide guidelines about length restrictions and anything else you consider important to mention, including a gently diplomatic explanation that acceptance for publication is not guaranteed.

5. You're the assistant to the Director of Human Resources at a medium-sized company. The crossing gate that prevents unauthorized entry to the employee parking lot can be raised only if the motorist inserts an encoded plastic card into a slot in the control box alongside the gate. Now the system is scheduled for an upgrade. A new box will be installed during this coming weekend, so everyone is required to obtain a new card from the Human Resources Office as soon as possible. To smooth the transition, the gate will be left open until next Wednesday, but after that every employee will need a new card to gain access. Write an e-mail alerting all employees to the situation.

CHAPTER 12

Business Letters

LEARNING OBJECTIVES

When you complete this chapter, you will be able to

► Write effective business letters in "full block" format
► Write business letters using orderly, three-part organization
► Achieve the appropriate tone for your audience

Unlike e-mail, which is used for both internal and external communication, business letters are almost always used for the latter. The business letter conveys a message from someone at Company X to someone elsewhere. And although e-mail is now being used in many situations that formerly required letters, the letter is still preferred for more formal exchanges, especially those in which speed of delivery is not a major factor. And for contacting individual customers and clients (some of whom may still rely on conventional mail), the business letter is obviously the better choice. At least for the immediate future, therefore, the letter will remain a relevant form of workplace correspondence, although its role will almost certainly undergo further redefinition as various forms of electronic communication become increasingly dominant. Ten of the more typical purposes of a letter are as follows:

► Sell a product or service (sales)
► Request payment (collection)
► Purchase a product or service (order)
► Voice a complaint (claim)
► Respond to a complaint (adjustment)
► Ask for information (inquiry)
► Provide information (reply)
► Thank someone (acknowledgement)
► Apply for a job (application)
► Recommend someone (reference)

FULL BLOCK FORMAT

Regardless of a letter's purpose, the preferred format today is the *full block* style, in which every line begins at the left margin. These two letters—a consumer claim letter and the adjustment letter in response—both illustrate this layout.

123 Duncan Avenue
Wailsburg, AZ 85000
November 10, 2017

Consumer Relations Department
Top Chef Foods, Inc.
666 Vidrio Street
Albuquerque, NM 87100

Dear Superior Foods:

Top Chef microwave dinners are excellent products that I have purchased regularly for several years. Recently, however, I had an unsettling experience with one of these meals.

While enjoying a liver and lima beans dinner, I discovered in the food what appears to be a thick splinter of glass. I'm sure this is an isolated incident, but I thought your quality control department would want to know about it.

I've enclosed the splinter, taped to the product wrapper, along with the sales receipt for the dinner. May I please be reimbursed $9.98 for the cost?

Sincerely,

G.M. Logan

George M. Logan

Enclosures

Top Chef Foods, Inc.

666 Vidrio Street, Albuquerque, NM 87100   *   (505) 277-1234

November 21, 2017

Mr. George M. Logan
123 Duncan Avenue
Wailsburg, AZ 85000

Dear Mr. Logan:

Thank you for purchasing our product and for taking the time to contact us about it. We apologize for the unsatisfactory condition of your Top Chef microwave dinner.

Quality is of paramount importance to all of us here at Top Chef Foods, and great care is taken in the preparation and packaging of all our products. Our quality assurance staff has been notified of the problem you reported. Although Top Chef Foods does not issue cash refunds, we have enclosed three coupons redeemable at your grocery store for complimentary Top Chef microwave dinners of your choice.

We appreciate this opportunity to be of service, and we hope you will continue to enjoy our products.

Sincerely,

Bernadette Mazur

Bernadette Mazur
Customer Services Department

Enclosures (3)

Notice that full block format employs several required features:

- ▶ Single spacing throughout (except between the "blocks" of print, where double-spacing is used)
- ▶ Margins of 1 to 1½ inches
- ▶ Writer's full address or company letterhead, at the top of the page, followed by the date
- ▶ Inside address (reader's full name and address)
- ▶ Salutation, followed by a colon (Avoid gender-biased salutations such as "Dear Sir" or "Gentlemen.")
- ▶ Complimentary close ("Sincerely" is best), followed by a comma
- ▶ Writer's signature
- ▶ Writer's full name and title
- ▶ Enclosure line (if necessary) to indicate items accompanying the letter

THREE-PART ORGANIZATION

Along with these standard features, all business letters—irrespective of purpose—embrace the same three-part pattern of organization:

1. Brief introductory paragraph establishing context (by referring to previous correspondence, perhaps, or by orienting the reader in some other way) and concisely stating the letter's purpose

2. Body paragraphs (as many as needed) fully conveying the message by providing all necessary details, presented in logical sequence

3. Brief concluding paragraph politely requesting action, thanking the reader, or mentioning any additional facts pertinent to the situation

APPROPRIATE TONE

Like all successful communication, a good letter must adopt an appropriate tone. A letter is more formal than an in-house e-mail because it's more public. Accordingly, a letter should uphold the image of the writer's company or organization by reflecting a high degree of professionalism. But although a letter's style should be polished, the language should be natural and easy to understand. The key to achieving a readable style—in a letter or in anything else you write—is to understand that you should not sound pompous or "official." As mentioned in Chapter 6, writing should sound much like ordinary speech, but polished up. Strive

fizkes/Shutterstock.com

for direct, conversational phrasing. Whatever you do, stay away from stilted, old-fashioned business clichés. Here's a list of overly bureaucratic expressions, paired with "plain English" alternatives:

Cliché	Alternative
As per your request	As you requested
Attached please find	Here is
At this point in time	Now

In lieu of	Instead of
In the event that	If
Please be advised that X	X
Pursuant to our agreement	As we agreed
Until such time as	Until
We are in receipt of	We have received
We regret to advise you that X	Regrettably, X

CHECKLIST: BUSINESS LETTER

A good business letter

- ▶ Follows full block format

- ▶ Includes certain features:

    Writer's complete address (but not the writer's name, which appears only at the bottom of the letter)

    Date

    Reader's full name and complete address (use abbreviations)

    Salutation, followed by a colon

    Complimentary close ("Sincerely" is best), followed by a comma

    Writer's signature and full name

    Enclosure notation, if necessary

- ▶ Is organized into paragraphs, covering the subject fully in an orderly way

    Introductory paragraph establishes context and states the purpose

    Body paragraphs provide all necessary details in logical sequence

    Concluding paragraph politely achieves closure

- ▶ Uses clear, simple, straightforward language—nothing fancy

- ▶ Maintains an appropriate tone, neither too formal nor too conversational

- ▶ Contains no typos or mechanical errors in spelling, punctuation, or grammar

EXERCISES

1. A product that you especially like is suddenly no longer available in retail stores in your area. Write the manufacturer an inquiry letter requesting information about how to place an order for the product.

2. Proceeding as if you've received the information requested in Exercise 1, write a letter ordering the product.

3. Pretend you've received the product ordered in Exercise 2, but it's somehow unsatisfactory. Write the manufacturer a claim letter expressing dissatisfaction and requesting an exchange or refund.

4. Team up with a classmate, exchange the claim letters you each wrote in response to Exercise 3, and then write adjustment letters to each other.

5. Write an acknowledgment letter to the editor of either your campus newspaper or a regional daily, expressing your approval of some meaningful contribution made by a local person or organization.

CHAPTER 13

Short Reports

LEARNING OBJECTIVES

When you complete this chapter, you will be able to

- ▶ Use basic principles of page design to create short reports that are visually appealing
- ▶ Write short reports of several different kinds: incident reports, progress reports, recommendation reports, travel reports, and lab reports

Andrey_Popov/Shutterstock.com

Like e-mail and letters, reports are an important form of on-the-job communication, and are often assigned in college courses as well. They can be internal or external documents and they follow certain standard conventions. In several respects, however, reports are quite different from e-mail and letters. For example, a report is rarely just a written account of information the reader already knows. Nearly always, the report's subject matter is new information. The reader may be acquainted with the general outlines of the situation the report explores but not with the details. Quite often, in fact, the reader will have requested the report just to get those details. And in the college setting, of course, the report's purpose is to demonstrate the results of an experiment or some other assigned exercise. In any case, reports communicate information that's too complicated for an e-mail or letter. Simply stated, there are two kinds of reports: short and long. This chapter focuses on the former.

PAGE DESIGN

As we have seen, the physical appearance of e-mail and letters is determined by established guidelines that vary only slightly. But reports, though also subject to certain conventions, are to a far greater extent the creation of individual writers who determine not only their content but also their physical appearance. This is significant because our ability to comprehend what we read is greatly influenced by how it looks on the page or screen. Therefore, a report should not appear difficult or intimidating. Instead, it should be visually appealing. This can be achieved by observing some basic design principles. Here they are:

- ▶ **Legible Type:** Although many different typefaces and type sizes exist, most readers respond best to 12-point type using both uppercase and lowercase letters, like this text. Anything smaller or larger is difficult to read, as is the all-capitals approach. Such variations are useful only in major headings or to emphasize a particular word or phrase.

- **Generous Margins:** Text should be framed by ample white space. Top and bottom margins should be at least 1 inch and side margins 1¼ inches. If the report is to be printed out and stapled or bound, the left-hand margins should be 2 inches. (If the report is to be duplicated back-to-back before stapling or binding, the 2-inch margin should be on the *right* side of the even-numbered pages.) The right margin should not be justified, but should be left ragged. This improves legibility by creating length variation from line to line.
- **Textual Divisions:** To organize a report's content, related paragraphs should be grouped together into separate sections, sequenced in a manner that logically reflects the nature of the information. Like those in an academic essay, paragraphs in a report should not exceed five or six sentences (unless some of the sentences are very short) and should be separated by ample white space. If the paragraphs are single spaced, insert double spacing between them. If the paragraphs are double spaced, insert triple spacing between them.
- **Headings:** Like mini-essays, the separate sections of text should be labeled with meaningful titles that orient the reader. Ordinarily, a heading consists of a word or phrase, not a complete sentence (unless the heading is phrased as a question). Its position depends on its relative importance. A major heading is set in boldface capitals and centered,

LIKE THIS

A secondary heading is set either in uppercase letters or in both uppercase and lowercase, is flush with the left-hand margin, and can be set in boldface print,

LIKE THIS

or

Like This

A subtopic heading is run into the text, separated by a period or a colon, and is sometimes indented. Set in both uppercase and lowercase letters, it can be set in bold print, like the subtopic headings in this section.

These guidelines are flexible. Various approaches to heading design and placement are used, some of them quite elaborate. Perhaps the most helpful recommendation is that a report should use no more than three levels of heading. More than that, and the page or screen looks cluttered and confusing.

- **Lists:** Sometimes a vertical list is more effective than an actual paragraph. If the purpose of the list is to reveal a definite hierarchy of importance, the items in the list should be numbered in descending order, with the most important first and the least important last. Similarly, if the list's purpose is to reflect a chronological sequence, the items should be numbered in sequential order. Numbers are not necessary, however, in a list of approximately equal items. In those cases, *bullets* (solid black dots or arrows, like those throughout this book) will suffice

KINDS OF REPORTS

Like e-mails and letters, reports are written in all kinds of situations and for a wide range of purposes. Many reports are unique in the sense that they are written in response to one-time occurrences. On the other hand, it's not uncommon for a given report to be part of an ongoing series of weekly, monthly, or annual reports on the same subject. Among the most common categories of reports are the following:

- **Incident Report**: Explains the circumstances surrounding a troublesome occurrence such as an accident, fire, equipment malfunction, or security breach.
- **Progress Report:** Outlines the status of an ongoing project or undertaking.
- **Recommendation Report:** Urges that certain procedures be adopted (or rejected).

- ▶ **Travel Report:** Identifies the purpose and summarizes the results of business-related travel.
- ▶ **Lab Report:** Summarizes the circumstances, procedures, and results of an experiment or other laboratory-based activity.

Of course, any report can serve more than one purpose. An incident report, for example, may conclude with a recommendations section intended to minimize the likelihood of recurrence, as in the example that follows. But as in every writing situation, the writer of a report must consider the purpose and intended audience, and use an appropriate tone. The content, terminology, degree of detail, and formatting must be appropriate to the circumstances.

FALLKILL AUTOMOTIVE SERVICES

MEMORANDUM

DATE: October 13, 2017

TO: Bill Shorter
                 Business Office Manager

FROM: Frank Rodgers
                 Service Manager

SUBJECT: Incident Report

Brian Johnson, a technician in the service department, backed into and damaged a customer's vehicle in the parking lot last weekend.

DESCRIPTION OF INCIDENT

At approximately 12:15 on Saturday, October 7, Johnson was leaving the premises after completing his shift. A 2008 Jeep Cherokee belonging to a customer named Yuri Soupinski was parked in the lot, having been serviced by Johnson earlier in the day. Johnson failed to notice the Jeep and backed into it, damaging its bumper, headlights, and hood. Johnson immediately notified and apologized to the customer, who was less upset and more understanding than might be expected. Because Johnson was off the clock at the time of the accident, the company incurred no liability, and Johnson's own insurance (The Hartford) has initiated proceedings to resolve the matter. Soupinski was given a "loaner" vehicle, a 2014 Kia. He has expressed satisfaction with this arrangement, and his Jeep is now being repaired at Buzzy's Auto Body, a nearby shop selected by the Hartford.

RECOMMENDATIONS

- ▶ Because Johnson is a valued employee with no history of problems of any kind, no disciplinary action should be taken at this time.
- ▶ To minimize the likelihood of other occurrences of this nature, all personnel should be emphatically reminded to exercise extreme caution when moving customers' vehicles or their own.
- ▶ Management should convey formal apologies to Soupinski and perhaps offer him some sort of token compensation—a free oil change or some such—to ensure his continued good will and patronage.

CHECKLIST: SHORT REPORT

A good short report

► Follows memo or e-mail format

► Includes certain features:

DATE line (appears automatically in e-mail)

TO line, which provides the name (and, on memos, the title and/or department) of the intended recipient

FROM line, which provides the name (appears automatically in e-mail) and, on a memo, the title and/or department of the sender; on a memo report, this line must be initialed by the sender before the report is sent

SUBJECT line, which is a clear, accurate but brief statement of what the report is about; usually a word or short phrase is enough

► Is organized into separate, labeled sections covering the subject fully in logical sequence

► Uses clear, simple, straightforward language—nothing fancy

► Maintains an appropriate tone, neither too formal nor too conversational

► Employs effective visuals—tables, graphs, charts, and the like—where necessary to clarify content

► Contains no typos or mechanical errors in spelling, punctuation, or grammar

EXERCISES

1. Write a short report to the academic dean at your college, urging that a particular college policy be modified. Be specific about your reasons. Justify the change and provide concrete suggestions about possible alternative policies.

2. Write a short report to your English professor, outlining your progress in class. Begin with a statement of what you've learned and provide an objective assessment of your performance thus far, including attendance, grades, and any other pertinent information. Conclude with a realistic estimate of the final grade you anticipate receiving.

3. Write a short report to the student services director or the physical plant supervisor at your college, evaluating a major campus building with respect to accessibility to the physically challenged. Discuss the presence or absence of special signs, doors, ramps, elevators, restroom facilities, and the like. Suggest additional accommodations that should be provided if such needs exist.

4. Write a short report to your classmates in which you evaluate a nearby store that specializes in a particular product (for example, athletic shoes, books and music, or clothing). Discuss selection, quality, price, and service.

5. Write a short report to your classmates in which you compare two local restaurants featuring similar cuisine (for example, Chinese, Italian, or Middle Eastern). Discuss quality, atmosphere, price, and service.

CHAPTER 14

Proposals

LEARNING OBJECTIVES

When you complete this chapter, you will be able to

▶ Write both external and internal proposals, whether solicited or unsolicited

▶ Write proposals that include all the required elements of proposal content

▶ Write proposals that employ an appropriate tone for the audience

fizkes/Shutterstock.com

Like correspondence and reports, proposals are a major form of workplace writing and may also be assigned in college-level English courses. Simply defined, a proposal is a persuasive offer intended to secure authorization to perform a task or provide products or services that will benefit the reader. There are basically two kinds of proposals: solicited and unsolicited (that is, requested and unrequested). Like most other kinds of business writing, a proposal—solicited or not—may be either an external or in-house document.

EXTERNAL PROPOSALS

Solicited external proposals are written in response to an RFP (request for proposal) issued by a business, agency, or organization that has identified a situation or problem it wishes to address. The RFP spells out the details of the project (for example, providing structural upgrades to a building) and provides detailed instructions for submitting bids. Often quite lengthy and complex, they commonly appear in trade publications, as government releases, and on the web. Anyone wishing to compete for the contract must follow the stated guidelines exactly, creating a proposal that will convincingly demonstrate its superiority to the others received.

An unsolicited external proposal, on the other hand, originates with the writer, who has perceived the problem or need that the resulting proposal seeks to address. Writing such a proposal is more difficult than responding to an RFP because the writer must convince the reader that the problem exists and should be solved. In short, an unsolicited proposal—usually in the form of a business letter, perhaps accompanied by supporting materials—must be more strategically persuasive than a solicited proposal.

Whether solicited or unsolicited, however, every external proposal is motivated primarily by the desire for financial reimbursement, and—because it includes a summary of the writer's qualifications for the project—can almost be seen as a form of employment application.

INTERNAL PROPOSALS

Internal proposals are often rather short (usually in the form of an e-mail or memo report) because the writers and readers are already known to each other and the context is mutually understood. Solicited in-house proposals are not usually written in response to a formal RFP, but rather to a direct assignment from a manager, supervisor, or other administrator. Unsolicited in-house proposals are motivated by an employee's own perception of need—for example, the belief that a particular policy or procedure be adopted, modified, or abandoned.

ELEMENTS OF PROPOSALS

Irrespective of whether a proposal is external or internal, solicited or unsolicited, short or long, it should include certain elements, some of which may overlap:

▶ A clear summary of the situation or problem the proposal is addressing. If unsolicited, the proposal must convince the reader that there is in fact an important unmet need.

▶ A detailed explanation of how the proposal will correct the situation or problem. This is sometimes called the "project description."

▶ Confirmation of the project's feasibility and the anticipated benefits of completing it, as well as possible negative consequences of not doing so.

▶ Convincing refutation of any probable objections.

▶ Summary of the writer's credentials and qualifications for the project.

▶ Identification of any necessary resources, equipment, or support.

▶ A reliable timetable for completion of the project.

▶ An honest, itemized estimate of the costs. Deliberately understating the timeline or the budget is not only unethical but also fraudulent. Doing so can incur legal liability.

▶ A strong conclusion that will motivate the reader to accept the proposal. A convincing cost/benefit analysis is helpful here.

APPROPRIATE TONE

As emphasized throughout this book, all writing must be sensitive to considerations of purpose, audience, and tone. But this is especially important in proposal writing because of its fundamentally persuasive nature. A proposal writer must be alert to the differing requirements of upward, lateral, and downward communication (see Chapter 3). The phrasing should be reader-centered, using the "you" approach. And because proposals often seek to improve conditions by solving problems, it's important that they maintain a positive and upbeat tone. The writer must refrain from assigning blame for existing difficulties and should instead focus on solutions. This is especially important when writing in-house, where a hostile climate can result if a writer neglects to consider people's needs and feelings, particularly if the proposal's recommendations might increase or otherwise alter the responsibilities of co-workers.

Like any piece of writing, a proposal will be far more favorably received if well-written. Nothing tarnishes credibility faster than careless typos and basic errors in spelling, punctuation, and grammar. In addition, a proposal should be clear and well-organized. Further, the wording should be simple, direct, and concise, using active verbs and everyday vocabulary, with no rambling, wordy expressions. As explained in Part 2, however, none of this can be achieved unless the writer employs the three-step approach: pre-writing, writing, and rewriting. The key is to revise, revise, and revise again. And proofread—carefully.

Here are two examples of well-executed proposals. The first, in letter format, is from a lawn care business offering its services to a local realty office. The second, in memo report format, is from a student to her instructor, regarding a topic for her research paper assignment.

ARDSLEY LAWNCARE

929 Alissa Road • Ardsley, WA 98100
(315) 555-1234

May 11, 2018

Jonathan Purdy
Purdy Realty
21 Bonita Avenue
Ardsley, WA 98100

Dear Mr. Purdy:

While servicing several properties in the vicinity of your business, we have noticed that your lawn might benefit from our attention, which would make your grounds even more attractive. Our proposal is as follows:

Five Lawn Treatments (Starting in Early Spring, Ending in Fall) @ $50 Each

- slow-release dry granular fertilizer
- pre-emergent crabgrass control
- balanced fertilizer
- broadleaf weed control
- surface insect control
- full clean-up after every treatment

We are a long-established, fully insured local business offering free service calls and a "No Damage," money-back guarantee. We use only premium-quality, EPA-approved fertilizers and pesticides. (Please see enclosed brochure.)

Certainly any business such as yours always benefits greatly from projecting a highly professional image, and the appearance of the grounds surrounding your office is a key part of conveying that positive impression to potential clients.

If you wish to discuss our proposal, please contact us at your earliest convenience. We look forward to welcoming Purdy Realty as another satisfied Ardsley customer!

Sincerely,

Lauren Brooks

Lauren Brooks
Office Manager
(e-mail: lbrooks@ardsleylawncarecom)

Enclosure

Hoboken Community College
Hoboken, New Jersey 07030

PROPOSAL

DATE: 16 October 2017

TO: Professor Alan Shulman

FROM: Rosalie D'Elia, Student
               English 101 (Section 36)

SUBJECT: Research Paper Proposal

As you know, I'm pursuing an A.A.S. degree in Art History and am enrolled in your English Composition class. We have been assigned to submit a short proposal identifying our choice of topic for the research-based term paper due at the end of the semester. The proposal must include a brief outline, a preliminary bibliography of print sources, and a timeline for completion. Here's my proposal. I hope it's satisfactory.

Topic: Five Major Art Museums in New York City

Outline: Introduction
               1 – Frick Collection
               2 – Guggenheim
               3 – Metropolitan Museum of Art
               4 – Museum of Modern Art
               5 – Whitney Museum
               Conclusion

Preliminary
Bibliography: Anderson, Maxwell L. *American Visionaries: Selections from the Whitney Museum of American Art*. Whitney Museum of American Art, 2001.

               Bailey, Colin B. *Building the Frick Collection: An Introduction to the House and Its Collections*. Frick Collection in Association with Scala, 2006.

               Elderfield, John. *Modern Painting and Sculpture: 1880 to the Present at the Museum of Modern Art*. Museum of Modern Art, 2004.

               The Metropolitan Museum of Art Guide. The Metropolitan Museum of Art, 2012.

               MOMA Collection Highlights: 350 Works from the Museum of Modern Art. Museum of Modern Art, 2012.

Timeline: Oct. 23–Nov. 6: Research
               Nov. 26: Individual Conference
               Nov. 26-Dec. 4: Writing
               Dec. 5-9: Editing/Revising
               Dec. 10: Paper Due

My paper will focus on the history of each museum, along with its holdings and special features. Having personally visited each of these museums at least once during the past several years, I am well acquainted with the topic and can illustrate the paper with photos from my own collection. In addition, I have numerous brochures, flyers, and other materials that I can use—along with each museum's Web site—to supplement my preliminary bibliography.

Given my longtime interest in the subject, I'm confident I can do a good job with this topic, and I'm hoping you'll approve it. Please contact me if you need any further information. My student e-mail account is rdelia.stu@hcc.edu, and of course I can discuss this with you after class or during your office hours in Bradford Hall.

CHECKLIST: PROPOSAL

A good proposal—

- ► is prepared in a format (e-mail, memo, or letter) appropriate to the situation;

- ► clearly identifies the problem and fully explains how the proposal addresses it;

- ► confirms the feasibility of the proposal, refuting any probable objections and establishing the writer's credentials and qualifications for the project;

- ► provides a reliable timeline for completion of the project;

- ► identifies any necessary resources, equipment, or support, and includes an itemized budget;

- ► closes with a strong, persuasive conclusion that will motivate the reader to accept the proposal;

- ► uses clear, simple, straightforward language—nothing fancy;

- ► maintains an appropriate tone, neither too formal nor too conversational;

- ► employs effective visuals—tables, graphs, charts, and the like—where necessary to clarify content;

- ► contains no typos or mechanical errors in spelling, punctuation, or grammar.

EXERCISES

1. Write a proposal seeking approval from your college's student activities director to create a new campus club or organization focused on an interest of yours.

2. Write a proposal to your college's athletic director to implement an addition or improvement to the intramural sports program.

3. Write a proposal seeking approval from the department head in your major field of study to take an elective course not among the program's recommended choices.

4. Write a proposal seeking approval from your workplace supervisor to implement a change in a particular policy or procedure you consider problematic.

5. Write a proposal seeking approval from your local library director to present a public lecture at the library on a topic you're knowledgeable about.

CHAPTER 15

Application Letters and Résumés

LEARNING OBJECTIVES

When you complete this chapter, you will be able to

- ▶ Write an effective job application letter using "full block" format and orderly, three-part organization to convey an accurate sense of your employment qualifications
- ▶ Write an effective job application letter that maintains an appropriately professional tone
- ▶ Design a visually attractive résumé that clearly details the several categories of information typically required by employers

fizkes/Shutterstock.com

Prepared in full block format and using three-part organization, a job application letter is in that sense no different from any other business letter. It should be neatly printed on 8½- by 11-inch white paper and framed by ample (1- to 1½-inch) margins. A job application letter is essentially a narrative summary of the applicant's qualifications, and in most cases should be no longer than one page. A résumé is a *detailed* list or outline of a job applicant's education, work history, and other credentials. It accompanies the application letter, complementing it by providing specifics about the information summarized in the letter. Although application letters and résumés are sometimes sent by traditional mail in response to job advertisements, many employers now prefer to receive them electronically, as e-mail attachments.

APPLICATION LETTER

When—as sometimes happens in job application situations—it's impossible to know the name of the person to whom you're writing, use "Dear Employer" as your salutation. This is a bit more original than such unimaginative greetings as the impersonal "To Whom It May Concern," the gender-biased "Dear Sir," or the old-fashioned "Dear Sir or Madam." And it will enable your letter to stand out from the others received, suggesting you're more resourceful than the other applicants.

Introduction

As explained in Chapter 12, the opening paragraph of any business letter creates context and states the letter's purpose. Since this is an employment application letter, you should say directly that you're applying for the job. Begin by coming right to the point, naming the position and how/where you heard about it. But start that first sentence with a descriptive phrase that creates context—and immediately gets the employer's attention—by identifying yourself as a qualified applicant, like this:

> As a recent County Community College graduate with an associate's degree in business, I am applying for the sales position described on your website.

Indeed, just one sentence like that would be enough as an opening paragraph.

Body Paragraphs

The middle section of any business letter must provide details. Accordingly, this is where you present a narrative summary of your qualifications: experience, education, and other credentials. Go into some depth, giving enough information to make the employer want to examine your résumé, which you should refer to specifically. But avoid *excessive* detail. Dates, addresses, and the like belong in the résumé, not the letter. Be sure to mention, however, any noteworthy attributes—specialized licenses, security clearances, computer skills, language fluency—that may set you apart from the competition. The purpose, of course, is to make the employer recognize your value as a prospective employee. Gear your letter accordingly. Without indulging in exaggeration or arrogant self-congratulation, explain why it would be in the employer's best interests to hire you. Sometimes a direct, straightforward statement such as this can be quite persuasive:

> With my college education now completed, I am eager to begin my career and will bring a high level of enthusiasm and commitment to this position.

Although there's no need to waste valuable résumé space listing references, you should mention in your letter that you can provide them. And you will be asked to do so if you become a finalist for the position. Therefore, when beginning your job search you'll need to find three people who are familiar with your work habits and are willing to write recommendation letters. Teachers and former employers are obvious possibilities. You must be certain, however, that anyone you choose will have nothing but good things to say. Tentative, halfhearted praise is worse than none at all. So you should ask to see a copy of any letter written on your behalf. Anyone reluctant to comply with such a request should almost certainly be replaced with someone more supportive.

Conclusion

The closing paragraph of any business letter, two or three sentences, just wraps things up, thanking the reader and providing a smooth conclusion that prevents the letter from ending abruptly. In an employment application letter this can be accomplished by mentioning that you're hoping for an interview. The fact is, nobody ever gets a job offer on the strength of a letter alone. The letter leads to the résumé, which (if you're lucky) leads to the interview, which (if you're *really* lucky) leads to a job offer. By mentioning the résumé and the interview in your letter, you reveal that you're a knowledgeable person familiar with the conventions of the hiring process.

Understand, however, that even one mechanical error in your letter may be enough to knock you out of the running. Make absolutely certain that there are no typos, spelling mistakes, faulty punctuation, or grammatical blunders—none whatsoever! Check and double-check to ensure that your letter (along with your résumé) is mechanically perfect. Here's an example of a good job application letter.

14 Broadman Parkway
Greenville, OR 97200
April 2, 2018

Ms. Carol Gagnon
Director of Human Resources
First National Bank of Greenville
925 Greenville Boulevard
Greenville, OR 97200

Dear Ms. Gagnon:

As an honor student about to graduate from County Community College with an AAS degree in Banking and Finance, I am applying for the teller trainee position advertised in *The Greenville Daily Sentinel.*

In college I have maintained a 3.8 grade-point average while serving as vice-president of the Mathematics Club and treasurer of the Asian-American Students Union. In keeping with my ongoing commitment to community service, last summer I joined a group of County Community College students working with senior citizens at the Greenville Acres Nursing Home, where we showed the residents how to create social media Web sites. My academic training, hands-on knowledge gained from extracurricular activities, and enhanced interpersonal skills acquired at Greenville Acres—not to mention my language skills in Korean and Spanish—equip me to become a valued member of your staff. Past and current employers, listed on the enclosed résumé, will attest to my strong work ethic. I can provide those individuals' names and contact information on request.

Thank you for considering my application. Please phone or e-mail me to arrange an interview at your convenience.

Sincerely,

Dustin Kim

Dustin Kim

Enclosure: résumé

RÉSUMÉ

As mentioned earlier, a résumé is a detailed listing of the job applicant's qualifications. The following categories of information typically appear:

- ► Contact Information
- ► Career Objective
- ► Education
- ► Work Experience
- ► Military Service
- ► Computer Literacy
- ► Specialized Skills or Credentials
- ► Honors and Awards
- ► Community Service

Of course, few résumés include *all* these categories. Not everyone has served in the military, for example, or received awards. Not everyone is active in the community or possesses special skills. But practically anyone can create an effective résumé. The trick is to carefully evaluate your background and emphasize your strengths. A person with a college degree but little work experience, for example, would highlight the education component. On the other hand, someone whose job experience outweighed the schooling would emphasize the employment history. Here are some pointers regarding the various sections of a résumé.

Contact Information

Provide *only* your name, address, phone number, and e-mail address, all at the top of the page. Note: If your e-mail address is in any way silly or juvenile, you must establish a professional e-mail account for job-search purposes. Ditto for your voice mail message. (And if your Facebook or other social networking sites contain anything that might displease potential employers, that must also be corrected.)

Career Objective

A brief but focused statement of your professional goals. Of course, if you wind up applying for a broad range of positions, this section must be revised to suit each situation.

Education

Using *reverse* chronological order (most recent first), provide the name and address of each school you've attended, and mention your program(s) of study and any degrees, diplomas, certificates, or honors received. Omit high school unless you're trying to beef up an otherwise skimpy résumé.

Work Experience

Like the education section, this is one of the most important parts of your résumé. Again using reverse chronological order, provide each job title, dates of employment, name and address of employer, and—if they're not obvious from the job title—the principal duties involved. If you've worked at many different jobs, some for short periods, it's wise to list only your most important positions and lump the others together in a one-sentence summary like this:

> Have also held part-time and temporary positions as a farm worker, retail sales clerk, and marina dock attendant.

Notice that in résumé writing it's not necessary to say "I." You are allowed to save space by using a somewhat telegraphic style that cuts right to the verb: "Did this, did that," rather than "I did this, I did that."

Military Service

If applicable, list the branch and dates of service, the highest rank achieved, and any noteworthy travel or duty. Applicants with no other significant employment history sometimes list military service under the work experience category.

Computer Literacy

A highly valued attribute—indeed, a necessary one—in today's technology-driven workplace. Mention specific word-processing and other software with which you're familiar (for example, Microsoft Word and Excel or Adobe Photoshop).

Specialized Skills or Credentials

Include licenses, certifications, security clearances, language competency, and proficiency with specific machines—in short, any "plus" that doesn't fit neatly elsewhere.

Honors and Awards

These can be academic or otherwise. In some cases—if you received a medal while in the military, for example, or made the college honor roll—it's best to include such distinctions under the appropriate categories. But if the Kiwanis Club awarded you its annual scholarship or you were cited for community leadership by the mayor, these honors would be highlighted in a separate category.

Community Service

Volunteer work or memberships in local clubs, organizations, or church groups are appropriate here. Most helpful are well-known activities such as Scouting, Little League, 4-H, and the like. Include details: dates of service or membership, offices held, special projects you initiated or coordinated. But don't claim involvement in organizations or activities you actually know little about. Such unethical falsification will become obvious if the interviewer asks about your outside interests.

As we have seen, all business letters—application letters included—are governed by standards that determine layout and organization: full block style, three-part structure. Once you understand those guidelines, writing a letter is really pretty easy. But résumés are another story. Many different approaches are in widespread use, and the design and appearance of a résumé are entirely up to the person writing it. This is good and bad. On the "plus" side, this flexibility gives the writer a great deal of freedom to experiment and innovate. On the "minus" side, however, this liberty often results in résumés that are visually cluttered and hard to read. To avoid that pitfall, follow these well-established guidelines:

- ► Like the application letter, the résumé should be printed on 8½- by 11-inch white paper, with ample margins. Use boldface, underlining, bullets, and other design options to create an inviting appearance. But don't overdo it. Use no more than two different fonts and three different type sizes.
- ► The various categories of information must be clearly labeled and distinct from one another so the employer can quickly review your background without having to labor over the page or screen. Indeed, most employers will simply discard a confusing résumé and move on to the next one.

- ▶ All necessary details must appear—names, addresses, dates, and so on—and must be presented in a uniform format throughout. For example, do not abbreviate words like *Avenue* and *Street* in one section and then spell them out elsewhere. Be consistent.
- ▶ Use *reverse* chronological order; list the most recent information first, then work backward through time.
- ▶ Do not allow your résumé to exceed two pages.
- ▶ Like your letter, your résumé must be mechanically perfect, with no errors in spelling, punctuation, or grammar. Carefully edit for careless blunders—typos, inconsistent spacing, and the like.

What follows is a sample résumé that observes the basic principles of good design. Prepared in standard, reverse-chronological format, it would accompany the letter shown earlier.

Dustin Kim

14 Broadman Parkway, Greenville OR 97200
(202) 556-2557 • dkim@cccstudent.edu

Career Objective

Secure, full-time position in banking.

Education

County Community College (2014–present)
1101 College Drive, Greenville OR

Will graduate in May 2018 with AAS degree in Banking and Finance. Have maintained 3.80 grade point average while serving as vice-president of the Mathematics Club and treasurer of the Asian-American Students Union.

Experience

- Counter Clerk (2015–present)
  Quik Stop Grocery, 34 Wade Street, Greenville OR

  Part-time position to help meet college expenses.

- Warehouse Worker (2012–2013)
  Cantor & Mitchell, Inc., 1 Meeker Avenue, Greenville OR

  Full-time job after high school, before deciding to pursue college education.

Language Proficiency

- Native fluency in Korean

- Conversational ability in Spanish (two years of college-level coursework)

Community Activities

- Volunteer, Greenville Acres Nursing Home (Summer, 2015)
  Taught computer skills (Facebook, etc.) to senior citizens.

- Assistant Baseball Coach, Greenville Little League (2016–present)

CHECKLIST: APPLICATION LETTER & RESUME

A good application letter

- ▶ Follows full block format

- ▶ Is organized into paragraphs

    First paragraph asks for the job by name and indicates where you learned of the opening

    Middle paragraphs briefly outline your credentials and refer the reader to your résumé

    Last paragraph politely achieves closure, mentioning that you would like an interview

- ▶ Does not exceed one page

- ▶ Uses clear, simple, straightforward language—nothing fancy

- ▶ Maintains an appropriate tone, neither too formal nor too conversational

- ▶ Contains no typos or mechanical errors in spelling, punctuation, or grammar

A good résumé

- ▶ *Looks* good, making effective use of white space, capitalization, bold print, and other format options

- ▶ Includes no irrelevant personal information

- ▶ Includes separate, labeled sections for education, experience, and other major categories of professional qualifications, providing all necessary details (dates, addresses, etc.)

- ▶ Maintains a consistent approach to abbreviation, spacing, and other design elements

- ▶ Does not exceed two pages

- ▶ Contains no typos or mechanical errors

EXERCISES

Three application letters accompanied by résumés follow. For a variety of reasons, all are badly flawed. Rewrite each to eliminate its particular weaknesses.

Jennifer Reaney
333 Fairmount Ave.
Jersey City, N.J. 03506
November 10, 2017

Mr. Morton Higgins
Glenwood Restaurant
144 West Side Avnue
Jersey City, New Jersey

Dear Sir;

I saw your add in The Jersey Journal and want to apply for the job.

I have inclosed my resume, I have all the qualifications for which you are looking for.

I look forward to hearing from you soon.

Your's truley,

Jennifer Reaney

RESUME

Name: Jennifer Reaney   Marital Status: divorced, two kids
Address: 333 Fairmount Ave.   Health: Excellent
Jersey City, New Jersey   Height: 5"3'
Phone: (201) 333–1234   Weight: 155 lbs
Religion: Cathlic   Citizenship: U.S.A.
Date of Birth: January 10, 1993   Military Service: none

Education

2017 to now   New Jersey City University
                                          Hospitality Manigemint Major

Class of 2011   Dickinson High School
                                          Jersey City, N.J.

Experience

20011   Dishwasher
                                          Mama Gina's Ristorante
                                          Jersey City, New Jersey

2012   Waitress
                                          Tania's Restaurant
                                          Jersey City, N.J.

2013   Dishwasher
                                          Pete & Dominics Restaurant
                                          Jersey City, NJ

20013–201   Waitress
                                          Pete & Dominic's Restaurant
                                          Jersey City, N.J.

2014   Hostess
                                          Pete and Dominics
                                          Jersey City, N.J.

2015–2016   Bartender
                                          Churchills Tavern
                                          Bayonne New Jersey

2016–now   Dining Room Manger
                                          Churchills
                                          Bayonne, NJ

Computers

I know how to use the POSiTouch computer systems.

References—Excelent refrences available on request

385 Leslie Street
Wallach, CA 92500
November 10, 2017

Ms. Mary Jane Reed, Branch Manager
Central Bank of Wallach
Wallach, CA 92500

Dear Ms. Reed:

As a May 2017 graduate of County Community College with an A.A.S. degree and a dual major in Business and Accounting, I am very much interested in the financial services position you have advertised in the November 6 edition of *The Smallville Courier*, and I would like you to consider me a serious candidate for that opening.

As mentioned above, I am a 2017 graduate of County Community College with an A.A.S. degree and a dual major in Business and Accounting, and I was on either the Dean's List (honors) or the President's List (high honors) every semester, compiling an overall GPA (grade-point average) of 3.87 and earning admission to the prestigious Phi Theta Kappa honor society. I completed such challenging classes as Business Law, Economics, Computer Applications, Principles of Management, Financial Management, Business Math, and Investment Science, along with General Education requirements such as English 101 & 102, Social Science (Psychology and Sociology), Lab Science (Biology 1 & 2), and Physical Education (Physical Fitness and First Aid), and several electives. While at CCC I served as Student Congress Treasurer for two semesters, maintaining a $3000 budget that funded thirty-five campus organizations; it was my responsibility to approve and verify all disbursements, including the Student Congress payroll. I also competed on the varsity tennis team during my second year, playing in both singles and doubles matches, compiling a 6 & 2 singles record and a 4 & 3 doubles record as the team achieved a winning season. In addition, I also completed an internship at the Sterling Insurance Company in nearby Elliston, California during the fall semester of 2016, contacting and meeting with prospective clients, answering client inquiries, and performing general office duties. During the summers of 2016, 2015, and 2014 I worked as a Trust Administrative Assistant at the First City Bank of Elliston, researching financial investment data, organizing trust account information, screening and answering customer inquiries, and composing routine business correspondence. Further, I was named the 2016 Red Cross "Volunteer of the Year" for this region.

Obviously, I am very highly qualified for the position you have advertised, and I can provide excellent references upon request. I look forward to meeting with you in an interview setting at your very earliest convenience. Thank you very much for considering me for this highly desirable position.

Sincerely,

Alexander Portnoy

Résumé

Alexander Portnoy
385 Leslie Street
Wallach, CA 92500
(805) 555-5555
Aportnoy2 email.net

OBJECTIVE

A permanent position in financial services.

EDUCATION

Associate in Applied Science
County Community College

EXPERIENCE

Student Congress Treasurer
County Community College
Intern

Sterling Insurance Company

Trust Administrative Assistant
First City Bank of Elliston

INTERESTS

Tennis

REFERENCES

Available upon request.

April 25, 2018

Shaniqua Gaines
Director of Security
Chesterton Mall
Chesterton, OH 44300

Dear Mrs. Gaines:

I will be graduating from college with a Certificate in Security Management next month, and would like to apply for the shopping center security position you have announced. My background—especially my education, my military service as an M.P., and my former employment as a college campus security guard—makes me well-qualified for this job. After you have had some time to review my enclosed resume I will contact you about arranging an interview.

Thank you,

Neil E. Whalen

Neil E. Whalen

RESUME

NAME: Neil E. Whalen

ADDRESS: 409 Kahler Road
                             Chesterton, OH 90406

PHONE: (805) 123-1234

CAREER OBJECTIVE: Full-Time Position as a Shopping Mall Security Guard

EDUCATION: Certificate in Security Management (2018)
                             John Jay College
                             New York, NY

EMPLOYMENT: Stockbroker's Assistant (2010–2012)
                             Carlisle & Jacquelin
                             2 Broadway
                             New York, NY 10005

RESPONSIBILITIES: Worked with stockbrokers on the trading floor of the New York Stock
                   Exchange, executing "odd lot" market orders.

EMPLOYMENT: Military Policeman (2012–2014)
                             United States Army War College
                             Carlisle Barracks
                             Carlisle, PA 17013

RESPONSIBILITIES: Performed such duties as radio car patrol, traffic control, and building security,
                   checking top-secret security passes.

EMPLOYMENT: Campus Security Officer (2014–2016)
                             County Community College
                             1101 College Drive
                             Binghamton, MO 64100

RESPONSIBILITIES: Enforced parking regulations, checked student i.d., monitored campus for
                   safety and security violations.

INTERESTS & ACTIVITIES: sports, martial arts, hunting

REFERENCES: None at present.

PART 6

Research-Based Writing

In most college courses (and in many high school classes as well), students are required to complete one or more research-based writing assignments. Sometimes the topic is given by the teacher, but at the college level students are often permitted to choose. In either case, you have to gather information by consulting reliable sources: books, magazines, newspapers, academic journals, and websites. But you can't simply copy other writers' ideas word-for-word and present them as if they were your own. That's plagiarism. Instead, you're required to use summary, paraphrase, and quotation correctly, and provide documentation to identify your sources and indicate where you've used them. In addition, research-based assignments sometimes involve writing collaboratively. These chapters show you how to handle all these aspects of research-based writing.

From *College English: The Basics, 2nd Edition* by George J. Searles. © 2017 by George J. Searles. Reprinted by permission of Kendall Hunt Publishing Company.

CHAPTER 16

Finding, Evaluating, and Integrating Sources of Information

LEARNING OBJECTIVES

When you complete this chapter, you will be able to

- ▶ Distinguish between reliable and unreliable sources of information
- ▶ Integrate information by using summary, paraphrase, and quotation correctly
- ▶ Function productively in collaborative writing situations

Rido/Shutterstock.com

Whether your professor assigns the topic of your research or allows you to select your own, you have to conduct research that enables you to gather enough information to cover the topic in depth, going beyond what you already know about it.

SOURCES

The basic sources of information appropriate for use in research-based writing are books, magazines, newspapers, academic journals, and websites.

Books

The most traditional source of in-depth information, books are published on an enormous range of topics. Whatever you're writing about, there are countless books that can provide you with abundant material that can enable you to develop your paper. But always look for books that have been published fairly recently. This helps you narrow your focus when searching your college library's holdings. More importantly, the recent titles are the most up-to-date and therefore reflect current thinking on the topic. In addition, it makes sense to choose books from university presses and long-established commercial publishers because these are more selective in choosing what to print. As a result, their books tend to be more accurate and reliable than those produced by lesser-known publishers. Here are a half-dozen of the most highly-regarded commercial houses, all based in New York:

- ▶ Farrar, Straus, and Giroux
- ▶ Harper Collins

- ► Houghton Mifflin
- ► Alfred A. Knopf
- ► W.W. Norton & Company
- ► Random House

Magazines

Even a brief glance at the display of magazines in any store that sells them reveals that countless such periodicals are published on a weekly or monthly basis. Some, like *Time* and *Sports Illustrated*, are quite well-known, others less so. But the mere fact that a magazine enjoys high visibility does not necessarily mean it's a good source. Many popular magazines are quite superficial, devoted to coverage of celebrity gossip and other trivial concerns. There are also many good but highly specialized magazines (like *Car & Driver*, *Psychology Today*, and *Wired*) that focus exclusively on one area of interest. Others, however, have broader appeal. Here's a short list of some of the best general audience magazines, all of which cover the arts and current events:

- ► *The Atlantic*
- ► *The Economist*
- ► *Harper's*
- ► *The Nation*
- ► *The New Republic*
- ► *The New Yorker*

Most college and university libraries maintain subscriptions to these magazines, along with many others. But it's advisable to check with your professor before using magazines as sources because some consider them too lightweight for serious research and will not accept them.

Newspapers

Although several major American newspapers have gone out of business in recent years, there are literally hundreds still being published. But only a few are typically cited as sources in academic writing. Here's the list, a short one:

- ► *The Los Angeles Times*
- ► *The Wall Street Journal*
- ► *The New York Times*
- ► *The Washington Post*

The New York Times and *The Washington Post* (<u>not</u> to be confused with the tabloid-format *New York Post*) are considered the most reputable. Indeed, *The New York Times* is one of the most respected newspapers not only in this country but in the world. Virtually all college and university libraries subscribe to *The New York Times* and *The Wall Street Journal*, along with local papers, and may maintain microfilm files going back many years. In addition, there are web archives that provide access to past issues.

Academic Journals

Every area of academic study supports many scholarly journals that publish highly specialized articles, almost always written by professors who teach in that field. Accordingly, these essays often discuss recent research or newly emerging theories. Given their familiarity with these journals, many professors require their students to consult such sources when completing research-based assignments.

Databases

To track down journal articles (or, for that matter, articles in magazines and newspapers as well), it's easiest to consult computerized databases that allow you to locate material related to your topic. Here are several very useful such resources, all available online from EBSCOhost, a service subscribed to by college and university libraries:

▶ **Academic Search Complete** is the most comprehensive database, covering articles in thousands of publications in all disciplines.

▶ **Associates Program Source** is geared to the needs of community college students, focusing on nearly 1,000 journals aligned with programs of study typical of the two-year schools.

▶ **Business Source Complete** is devoted exclusively to indexing and abstracts of business articles as far back as the 1880s.

▶ **CINAHL Plus with Full Text** is the best database for articles about nursing and allied health services, covering more than 750 scholarly journals in those fields.

▶ **Computer Source** provides up-to-date information on articles about trends and developments in the field of high technology.

▶ **ERIC** is the Education Resource Information Center database, containing links to more than 300,000 articles dating back to the 1960s.

▶ **GreenFILE** covers the environment, with information on nearly 5,000 articles about global warming, green building, pollution, sustainable agriculture, renewable energy, recycling, and the like.

▶ **Humanities International Complete** includes data on more than 2,000 journals devoted to the humanities (art, music, literature, film, etc.)

▶ **Newspaper Source Plus** covers more than 700 newspapers along with more than a half-million television and radio news transcripts.

▶ **Vocational and Career Collection** serves community colleges and trade schools by providing information on articles in more than 300 trade and industry-related periodicals.

Websites

As anyone who has ever clicked a mouse has immediately discovered, the amount of information available on the web is seemingly unlimited. A Google search for virtually any topic results in hundreds if not thousands of results. But the quality of this material varies greatly. The eighth edition of the *MLA Handbook for Writers of Research Papers* says it quite well:

> Assessing Internet resources is a particular challenge. Whereas the print publications that researchers depend on are generally issued by reputable publishers, like university presses, that accept responsibility for the quality and reliability of the works they distribute, relatively few electronic publications currently have comparable authority. Some Internet publications are peer-reviewed, but others are not. Online materials are often self-published, without any outside review. (34)

Therefore, you must be very selective when gathering information online. Here are some questions to ask yourself when evaluating electronic sources:

▶ Who has posted or sponsored this site? An individual? An organization? A special interest or advocacy group? What are their credentials or qualifications? The final suffix in the URL will reveal a site's origins:

.com   commercial enterprise
.org   nonprofit organization

.edu   college, university, or other educational institution
.gov   government agency
.mil   military group

▶ Sometimes it's helpful to enter the individual's or group's name in a search engine to see what other sites emerge. This can reveal affiliations and biases that have an impact on credibility.

▶ Does the site itself provide links to related sites? Does it credit its own sources?

▶ Is the information presented in a reasonably objective fashion or does the site seem to favor or promote a particular viewpoint or perspective?

▶ Does the site provide an e-mail address or other contact information that you can use to seek more background?

▶ What is the date of the posting? Is the information current?

▶ How well-written is the site? How well designed? In short, does it seem to be the work of amateurs or professionals?

Be aware that, despite its wide range and resulting popularity among Internet users, *Wikipedia, the free encyclopedia* is not considered an acceptable source for academic research. For that matter, most professors do not accept print encyclopedias either. But encyclopedias—*Wikipedia* included—can lead you to more highly regarded sources because encyclopedia entries commonly include a bibliography of related works.

INTEGRATING INFORMATION

When developing your paper by inserting information you've gathered from your research, there are basically three approaches you can use: summary, paraphrase, and quotation. Most research-based writing relies on all three. But they are quite different from one another.

Rachata Teyparsit/Shutterstock.com

Summary

In the very broadest sense, all writing is a form of summary. Whenever we put words on paper or computer screen, we condense ideas and information to make them clear to the reader. Ordinarily, however, the term *summary* refers to a brief but accurate statement of the essential content of something heard, seen, or read. For any kind of summary, the writer reduces a body of material to its bare essentials. Summarizing is therefore an exercise in compression, requiring simple and concrete language. Summarizing requires an especially keen sense not only of what to include, but also what to *leave out*. The goal is to highlight key points and not burden the reader with unnecessary details. Because of its innately compact nature, a summary is always a shorter version of the original wording. If any original wording is retained, it must be enclosed in quotation marks. (See "Quotation," below.)

Paraphrase

Like summary, paraphrase involves rewording. But, *unlike* summary, it's often *longer* than the original. That's because its purpose is not only to present the original information but also to clarify it. Sometimes this is accomplished by choosing words that are more familiar. Often it involves providing explanations or re-sequencing the original information to make it easier to understand. Paraphrase is especially useful when you're attempting to deal with technical or otherwise specialized subject matter.

Quotation

Sometimes called "direct quotation," this involves using the exact same phrasing that appears in the original, repeating it *verbatim* (word-for-word), and enclosing it within quotation marks. Indeed, that's the main purpose of quotation marks—to indicate that what appears between them is an exact copy. Sometimes a quotation will include *ellipses* (four periods). They indicate that an entire sentence or more has been removed from the original at that point. When something is removed *within* a quoted sentence, the ellipsis consists of only three periods.

If you wish to use a longer, paragraph-length quotation, you can insert it into your paper using "block" quotation, as in the example below, a passage from *New York Safe Boating*, a publication of the New York State Office of Parks, Recreation and Historic Preservation:

> The standard outboard engine is a complete propulsion unit. Boats that use outboard engines don't have rudders, so the boat turns in response to operator's turning of the outboard engine. Most outboard engines are mounted on the transom of the boat. The outboard engine has many advantages. In general, outboards have an excellent power to weight ratio so the operator can get a lot of power and speed out of a small engine. These engines are easy to service and replace. They don't take up space in the boat, leaving more room for passengers and gear. On the downside, they are not as efficient or economical to operate as other types of engines. (9)

Note that block quotation does not require quotation marks. This is because the block format itself indicates that the passage is a quote. Although quotation certainly has value, not least because it exactly captures the content and tone of the source, do not depend on it too heavily. Good research-based writing is never simply an exercise in stringing quotes together. No more than 20 percent of your paper should consist of quotation.

COLLABORATION

Most writing is done by one person working alone. This is true of e-mail, business letters, short reports, and certainly the academic essay. And it's often true of long papers as well. However, since the subject matter of long papers is usually complex, they are sometimes group-written. Indeed, most college students—and nearly all workplace writers—are called upon to cooperate on writing projects at least occasionally. This kind of teamwork is common because it affords certain real advantages.

For example, a group that works well together can produce a long paper faster than one person working alone. In addition, a team possesses a broader perspective and greater range of knowledge and expertise than an individual. To slightly amend the old saying, two heads—or more—are better than one. In addition, with the increasing sophistication of groupware (word-processing and document design programs created specifically for collaborative use) such as Google Docs, teamworking has become easier and faster than ever.

Nevertheless, collaboration can pose problems if the members of the group have difficulty interacting smoothly. Teamwork requires everyone involved to exercise tact, courtesy, and responsibility. The following factors are essential to successful collaboration:

1. Everyone on the team must fully understand the purpose, goals, and intended audience of the project.

2. Team members must agree to set aside individual preferences in favor of the group's collective judgment.

3. The team must have a leader—someone whom the other members are willing to recognize as the coordinator. Ideally, the leader is elected from within the group, rather than self-appointed. The leader must not only be knowledgeable and competent, but should also be a "people person" with good interpersonal skills. The leader has many responsibilities:

- ▶ Helps establish procedural guidelines, especially regarding progress assessment
- ▶ Monitors team members' involvement, providing encouragement and assistance
- ▶ Promotes consensus and referees disagreements
- ▶ Maintains an accurate master file of the evolving document

In short, the leader functions as team manager, ensuring a successful outcome by keeping everyone on task and holding the whole effort together.

4. The team must create clearly defined roles for the other members, assigning responsibilities according to everyone's talents and strengths. For example, the group's most competent researcher takes charge of information retrieval. Someone trained in drafting or computer-assisted design agrees to format the report and create visuals. The member with the best keyboarding skills actually produces the document. The best writer is the overall editor, making final judgments on matters of organization, style, mechanics, and the like. If an oral presentation is required, the group's most confident public speaker assumes that responsibility. In some cases a given individual might play more than one role, but everyone must feel satisfied that the work has been fairly distributed.

5. Once the project has begun, the team continuously assesses its progress, prevents duplication of effort, and resolves any problems that may arise. All disagreements or differences of opinion are reconciled in a productive manner. In any group undertaking, a certain amount of conflict is inevitable and indeed necessary to achieve consensus. This interplay, however, should be a source of creative energy, not antagonism. Issues must be dealt with on an objectively intellectual level, not in a personal or emotional manner.

6. All members of the group must complete their fair share of the work in a conscientious manner and observe all deadlines. Nothing is more disruptive to a team's progress than an irresponsible member who fails to complete work punctually or "vanishes" for long periods of time. To maintain contact, group members should exchange phone numbers and/or e-mail addresses. Another option is to use file transfer protocol (FTP) to create a common website to which group members can post drafts for review by their teammates. In any case, electronic communication should be seen simply as a way to keep in touch, not as a substitute for frequent face-to-face interaction.

Theoretically, a group can handle the actual writing of the paper in one of three ways:

- ▶ The whole team writes the paper collectively, then the editor revises the draft and submits it to the group for final approval or additional revisions.
- ▶ One person writes the entire paper, and then the group—led by the editor—revises it collectively.
- ▶ Each team member writes one part of the paper individually, and then the editor revises each part and submits the complete draft to the whole group for final approval or additional revisions.

Of these alternatives, the first is the most truly collaborative but is also extremely difficult and time-consuming, requiring exceptional harmony within the group. The second method is preferable but places too great a burden on one writer. The third approach is the most common and is certainly the best, provided the editor seeks clarification from individuals whenever necessary during the editing process. For this reason, the third approach is the one that underlies most of what's been said here. Note, however, that in all three approaches the whole group gets to see the proposed final version and provide additional fine-tuning if necessary. In the workplace, everybody on the team will be equally responsible for the outcome. And in the college setting, everybody usually receives the same grade on the assignment. Therefore, no one should be dissatisfied with the final product. Collaboration is, after all, a team effort with the goal of producing a polished document approved by all members of the team.

EXERCISES

1. Pretend you are writing a research paper on the topic of cigarette smoking among doctors and nurses. Using your college library's resources and the Internet, track down five sources of information on this subject:

   ► a chapter in an edited book

   _____

   ► an article in a popular magazine

   _____

   ► an article in a medical journal

   _____

   ► an article in a major newspaper

   _____

   ► a discussion on a website

   _____

2. Find an obviously biased (and therefore unreliable) website devoted to a controversial topic such as gun control, global warming, or capital punishment. Write a short explanation of why you think the site is questionable.

   _____

   _____

   _____

3. Find an apparently objective (and therefore reliable) website devoted to a controversial topic such as those mentioned in Exercise 2. Write a short explanation of why you think the site is legitimate.

   _____

   _____

   _____

4. Write a summary of the Gettysburg Address.

5. Write a paraphrase of the Gettysburg Address.

6. Team up with two or three other students and produce a detailed list of the classrooms, labs, and other instructional spaces in one campus building. Be sure to include the location of each, along with all furnishings and equipment (e.g., computers, projectors, interactive whiteboards, etc.). Then write a collaborative essay in which you discuss whether the building is well suited to its purposes.

CHAPTER 17

Documentation

LEARNING OBJECTIVES

When you complete this chapter, you will be able to

- ► Avoid plagiarism
- ► Create correctly formatted bibliographies using both MLA and APA styles
- ► Create correct in-text citations using both MLA and APA styles

Whatever sources you finally use in a research assignment, you must provide documentation. That is, you must identify those sources and indicate where you have used them. In everyday writing this is often accomplished by inserting the relevant information directly into the text, as in this example.

> As journalist Verlyn Klinkenborg says in his article "How to Destroy Species, Including Us," in the March 20, 2014, issue of *The New York Review of Books*, "The last time species died out as fast as they're doing now was 65 million years ago, when an asteroid crashed into earth at a low angle, leaving an enormous crater near what is now the Yucatán and causing a long-lasting global winter."

This straightforward approach eliminates the need for a bibliography (list of sources) at the end of the piece. In academic writing, however, documentation nearly always includes both a bibliography and parenthetical citations identifying the origin of each quotation, statistic, paraphrase, or visual when it appears within the text.

PLAGIARISM

Documentation is necessary to avoid *plagiarism*, which the new (eighth) edition of the *MLA Handbook* defines as, "presenting another person's ideas, information, expressions, or entire work as one's own...a kind of fraud...always a serious moral and ethical offense" (7). The previous (eighth) edition of the *Handbook* provided useful guidelines for recognizing and avoiding plagiarism:

From *College English: The Basics, 2nd Edition* by George J. Searles. © 2017 by George J. Searles. Reprinted by permission of Kendall Hunt Publishing Company.

"You have plagiarized if:

- you took notes that did not distinguish summary and paraphrase from quotation and then you presented wording from the notes as if it were all your own.
- while browsing the Web, you copied text and pasted it into your paper without quotation marks or without citing the source.
- you repeated or paraphrased someone's wording without acknowledgment.
- you took someone's unique or particularly apt phrase without acknowledgment.
- you paraphrased someone's argument or presented someone's line of thought without acknowledgment.
- you bought or otherwise acquired a research paper and handed in part or all of it as your own.

You can avoid plagiarism by:

- making a list of the writers and viewpoints you discovered in your research and using this list to double-check the presentation of material in your paper.
- keeping the following three categories distinct in your notes: your ideas, your summaries of others' material, and exact wording you copy.
- identifying the sources of all material you borrow—exact wording, paraphrases, ideas, arguments, and facts.
- checking with your instructor when you are uncertain about your use of sources." (*MLA Handbook for Writers of Research Papers*, 7th ed., pp. 60–61)

CHECKLIST: RESEARCH-BASED ESSAY

A good research-based essay

- ▶ Has a meaningful title that clearly identifies the topic

- ▶ Opens with an interesting, attention-getting introduction that establishes the significance of the topic, and provides a firm thesis statement

- ▶ Is organized into several body paragraphs, enough to fully cover the topic, and proceeds in a coherent, step-by-step way, focusing on one main idea at a time

- ▶ Draws upon reliable sources of information

- ▶ Employs paraphrase, summary, and quotation correctly, avoiding plagiarism

- ▶ Closes with a smooth, meaningful conclusion that gracefully resolves the discussion by somehow relating back to the introduction

- ▶ Includes full documentation—bibliography and parenthetical citations—prepared in either MLA or APA format

- ▶ Uses clear, simple, straightforward language—nothing fancy

- ▶ Maintains an appropriate tone, neither too formal nor too conversational

- ▶ Contains no inappropriate material

- ▶ Contains no typos or mechanical errors in spelling, capitalization, punctuation, or grammar

- ▶ Satisfies the length requirements of the assignment

MODEL RESEARCH-BASED ESSAY

Sara Nac

Professor Rosemary Smith

English 101

December 11, 2017

News Events on My Birthday: November 10, 1995

I was born at St. Elizabeth's Hospital in Utica, New York, at 2:00 P.M. on Friday, November 10, 1995, weighing in at twelve pounds. My parents took me home to Edward Street, where they still reside today. This research-based essay will summarize some of the major news events that were reported in the media on the day of my birth, focusing on world, national, and local stories, along with sports and entertainment. I will also update each of the stories, placing them in contemporary perspective.

In world news, Ukraine and Macedonia ratified the European Convention on Human Rights, joining thirty-six other countries as members of the Council of Europe, an organization that "promotes democracy, monitors human rights and fosters cultural diversity" ("2 Nations" D1). Based in Strasbourg, France, the Council still exists today, and now has forty-seven member nations. ("47")

One highly controversial national story involved Jack Kevorkian, a Michigan physician who had become famous as "Dr. Death" for helping terminally ill people commit suicide. He was charged with the murder of Patricia Cashman, 58, of San Marcos, California, after helping her inhale lethal exhaust fumes from her car ("After" A20). She was the twenty-sixth person known to have sought his assistance since 1990 (Borg). Kevorkian was acquitted, as he had been many times before, but was finally convicted in 1999 after participating in yet another voluntary suicide, that of Thomas Youk, 51, of Detroit, and was sentenced to ten to twenty-five years in prison ("Kevorkian Case"). In 2007, however, he was released after earning "time off for good behavior" ("Kevorkian Released"). An HBO movie about him, *You Don't Know Jack*, starring Al Pacino, was released in 2010 ("You").

He died in 2011 at age 83. (Schneider A1)

On the local scene, Democrat Ed Hanna, who had been Utica's mayor from 1974

to 1977, returned to that office by winning a close three-way race, defeating four-term

incumbent Republican Louis LaPolla and Independent Barbara Klein (Crockett 1A). Four

years later he was reelected, getting 75% of the vote, but resigned in 2000 because of health

issues and was replaced by common council president Tim Julian, who remained in office

until 2007. Hanna ran against Julian in 2007, but both lost to David Roefaro (Dufresne).

Hanna died in 2009 at the age of 86. As Julian said, "His methods were sometimes

unconventional, but he had a certain knack of getting the people to rally behind him"

("Hanna"). Today Utica's mayor is Robert Palmieri.

In sports, the Chicago Bulls remained undefeated, winning their fourth straight

basketball game, a 106-88 drubbing of the Cleveland Cavaliers. As usual, the Bulls' high-

scorer was All-Star Michael Jordan, with 29 points. But Jordan's teammate Scottie Pippen

also sparkled, recording a rare triple-double, with 18 points, 13 rebounds, and 12 assists

("Triple-Double" B14). The Bulls were the most dominant NBA team of the 1990s, winning

six championships as Jordan established himself as one of the very greatest players of all

time ("History"). Jordan and Pippen are now retired, and both are in the Basketball Hall of

Fame. ("Hall")

Among the Hollywood movies in the theaters on my birthday was *The American*

President, a "comedy-drama about a widowed United States president and a lobbyist who

fall in love." Michael Douglas plays the president and Annette Bening the lobbyist. Directed

by Rob Reiner, the movie was rated PG-13 ("The American"). Douglas, one of America's

most celebrated actors, has starred in a great many other films. Bening has also won

many awards, including The Screen Actors Guild "Best Female Actress in a Leading Role"

recognition for her performance in *American Beauty*. ("Annette")

So there you have it: a selection of some of the highlights of my birthday twenty-

two years ago. To my parents, however, probably none of these occurrences seemed very

important, as they were undoubtedly more focused on my arrival!

Works Cited

"After Kevorkian-Aided Suicide, Clash Over How Ill Woman Was." *The New York Times*, 10 Nov. 1995, p. A20. *ProQuest Historical Newspapers: The New York Times with Index*. Accessed 20 Nov. 2017.

"The American President." *IMNb: The Internet Movie Database*. www.imdb.com. Accessed 20 Nov. 2017.

"Annette Bening." *Moviefone*. www.moviefone.com. Accessed 20 Nov. 2017.

Borg, Gary. "Kevorkian Uses His 'Machine' To Assist in Latest Aided Suicide." *Chicago Tribune*, 13 Nov. 1995. www.chicagotribune.org. Accessed 20 Nov. 2017.

Crockett, Alan D. "It's Hanna: Vote Recount Makes Him Utica Mayor, Again." *Observer-Dispatch*, 10 Nov. 1995. www.uticaod.com. Accessed 20 Nov. 2017.

Dufresne, Debbie. "Timeline of the Life and Career of Edward A. Hanna." *Observer-Dispatch*, 14 Mar. 2009. wwwuticaod.com. Accessed 20 Nov. 2017.

"47 Member States." *Council of Europe*. www.coe.int. Accessed 20 Nov. 2017.

"Hall of Famers." *Naismith Memorial Basketball Hall of Fame*. www.hoophall.com. Accessed 20 Nov. 2017.

"Hanna Dead at 86; Funeral Arrangements Set." *Observer-Dispatch*, 13 Mar. 2009. www.uticaod.com. Accessed 20 Nov. 2017.

"History of the Chicago Bulls." *The Official Site of the Chicago Bulls*. www.bulls.com. Accessed 20 Nov. 2017.

"Kervorkian Case: Kevorkian Sentenced to 10 to 25 Years." *CNN*, 31 Dec. 2007. www.cnn.org. Accessed 20 Nov. 2017.

"Kevorkian Released After 8 Years: Suicide Activist Says He Will Obey the Law but Try to Change It." *Washington Post*, 2 June 2007. www.washingtonpost.com. Accessed 20 Nov. 2017.

Schneider, Keith. "Jack Kevorkian, 1928-2011: Doctor Who Helped End Lives." *The New York Times*, 4 June 2011, p. A1. *ProQuest Historical Newspapers: The New York Times with Index.* Accessed 20 Nov. 2017.

"Triple-Double for Pippen." *The New York Times*, 10 Nov. 1995, p. B14. *ProQuest Historical Newspapers: The New York Times with Index.* Accessed 20 Nov. 2017.

"2 Nations Join Panel for Rights in Europe." *The New York Times*, 10 Nov. 1995, p. A12. *ProQuest Historical Newspapers: The New York Times with Index.* Accessed 20 Nov. 2017.

"You Don't Know Jack." *HBO Movies.* www.hbo.com. Accessed 20 Nov. 2017.

CHAPTER 18

Workbook

If you think over what you have read or written but you don't write about it, you leave no record of your thoughts. To make the most efficient use of your thinking, you need to record your thoughts in print. Failing to record your thoughts and ideas can be quite expensive. Often, important insights and ideas arise fleetingly, even while you are doing something else and not even aware you are thinking about them, and then, if you do not do something to remind yourself of them, they disappear.

You can keep a reading journal to help you make use of these important ideas, but writing that also addresses the work you yourself do to complete the assignment can give you a record of your thinking and also places to return to with new avenues to explore in your thinking. The more you help yourself by seeing how you think, the less likely you will run out of things to say.

The intent of these pages is to present you with the exact opposite of busywork. The questions here aim to provoke your thinking, to get you to turn ideas about in your mind, and to help you realize that the first words you put on paper represent only the beginning of your thinking, and there is much more to come from you if you give it time and have a systematic way of understanding what you have to say.

The first worksheet you will find in this section for the assignments in this textbook are intended for you in working with yourself. Nothing you write on these worksheets needs to be shared with anyone else (ask in advance if your instructor requires you to turn these in) and should be a place where ideas that may never appear in your essay have a chance to take form on paper in order to help you get where you need to go in your writing.

The second worksheet is a peer response worksheet and provides a pair or group of students working together prompts to discuss each other's writing. It is important in working with both worksheets that you observe, record, and observe again what you have written in order to discuss it, but you must not judge. If you judge your own writing or someone else's writing during these important steps of the process, you sabotage any chance of recognizing important ideas or earning insight. Restrain yourself from commenting about the quality you perceive in your own or someone else's work and instead concentrate on seeing what is really there. So often we write what we think we mean but mean more than we say. If we expect others to understand us, we have to clarify to ourselves exactly what we mean and then anticipate the questions our readers may ask. Those questions others have when they read our writing often come very close to the questions we ask ourselves. After all, language is shared, and reading and writing are far from the solitary activities they seem to be at times. These distinctly human activities include all of us who share a language, and our words have the power to affect anyone who takes a moment to listen and to read.

Name _____ Date _____

WORKSHEET ON RESPONSE ANALYSIS ESSAY

To expand your response, first write a summary and response Reading Journal for the essay you want to work with. Then:

1.   Write here the most interesting detail from the essay you are responding to:

2.   Tell a story about an experience you have had that you can associate with this detail.

3.   Write a question, as if you were asking the author directly, about this or other details from his or her essay.

4.   Associate the detail you are responding to with a detail from something else you have read. Where have you seen this idea before?

5.   Write about why this detail is important to you. What do you think about when you read this work?

Name _____ Date _____

PEER RESPONSE WORKSHEET ON RESPONSE ANALYSIS ESSAY

The Response Analysis Essay assignment asks you to respond to a work and then to analyze your own response. In other words, you are being asked to read subjectively and then to turn toward your own writing objectively. To read subjectively is to think about what something means to us, how we respond, and where we find ourselves in our reading. To read objectively means to look at the text in order to analyze or evaluate it to answer questions other readers might have as well.

1.   What detail(s) from the reading do you respond to in your essay?

2.   What are the three most important statements you make about those details?

3.   Why did you pick the work you have chosen and not another work instead?

4.   In one to two sentences, tell where your response comes from, if you could locate just one source of your response.

5.   What do you say in your essay that only you could have said about your relationship to the work you are reading?

6.   What point do you make about reading the work? How do your experiences, previous reading, and prior understanding of the topic affect how you read the work?

Name _____ Date _____

WORKSHEET ON CLOSE READING ESSAY

1. Choose a passage from one of the essays in this textbook in which the writer says something that interests you. The passage should be a few sentences to several sentences in length.

2. Identify vocabulary that is unfamiliar to you or used in an unfamiliar way, below, and then give the definitions to those words. Be sure to look in more than one dictionary and at multiple word definitions before you commit to the definition you think the word should have in its context in the passage.

3. If you look at just the vocabulary you isolated in #2, above, what conclusions can you draw about the passage? About the work as a whole?

4. Find other instances in the essay where the words in your vocabulary list are used again. How is the context for their use similar? Different? Do the words require redefining?

Name _____ Date _____

PEER RESPONSE WORKSHEET ON CLOSE READING ESSAY

1. Why did you want to work with the passage you chose for your paper? What questions did you have initially when you read it? What ideas did the passage inspire you to think about?

2. Choose three words from the passage and describe how they are central to the meaning of the passage or the work as a whole:

    a.

    b.

    c.

3. How do you make connections between the passage and the work as a whole in your paper? What ideas tie them together?

4. Do you think the author could have written this passage more clearly than it appears in the text? How does the author's choice of words help clarify the ideas or on the other hand prevent a clear understanding of the ideas? Is it possible the language of the passage does both?

5. Write a note to the author asking for clarification of the passage. Then write back in the voice of the author giving you that clarification. What can you find from this game that gives you some insight into the vocabulary, organization, and ideas?

Name _____ Date _____

WORKSHEET ON INTERPRETIVE ANALYSIS ESSAY

A successful interpretive analysis essay will have a clear introduction that orients the reader to the subject of the essay, to the urgency of addressing the subject (why it is important), and to the limits of the thesis (what will be considered and what will not be).

I.   Introduction/Thesis

In "Total Eclipse" Annie Dillard gives us the picture of her experience as she recalls the impossible, the world coming to an end. While the world does not in fact end, Dillard's existential encounter with the total eclipse makes it seems so. Though she responds intellectually and emotionally to the phenomenon, Dillard does not assess it scientifically because to do so would be to avoid a direct experience of the eclipse. Dillard attempts to show that a basic, if rare, event can bring us to full consciousness, even if only momentarily.

II. Analysis of the Thesis

a. Acute observation

In "Total Eclipse" Annie Dillard gives us the picture of her experience as she recalls the impossible, the world coming to an end.

b. Focus of observation

While the world does not in fact end, Dillard's existential encounter with the total eclipse makes it seem so. Though she responds intellectually and emotionally to the phenomenon, Dillard does not assess it scientifically.

c. "Because" clause

Because to do so would be to avoid a direct experience of the eclipse.

d. Context/relevance

Dillard attempts to show that a basic, if rare, event can bring us to full consciousness, even if only momentarily.

Write an introduction/thesis to one or more of the essays you have read in this course. Use the model introduction/thesis above to word your own, or work piece by piece, constructing your introduction/thesis according to the four segments (a, b, c, d) outlined above.

Name _____ Date _____

PEER RESPONSE WORKSHEET ON INTERPRETIVE ANALYSIS ESSAY

Exchange drafts with a classmate or look over your own paper. Address the following questions with detailed answers.

1. What does the introduction, as it is currently written, help you understand? How does it guide your attention?

2. What is the proposed "context" for examining this essay? That is, how or why, according to your paper, is the essay relevant?

3. What do you say are the point and purpose of the essay about which you are writing?

4. Look carefully at the organization of your paper. Do the paragraphs lead logically from one to the next? Explain how.

5. Look for the quality of references to the original essay. How many references does this draft make? What does the student *do* with those references?

Name _____ Date _____

WORKSHEET ON ANNOTATED WORKS CITED ESSAY, PART I

A theme is a unifying idea or a motif in a work. One way to find a theme is by describing a work's topic—what the work occupies itself with—and what it says about its topic.

For a work you have chosen as an anchor for your annotated works cited page, make a list of themes you find in the work:

1.

2.

3.

4.

5.

6.

7.

8.

For each of the themes you listed above, locate at least three page numbers or paragraphs in the work where you find the theme illustrated (i.e., examples of the theme):

1.   Location a:
         Location b:
         Location c:

2.   Location a:
         Location b:
         Location c:

3.   Location a:
         Location b:
         Location c:

4.   Location a:
         Location b:
         Location c:

5.   Location a:
         Location b:
         Location c:

6.   Location a:
          Location b:
          Location c:

7.   Location a:
          Location b:
          Location c:

8.   Location a:
          Location b:
          Location c:

Next, list the works or sources you can think of that carry each theme. The theme may be a major component of the works you list or simply a motif that you notice in the work. Begin by listing essays in this book that share the theme you want to work with:

1.

2.

3.

4.

5.

6.

Continue to list sources separately for each theme you may be interested in. As you do your work, look for sources that overlap. If you were interested in the theme, for instance, "violence in nature," you might associate "Total Eclipse," "The Solace of Open Spaces," "Havasu," among other sources with that theme. If "finding a purpose" were another theme you listed, at least one of the sources you listed for "violence in nature" would address "finding a purpose" as well. The point of cross-listing sources like this is to remind yourself of the latitude you have in finding and incorporating new sources that fit your theme.

Name _____ Date _____

WORKSHEET ON ANNOTATED WORKS CITED ESSAY, PART II

Practice in Constructing a Works Cited Page

Put the list of sources below in the correct format for MLA, APA, CMS, or any other style guide your instructor prefers. You can find many guides on the web for free, including the excellent free access site at Johns Hopkins University, http://guides.library.jhu.edu/citing, and your school may also have a bibliography or citation guide online. Pay special attention to alphabetizing the list and punctuating the entries correctly. If a source is missing information needed to complete the bibliographic entry, note that that piece of information is missing below the entry.

1. A Rhetoric of Motives by Kenneth Burke (book). Published by University of California Press in Berkeley. This edition dated 1969.
2. Metaphors We Live By by George Lakoff and Mark Johnson (book). This second edition is published by the University of Chicago Press in 2003.
3. The Translator's Preface by Cary F. Baynes in Modern Man in Search of a Soul by C. G. Jung, translated by W. S. Dell and Cary F. Baynes. Published by Harcourt Brace Jovanovich in New York in 1955.
4. "An Ideal Craftsman" by Walter De La Mare, which is a short story on pp. 202–218 in The Oxford Book of Short Stories, which is edited by V. S. Pritchett and published in New York by Oxford University Press in 1981. Also, from the same collection of stories, "The Secret Sharer" by Joseph Conrad on pp. 109–146.
5. Kant, the name of a book by Karl Jaspers, edited by Hannah Arendt and translated by Ralph Manheim.
6. Lachrimae, which is a cycle of poems published in a book titled Collected Poems by Geoffrey Hill in New York by Oxford University Press in 1986.
7. M. Butterfly, a play by David Henry Hwang published by the Dramatists Play Service, Inc., in 1998 in New York.
8. A journal article titled The "Halakhic Kernel" as a Criterion for Dating Babylonian Aggadah: Bavli Hullin 110a–b and Parallels, which is written by Aaron Amit in the AJS Review, Vol. 36, No. 2 (NOVEMBER 2012) (pp. 187–205).
9. Donald Kohn's lecture titled Bone Marrow Stem Cells: Developing New Therapies in the Fight Against Disease, from the public lecture series at UCLA on January 19, 2011.
10. Sheet music by Ludwig Beethoven call Fur Elise, written in 1810 and published by Random House in New York in 2002.

Name _____ Date _____

PEER RESPONSE WORKSHEET ON ANNOTATED WORKS CITED ESSAY

1. What is missing from your draft that you need to include? Be specific about what you need to achieve in terms of information, organization, synthesis of ideas, development of your theme, MLA style, etc.

2. What work have you done in the course of working on this assignment that has surprised you? That you are proud of?

3. Have you given your theme a treatment that goes beyond the obvious or cliché? How did you, or how will you accomplish this?

4. Do your annotations, when taken together, give a unified picture of your sources? That is, does it appear that your sources, despite being about different subjects, all seem somehow related? If so, how? If not, what is missing from them?

5. Write two paragraphs explaining the connection between your anchor work and the sources you have identified.

6. How would you score your own essay? Why? What do you think your instructor will notice about your work? What do you want your instructor to notice about your work?

WORKSHEET ON ANALYSIS OF STYLE ESSAY

Identifying Convergent Themes and Divergent Styles

You can complete the following in small groups or individually, according to your preferences or the preferences of your instructor:

1. List the important themes in the two essays you intend to write about. Write these themes in phrases or sentences (rather than in one word) to get a good notion of the idea. Where do the themes of these essays intersect?

2. Consider the thesis for each essay (the central, guiding statement about the most important idea in the essay) and write it down. In what ways are the theses similar between the essays? Do they differ or vary only on the basis of the subject matter or on more important points?

3. Begin to address style by choosing *one* element of style for each essay and list the most important evidence of that element. If you choose to examine imagery in "Carnal Acts," for example, list the images that seem particularly important to the style or themes of the essay.

You should complete the following on your own:

4. Write two paragraphs in which you explain how the style of the writing in one of these essays supports, contributes to, or reflects an important theme in the essay.

Name _____ Date _____

PEER RESPONSE WORKSHEET ON ANALYSIS OF STYLE ESSAY

1. How does your paper answer the primary question, how the styles of the essays affect the content of the essays? In other words, how do metaphors, images, diction, or any element of style you chose to examine help create the ideas in the essays and give them their meaning?

2. What theme do you find in common between the two essays? Describe the theme in two to five sentences.

3. Do you focus on a specific element of style deemed important in each essay? How or why did you choose that element of style to analyze? What examples do you offer of specific instances of that element of style?

4. How, according to your paper, does the style of each essay contribute to its theme? What is *significant* or important about noticing and analyzing the style of these essays?

5. What is the main point or thesis of the paper so far? Do not anticipate what the finished paper will say; instead, identify the thesis of the writing at this point.

6. What reasons could you have for identifying and analyzing elements of style in writing? What could such work give you that you would otherwise miss?

Close Reading and Explication

EXPLICATION

Explication is a running commentary on a text, addressing and explaining details as they arise. Explication is based on a close reading of a text; that is, it requires patient explanation of the subtle details that come forward as you read and think about the reading. Explication is empirical reading put into practice.

Any simple utterance such as the phrase "Shut the door" seems to carry an obvious meaning not subject to interpretation. It comes with an instruction (to shut), an implied agent (you), and an object in need of shutting. What could be difficult? But as we all know, infinitely subtle characteristics of this utterance can color and shape it to mean immensely different things. If spoken through gritted teeth, one might suppose, we would worry that we had gotten ourselves into some trouble. In another circumstance, the three words may be the prelude to a serious talk. Or to getting fired from a job. Or, if spoken in a whisper drenched in intimate tones, it may mean something else entirely. We know generally what to make of simple utterances, but the tone is not always clear. Our *precise* response depends on more than the denotation, or dictionary definition, of the words. In writing especially, because we do not have the benefit of body language, facial gestures, and tone of voice to help us understand meaning, the vocabulary may stretch beyond our common use of words, which would require not only that we understand the connotation expressed by each word and each phrase, but the various denotative qualities of each word, which necessarily vary across usages and over time.

The essays you find in this chapter span 130 years and approach disparate subjects, yet they have much in common. Finding those commonalities requires careful attention to what they say, and sometimes our interest can get taxed by the demands of language that looks different from our own. Though we all in speaking and writing English share a language, the fact that the way we speak and write changes a great deal over time can challenge our understanding of what we read. The linguist Ed Finnegan made the point once that Shakespeare's language, which some high school students find to be nearly a foreign language, is 400 years old. While that's undeniably a long time ago, Finnegan remarked, Shakespeare lived only eight 50-year periods ago. Think then how much language changes in a relatively brief amount of time. It is really quite astounding. Developing skills in close reading helps us to pin down meanings of language that so fluidly wriggle from our grasp.

REVISITING WHAT YOU READ

As you read the essays in this chapter, notice when the writing turns opaque for you—when you cannot feel sure about what the author wants to tell you. Returning to that place almost guarantees you will gain mastery

From *Writing Like You Own it: A Course in College Composition*, by Charles Grogg. © 2014 by Charles Grogg. Reprinted by permission of Kendall Hunt Publishing Company

over it if you follow a few protocols. There is simply no way around the tedium associated with the often surprising act of looking up a word. With multiple Internet dictionaries at our disposal, finding word definitions has never been easier, and while we can (and want to believe we can) ascertain an aspect of a word's definition from its context, settling for this understanding will give us little more than an ability to read on without being hopelessly stuck. While a quick fix is helpful, it is not exactly something to aim for, especially when we run up on a phrase or entire paragraph that seems impenetrable. Explication forces us to slow down when we read.

Think about the things you read when you are not in a hurry. If you read for pleasure—a novel, a magazine article, a love letter—you may find yourself reading slowly and savoring each word for what it does for you. The words may move you, help you to imagine something, or give you something to dream about. You decide you will take your time. Yet when we read other things, for instance the caution statements printed and packaged with a new toaster, on whose understanding our lives might depend, we skim or ignore the exact words. Yes, yes, don't throw a plugged in toaster into the kitchen sink. Clear enough. The actual words do not give us any more than the instruction to perform or refrain from performing a particular action. We read with very little attention, and yet (usually) we understand the imperative. What makes the experience of reading love letters so different? We are not merely looking for information. Instead we want to give ourselves to the words, to the source of the words. We want to *connect,* and the willingness to make a connection makes us fall in love with words. Bizarre as it may sound at first, falling in love is the first requirement to understanding.

Following the readings in this chapter you will find help in navigating challenging passages that will open up new worlds to you if you open yourself up to them.

LEARNING TO NAVIGATE CHALLENGING PASSAGES

Inevitably not only words but whole passages of writing can seem impenetrable on first reading. To form a strong mental picture, understanding exactly what an author is saying and how the details cohere, it helps to identify the main idea, the supporting details, the purpose of the writing, and any unusual words or terms that confound a quick understanding of the material. Words are like stones in a slingshot. When a word is used, its whole history—all its etymology, its previous uses, other contexts and connotations—spring forward with great force into its current use. For this reason, sometimes writing can seem unclear if we cannot account for the history of a word that accompanies it into the text before us. Consider this passage from part II of "The American Scholar."

> Books are the best of things, well used; abused, among the worst. What is the right use? What is the one end which all means go to effect? They are for nothing but to inspire. I had better never see a book than to be warped by its attraction clean out of my own orbit, and made a satellite instead of a system. The one thing in the world of value is the active soul,—the soul, free, sovereign, active. This every man is entitled to; this every man contains within him, although in almost all men obstructed, and as yet unborn.

What is Emerson saying? What does he want us to understand? To whom is he speaking exactly (in his own time—is it possible he imagines us as well, more than 175 years later, reading his words)? What is his tone exactly? Emerson delivered this passage in a speech in 1837. Imagine how much language has changed over that time. Just over twice that amount of time, people spoke English the way Shakespeare wrote it, and for many people, that language looks nearly foreign to contemporary English. Language changes fairly rapidly, taking on new words while some older words become archaic, and the ways we relate to each other over new technologies change how we communicate as well. In an age of ever-increasing ease and immediacy of communication, getting the exact point of what someone says to us becomes increasingly important. Notice that in the passage above, you can find every word used in a common dictionary. None has fallen out of use. And yet the usage, strange to our ears, can defy our immediate understanding. Skirting the passage to rely on the context alone will not help us, though the context will help us later. We have to stop and read closely.

To give the passage above a close reading, we would need to understand the limitations of our understanding first, and then we can decide what steps we can take most efficiently to get at the meaning. Simply knowing the vocabulary and substituting words can give insight to meaning, but we can use the definitions to help clarify our understanding even more.

1. Defining the key words or terms or any unusual words:

inspire, warped, attraction, orbit, satellite, system, sovereign, obstructed

You may recognize all these words and may even be able to give a definition for each without much thought. The point here however is to push yourself to look at the definitions of these words in order to see something not already apparent when you read the passage. Reading definitions of words can spark ideas about them, and this action can enrich and clarify your reading experience by producing avenues of inquiry you otherwise might have missed.

2. Substituting words for the key words.

If you substitute the definitions you find that seem plausible for the context of the passage, you might end up with something like this:

> Books are the best of things, well used; abused, among the worst. What is the right use? What is the one end which all means go to effect? They are for nothing but to [**fill with an animating influence**]. I had better never see a book than to be [**distorted from the truth**] by its [**magnetic charm**] clean out of my own [**sphere or power of influence**], and made a [**subservient attendant**] instead of a [**comprehensive assemblage of knowledge**]. The one thing in the world of value is the active soul,—the soul, free, [**with supreme power or authority**], active. This every man is entitled to; this every man contains within him, although in almost all men [**closed up with an obstacle**], and as yet unborn.

3. Paraphrasing the passage.

By substituting words we have wrecked the poetry of the passage. In the substituted passage the language is clunky, stilted, arrested in its rhythm. At the same time we have forced ourselves to think through the meanings of the words, something our minds usually do automatically for us for better or worse. Here we have awakened ourselves to various levels of meaning, to the metaphor that encompasses Emerson's writing in this passage, where the poetry of the original no longer has the power to lure us into its influence without our first understanding what the words say. Staying awake to the meanings of words keeps us from making quick assumptions or jumping to conclusions about what we read. We are purposely slowing ourselves down, and the effect will be one of recognizing and failing to recognize the meaning. This process can be called **defamiliarization**, and it forces our conscious attention. Here is what the passage might look like were we to paraphrase it with the newly found definitions in mind:

> [Books are great if you use them the right way, but they can be bad for you if you don't know how to regard them. What is the right way? What should books do for us for all our careful reading and thinking about them? They should influence us and make us feel alive. I do not want a book to distort the truth of what I know by charming me out of my own power and making me a servant to what it has to say instead of my own comprehensive assemblage of knowledge. I would rather never read a book if that's what books do. An active mind is very important. We can't fall asleep in front of what we are reading. We have to be vigilant. We have to be active readers. Our understanding has to come from us, not books. We are all capable of this way of understanding, but most of us have not awakened to it.]

4. Gaining the Context

Again, our purpose is not to wax poetic but to understand what is being said with some degree of certainty beyond what a cursory glance can yield. Is this paraphrase clear? It doesn't seem to be much clearer than the original passage in terms of its central idea, but our paraphrase does help us hone in on what that central idea might be. If we stop to ask what could be the theme of this passage, we can help ourselves out by looking at what immediately precedes the passage and what immediately follows. Emerson concerns himself with locating authority within the scholar or the reader. Books, he argues, do not have the final word about anything but give us the thinking of authors who came before us, authors who read other authors and made up their own minds about what they see. At the time Emerson delivered this speech, America was yet a new nation, and Emerson was of a mind that European ways and European thinking still influenced American ways and thinking to a great degree, something he thought needed to change. A new country, after all, needs its own traditions and its own ways that grow out of its ground organically. Whether this is possible or likely is a separate matter, but this at least on some level concerned Emerson at the time.

SPENDING TIME WITH WORDS

When we find ambiguity in writing, we have choices to make about how to deal with it. Some ambiguities, such as the various connotations of a word, we might skip over in favor of getting the general idea of a passage, or we might not want to be disturbed at present to reread a passage to get at all the possible meanings implied in it. There is nothing inherently wrong with this. If you think about where you gained your vocabulary (perhaps ranging between 10,000 and 20,000 words), it is doubtful you will credit word lists or looking up words in the dictionary as the source. You probably did not look up new words when around two years old, you began speaking in sentences longer than you had previously been capable of forming. And few people will say they use a dictionary often. All the people surveyed to complete this sentence in this textbook estimated they had looked up a word in a dictionary fewer than 100 times in their lives. Obviously our vocabulary comes from elsewhere, namely from reading and from hearing unfamiliar words and from hearing and seeing familiar words used in new contexts. Over time, we assimilate these words into our cache.

AshTproductions/Shutterstock.com

In an amusing piece for *The New York Times* (March 11, 2010) about vocabulary sizes and the age-old industries that have grown around trying to convince people they need to have bigger vocabularies, Ammon Shea notes that "Brandishing 25-cent words unnecessarily will mark you as a blowhard, not an effective communicator." Nice advice. Verbal acuity comes from knowing how to use words and how to decipher them in varied contexts, not simply by building the number of words you can use comfortably in conversation (or elsewhere).

Yet texts often present us with ideas and expressions that are new to us, and the point is that dealing with some ambiguities requires that we spend time with words.

The American Scholar

Ralph Waldo Emerson

This address was delivered at Cambridge in 1837, before the Harvard Chapter of the Phi Beta Kappa Society, a college fraternity composed of the first twenty-five men in each graduating class. The society has annual meetings, which have been the occasion for addresses from the most distinguished scholars and thinkers of the day.

MR. PRESIDENT AND GENTLEMEN,

I greet you on the recommencement of our literary year. Our anniversary is one of hope, and, perhaps, not enough of labor. We do not meet for games of strength[1] or skill, for the recitation of histories, tragedies, and odes, like the ancient Greeks; for parliaments of love and poesy, like the Troubadours;[2] nor for the advancement of science, like our co-temporaries in the British and European capitals. Thus far, our holiday has been simply a friendly sign of the survival of the love of letters amongst a people too busy to give to letters any more. As such it is precious as the sign of an indestructible instinct. Perhaps the time is already come when it ought to be, and will be, something else; when the sluggard intellect of this continent will look from under its iron lids and fill the postponed expectation of the world with something better than the exertions of mechanical skill. Our day of dependence, our long apprenticeship to the learning of other lands, draws to a close. The millions that around us are rushing into life cannot always be fed on the sere remains of foreign harvests.[3] Events, actions arise that must be sung, that will sing themselves. Who can doubt that poetry will revive and lead in a new age, as the star in the constellation Harp, which now flames in our zenith, astronomers announce, shall one day be the pole-star[4] for a thousand years?

In the light of this hope I accept the topic which not only usage but the nature of our association seem to prescribe to this day,—the AMERICAN SCHOLAR. Year by year we come up hither to read one more chapter of his biography. Let us inquire what new lights, new events, and more days have thrown on his character, his duties, and his hopes.

It is one of those fables which out of an unknown antiquity convey an unlooked-for wisdom, that the gods, in the beginning, divided Man into men, that he might be more helpful to himself; just as the hand was divided into fingers, the better to answer its end.[5]

The old fable covers a doctrine ever new and sublime; that there is One Man,—present to all particular men only partially, or through one faculty; and that you must take the whole society to find the whole man. Man is not a farmer, or a professor, or an engineer, but he is all. Man is priest, and scholar, and statesman, and producer, and soldier. In the *divided* or social state these functions are parceled out to individuals, each of whom aims to do his stint[6] of the joint work, whilst each other performs his. The fable implies that the individual, to possess himself, must sometimes return from his own labor to embrace all the other laborers. But, unfortunately, this original unit, this fountain of power, has been so distributed to multitudes, has been so minutely subdivided and peddled out, that it is spilled into drops, and cannot be gathered. The state of society is one in which the members have suffered amputation from the trunk and strut about so many walking monsters,—a good finger, a neck, a stomach, an elbow, but never a man.

Man is thus metamorphosed into a thing, into many things. The planter, who is Man sent out into the field to gather food, is seldom cheered by any idea of the true dignity of his ministry. He sees his bushel and his cart, and nothing beyond, and sinks into the farmer, instead of Man on the farm. The tradesman scarcely ever gives an ideal worth to his work, but is ridden[7] by the routine of his craft, and the soul is subject to dollars. The priest becomes a form; the attorney a statute-book; the mechanic a machine; the sailor a rope of the ship.

In this distribution of functions the scholar is the delegated intellect. In the right state he is *Man Thinking*. In the degenerate state, when the victim of society, he tends to become a mere thinker, or, still worse, the parrot of other men's thinking.

In this view of him, as Man Thinking, the whole theory of his office is contained. Him Nature solicits with all her placid, all her monitory pictures.[8] Him the past instructs. Him the future invites. Is not indeed every man a student, and do not all things exist for the student's behoof? And, finally, is not the true scholar the only true master? But as the old oracle said, "All things have two handles: Beware of the wrong one."[9] In life, too often, the scholar errs with mankind and forfeits his privilege. Let us see him in his school, and consider him in reference to the main influences he receives.

* * * * *

I. The first in time and the first in importance of the influences upon the mind is that of nature. Every day, the sun;[10] and, after sunset, Night and her stars. Ever the winds blow; ever the grass grows. Every day, men and women, conversing, beholding and beholden.[11] The scholar must needs stand wistful and admiring before this great spectacle. He must settle its value in his mind. What is nature to him? There is never a beginning, there is never an end, to the inexplicable continuity of this web of God, but always circular power returning into itself. [12] Therein it resembles his own spirit, whose beginning, whose ending, he never can find,— so entire, so boundless. Far too as her splendors shine, system on system shooting like rays, upward, downward, without center, without circumference,—in the mass and in the particle, Nature hastens to render account of herself to the mind. Classification begins. To the young mind everything is individual, stands by itself. By and by it finds how to join two things and see in them one nature; then three, then three thousand; and so, tyrannized over by its own unifying instinct, it goes on tying things together, diminishing anomalies, discovering roots running under ground whereby contrary and remote things cohere and flower out from one stem. It presently learns that since the dawn of history there has been a constant accumulation and classifying of facts. But what is classification but the perceiving that these objects are not chaotic, and are not foreign, but have a law which is also a law of the human mind? The astronomer discovers that geometry, a pure abstraction of the human mind, is the measure of planetary motion. The chemist finds proportions and intelligible method throughout matter; and science is nothing but the finding of analogy, identity, in the most remote parts. The ambitious soul sits down before each refractory fact; one after another reduces all strange constitutions, all new powers, to their class and their law, and goes on forever to animate the last fiber of organization, the outskirts of nature, by insight.

Thus to him, to this school-boy under the bending dome of day, is suggested that he and it proceed from one Root; one is leaf and one is flower; relation, sympathy, stirring in every vein. And what is that root? Is not that the soul of his soul?—A thought too bold?—A dream too wild? Yet when this spiritual light shall have revealed the law of more earthly natures,—when he has learned to worship the soul, and to see that the natural philosophy that now is, is only the first gropings of its gigantic hand,—he shall look forward to an ever-expanding knowledge as to a becoming creator.[13] He shall see that nature is the opposite of the soul, answering to it part for part. One is seal and one is print. Its beauty is the beauty of his own mind. Its laws are the laws of his own mind. Nature then becomes to him the measure of his attainments. So much of nature as he is ignorant of, so much of his own mind does he not yet possess. And, in fine, the ancient precept, "Know thyself,"[14] and the modern precept, "Study nature," become at last one maxim.

* * * * *

II. The next great influence into the spirit of the scholar is the mind of the Past,—in whatever form, whether of literature, of art, of institutions, that mind is inscribed. Books are the best type of the influence of the past, and perhaps we shall get at the truth,—learn the amount of this influence more conveniently,—by considering their value alone.

The theory of books is noble. The scholar of the first age received into him the world around; brooded thereon; gave it the new arrangement of his own mind, and uttered it again. It came into him life; it went out from him truth. It came to him short-lived actions; it went out from him immortal thoughts. It came to him business; it went from him poetry. It was dead fact; now, it is quick thought. It can stand, and it can go. It now endures, it now flies, it now inspires. [15] Precisely in proportion to the depth of mind from which it issued, so high does it soar, so long does it sing.

Or, I might say, it depends on how far the process had gone, of transmuting life into truth. In proportion to the completeness of the distillation, so will the purity and imperishableness of the product be. But none is quite perfect. As no air-pump can by any means make a perfect vacuum,[16] so neither can any artist entirely exclude the conventional, the local, the perishable from his book, or write a book of pure thought, that shall be as efficient, in all respects, to a remote posterity, as to contemporaries, or rather to the second age. Each age, it is found, must write its own books; or rather, each generation for the next succeeding. The books of an older period will not fit this.

Yet hence arises a grave mischief. The sacredness which attaches to the act of creation, the act of thought, is instantly transferred to the record. The poet chanting was felt to be a divine man. Henceforth the chant is divine also. The writer was a just and wise spirit. Henceforward it is settled the book is perfect; as love of the hero corrupts into worship of his statue. Instantly the book becomes noxious.[17] The guide is a tyrant. We sought a brother, and lo, a governor. The sluggish and perverted mind of the multitude, always slow to open to the incursions of Reason, having once so opened, having once received this book, stands upon it, and makes an outcry if it is disparaged. Colleges are built on it. Books are written on it by thinkers, not by Man Thinking, by men of talent, that is, who start wrong, who set out from accepted dogmas, not from their own sight of principles. Meek young men grow up in libraries, believing it their duty to accept the views which Cicero, which Locke,[18] which Bacon,[19] have given; forgetful that Cicero, Locke and Bacon were only young men in libraries when they wrote these books.

Hence, instead of Man Thinking, we have the bookworm. Hence the book-learned class, who value books, as such; not as related to nature and the human constitution, but as making a sort of Third Estate[20] with the world and soul. Hence the restorers of readings,[21] the emendators,[22] the bibliomaniacs[23] of all degrees. This is bad; this is worse than it seems.

Books are the best of things, well used; abused, among the worst. What is the right use? What is the one end which all means go to effect? They are for nothing but to inspire.[24] I had better never see a book than to be warped by its attraction clean out of my own orbit, and made a satellite instead of a system. The one thing in the world of value is the active soul,—the soul, free, sovereign, active. This every man is entitled to; this every man contains within him, although in almost all men obstructed, and as yet unborn. The soul active sees absolute truth and utters truth, or creates. In this action it is genius; not the privilege of here and there a favorite, but the sound estate of every man.[25] In its essence it is progressive. The book, the college, the school of art, the institution of any kind, stop with some past utterance of genius. This is good, say they,—let us hold by this. They pin me down.[26] They look backward and not forward. But genius always looks forward. The eyes of man are set in his forehead, not in his hindhead. Man hopes. Genius creates. To create,—to create,—is the proof of a divine presence. Whatever talents may be, if the man create not, the pure efflux of the Deity is not his;[27]—cinders and smoke there may be, but not yet flame. There are creative manners, there are creative actions, and creative words; manners, actions, words, that is, indicative of no custom or authority, but springing spontaneous from the mind's own sense of good and fair.

On the other part, instead of being its own seer, let it receive always from another mind its truth, though it were in torrents of light, without periods of solitude, inquest, and self-recovery; and a fatal disservice[28] is done. Genius is always sufficiently the enemy of genius by over-influence.[29] The literature of every nation bear me witness. The English dramatic poets have Shakespearized now for two hundred years.[30]

Undoubtedly there is a right way of reading, so it be sternly subordinated. Man Thinking must not be subdued by his instruments. Books are for the scholar's idle times. When he can read God directly, the hour is too precious to be wasted in other men's transcripts of their readings. [31] But when the intervals of darkness come, as come they must,—when the soul seeth not, when the sun is hid and the stars withdraw their shining,—we repair to the lamps which were kindled by their ray, to guide our steps to the East again, where the dawn is.[32] We hear, that we may speak. The Arabian proverb says, "A fig-tree, looking on a fig-tree, becometh fruitful."

It is remarkable, the character of the pleasure we derive from the best books. They impress us ever with the conviction that one nature wrote and the same reads. We read the verses of one of the great English poets, of Chaucer,[33] of Marvell,[34] of Dryden,[35] with the most modern joy,—with a pleasure, I mean, which is in great part caused by the abstraction of all *time* from their verses. There is some awe mixed with the joy of our surprise, when this poet, who lived in some past world, two or three hundred years ago, says that which lies close to my own soul, that which I also had well-nigh thought and said. But for the evidence thence afforded to the philosophical doctrine of the identity of all minds, we should suppose some pre-established harmony, some foresight of souls that were to be, and some preparation of stores for their future wants, like the fact observed in insects, who lay up food before death for the young grub they shall never see.

I would not be hurried by any love of system, by any exaggeration of instincts, to underrate the Book. We all know that as the human body can be nourished on any food, though it were boiled grass and the broth of shoes, so the human mind can be fed by any knowledge. And great and heroic men have existed who had almost no other information than by the printed page. I only would say that it needs a strong head to bear that diet. One must be an inventor to read well. As the proverb says, "He that would bring home the wealth of the Indies must carry out the wealth of the Indies." There is then creative reading as well as creative writing. When the mind is braced by labor and invention, the page of whatever book we read becomes luminous with manifold allusion. Every sentence is doubly significant, and the sense of our author is as broad as the world. We then see, what is always true, that as the seer's hour of vision is short and rare among heavy days and months, so is its record, perchance, the least part of his volume. The discerning will read, in his Plato[36] or Shakespeare, only that least part,—only the authentic utterances of the oracle;—all the rest he rejects, were it never so many times Plato's and Shakespeare's.

Of course there is a portion of reading quite indispensable to a wise man. History and exact science he must learn by laborious reading. Colleges, in like manner, have their indispensable office,—to teach elements. But they can only highly serve us when they aim not to drill, but to create; when they gather from far every ray of various genius to their hospitable halls, and by the concentrated fires set the hearts of their youth on flame. Thought and knowledge are natures in which apparatus and pretension avail nothing. Gowns[37] and pecuniary foundations,[38] though of towns of gold, can never countervail the least sentence or syllable of wit. [39] Forget this, and our American colleges will recede in their public importance, whilst they grow richer every year.

* * * * *

III. There goes in the world a notion that the scholar should be a recluse, a valetudinarian,[40]—as unfit for any handiwork or public labor as a penknife for an axe. The so-called "practical men" sneer at speculative men, as if, because they speculate or *see*, they could do nothing. I have heard it said that the clergy—who are always, more universally than any other class, the scholars of their day—are addressed as women; that the rough, spontaneous conversation of men they do not hear, but only a mincing[41] and diluted speech. They are often virtually disfranchised; and indeed there are advocates for their celibacy. As far as this is true of the studious classes, it is not just and wise. Action is with the scholar subordinate, but it is essential. Without it he is not yet man. Without it thought can never ripen into truth. Whilst the world hangs before the eye as a cloud of beauty, we cannot even see its beauty. Inaction is cowardice, but there can be no scholar without the heroic mind. The preamble[42] of thought, the transition through which it passes from the unconscious to the conscious, is action. Only so much do I know, as I have lived. Instantly we know whose words are loaded with life, and whose not.

The world—this shadow of the soul, or *other me*, lies wide around. Its attractions are the keys which unlock my thoughts and make me acquainted with myself. I launch eagerly into this resounding tumult. I grasp the hands of those next to me, and take my place in the ring to suffer and to work, taught by an instinct that so shall the dumb abyss[43] be vocal with speech. I pierce its order; I dissipate its fear;[44] I dispose of it within the circuit of my expanding life. So much only of life as I know by experience, so much of the wilderness have I vanquished and planted, or so far have I extended my being, my dominion. I do not see how any man can afford, for the sake of his nerves and his nap, to spare any action in which he can partake. It is pearls and rubies to his discourse. Drudgery, calamity, exasperation, want, are instructors in eloquence and wisdom. The true scholar grudges every opportunity of action passed by, as a loss of power.

It is the raw material out of which the intellect molds her splendid products. A strange process too, this by which experience is converted into thought, as a mulberry-leaf is converted into satin.[45] The manufacture goes forward at all hours.

The actions and events of our childhood and youth are now matters of calmest observation. They lie like fair pictures in the air. Not so with our recent actions,—with the business which we now have in hand. On this we are quite unable to speculate. Our affections as yet circulate through it. We no more feel or know it than we feel the feet, or the hand, or the brain of our body. The new deed is yet a part of life,—remains for a time immersed in our unconscious life. In some contemplative hour it detaches itself from the life like a ripe fruit,[46] to become a thought of the mind. Instantly it is raised, transfigured; the corruptible has put on incorruption.[47] Henceforth it is an object of beauty, however base its origin and neighborhood. Observe, too, the impossibility of antedating this act. In its grub state it cannot fly, it cannot shine, it is a dull grub. But suddenly, without observation, the selfsame thing unfurls beautiful wings, and is an angel of wisdom. So is there no fact, no event, in our private history, which shall not, sooner or later, lose its adhesive, inert form, and astonish us by soaring from our body into the empyrean.[48] Cradle and infancy, school and playground, the fear of boys, and dogs, and ferules,[49] the love of little maids and berries, and many another fact that once filled the whole sky, are gone already; friend and relative, profession and party, town and country, nation and world, must also soar and sing.[50]

Of course, he who has put forth his total strength in fit actions has the richest return of wisdom. I will not shut myself out of this globe of action, and transplant an oak into a flower-pot, there to hunger and pine; nor trust the revenue of some single faculty, and exhaust one vein of thought, much like those Savoyards,[51] who, getting their livelihood by carving shepherds, shepherdesses, and smoking Dutchmen, for all Europe, went out one day to the mountain to find stock, and discovered that they had whittled up the last of their pine-trees. Authors we have, in numbers, who have written out their vein, and who, moved by a commendable prudence, sail for Greece or Palestine, follow the trapper into the prairie, or ramble round Algiers, to replenish their merchantable stock.

If it were only for a vocabulary, the scholar would be covetous of action. Life is our dictionary. [52] Years are well spent in country labors; in town; in the insight into trades and manufactures; in frank intercourse with many men and women; in science; in art; to the one end of mastering in all their facts a language by which to illustrate and embody our perceptions. I learn immediately from any speaker how much he has already lived, through the poverty or the splendor of his speech. Life lies behind us as the quarry from whence we get tiles and copestones for the masonry of to-day. This is the way to learn grammar. Colleges and books only copy the language which the field and the work-yard made.

But the final value of action, like that of books, and better than books, is that it is a resource. That great principle of Undulation in nature, that shows itself in the inspiring and expiring of the breath; in desire and satiety; in the ebb and flow of the sea; in day and night; in heat and cold; and, as yet more deeply ingrained in every atom and every fluid, is known to us under the name of Polarity,—these "fits of easy transmission and reflection," as Newton[53] called them, are the law of nature because they are the law of spirit.

The mind now thinks, now acts, and each fit reproduces the other. When the artist has exhausted his materials, when the fancy no longer paints, when thoughts are no longer apprehended and books are a weariness,—he has always the resource *to live*. Character is higher than intellect. Thinking is the function. Living is the functionary. The stream retreats to its source. A great soul will be strong to live, as well as strong to think. Does he lack organ or medium to impart his truth? He can still fall back on this elemental force of living them. This is a total act. Thinking is a partial act. Let the grandeur of justice shine in his affairs. Let the beauty of affection cheer his lowly roof. Those "far from fame," who dwell and act with him, will feel the force of his constitution in the doings and passages of the day better than it can be measured by any public and designed display. Time shall teach him that the scholar loses no hour which the man lives. Herein he unfolds the sacred germ of his instinct, screened from influence. What is lost in seemliness is gained in strength. Not out of those on whom systems of education have exhausted their culture comes the helpful giant to destroy the old or to build the new, but out of unhandselled[54] savage nature; out of terrible Druids[55] and Berserkers[56] come at last Alfred[57] and Shakespeare. I hear therefore with joy whatever is beginning to be said of the dignity and necessity of labor to every citizen. There is virtue yet in the hoe and the spade,[58] for learned as well as for unlearned hands. And labor is everywhere welcome; always we are invited to work; only be this limitation observed, that a man shall not for the sake of wider activity sacrifice any opinion to the popular judgments and modes of action.

* * * * *

I have now spoken of the education of the scholar by nature, by books, and by action. It remains to say somewhat of his duties.

They are such as become Man Thinking. They may all be comprised in self-trust. The office of the scholar is to cheer, to raise, and to guide men by showing them facts amidst appearances. He plies the slow, unhonored, and unpaid task of observation. Flamsteed[59] and Herschel,[60] in their glazed observatories, may catalogue the stars with the praise of all men, and, the results being splendid and useful, honor is sure. But he, in his private observatory, cataloguing obscure and nebulous[61] stars of the human mind, which as yet no man has thought of as such,—watching days and months sometimes for a few facts; correcting still his old records,—must relinquish display and immediate fame. In the long period of his preparation he must betray often an ignorance and shiftlessness in popular arts, incurring the disdain of the able who shoulder him aside. Long he must stammer in his speech; often forego the living for the dead. Worse yet, he must accept—how often!—poverty and solitude. For the ease and pleasure of treading the old road, accepting the fashions, the education, the religion of society, he takes the cross of making his own, and, of course, the self-accusation, the faint heart, the frequent uncertainty and loss of time, which are the nettles and tangling vines in the way of the self-relying and self-directed; and the state of virtual hostility in which he seems to stand to society, and especially to educated society. For all this loss and scorn, what offset? He is to find consolation in exercising the highest functions of human nature. He is one who raises himself from private considerations and breathes and lives on public and illustrious thoughts. He is the world's eye. He is the world's heart. He is to resist the vulgar prosperity that retrogrades ever to barbarism, by preserving and communicating heroic sentiments, noble biographies, melodious verse, and the conclusions of history. Whatsoever oracles the human heart, in all emergencies, in all solemn hours, has uttered as its commentary on the world of actions,—these he shall receive and impart. And whatsoever new verdict Reason from her inviolable seat pronounces on the passing men and events of to-day,—this he shall hear and promulgate.

These being his functions, it becomes him to feel all confidence in himself, and to defer never to the popular cry. He and he only knows the world. The world of any moment is the merest appearance. Some great decorum, some fetich[62] of a government, some ephemeral trade, or war, or man, is cried up[63] by half mankind and cried down by the other half, as if all depended on this particular up or down. The odds are that the whole question is not worth the poorest thought which the scholar has lost in listening to the controversy. Let him not quit his belief that a popgun is a popgun, though the ancient and honorable[64] of the earth affirm it to be the crack of doom. In silence, in steadiness, in severe abstraction, let him hold by himself; add observation to observation, patient of neglect, patient of reproach, and bide his own time,—happy enough if he can satisfy himself alone that this day he has seen something truly. Success treads on every right step. For the instinct is sure that prompts him to tell his brother what he thinks. He then learns that in going down into the secrets of his own mind he has descended into the secrets of all minds. He learns that he who has mastered any law in his private thoughts is master to that extent of all men whose language he speaks, and of all into whose language his own can be translated. The poet, in utter solitude remembering his spontaneous thoughts and recording them, is found to have recorded that which men in cities vast find true for them also. The orator distrusts at first the fitness of his frank confessions, his want of knowledge of the persons he addresses, until he finds that he is the complement[65] of his hearers;—that they drink his words because he fulfills for them their own nature; the deeper he dives into his privatest, secretest presentiment, to his wonder he finds this is the most acceptable, most public and universally true. The people delight in it; the better part of every man feels—This is my music; this is myself.

In self-trust all the virtues are comprehended. Free should the scholar be,—free and brave. Free even to the definition of freedom, "without any hindrance that does not arise out of his own constitution." Brave; for fear is a thing which a scholar by his very function puts behind him. Fear always springs from ignorance. It is a shame to him if his tranquility, amid dangerous times, arise from the presumption that like children and women his is a protected class; or if he seek a temporary peace by the diversion of his thoughts from politics or vexed questions, hiding his head like an ostrich in the flowering bushes, peeping into microscopes, and turning rhymes, as a boy whistles to keep his courage up. So is the danger a danger still; so is the fear worse. Manlike let him turn and face it. Let him look into its eye and search its nature, inspect its origin,—see the whelping of this lion,—which lies no great way back; he will then find in himself a perfect comprehension of its nature and extent; he will have made his hands meet on the other side, and can henceforth defy it and pass on superior. The world is his who can see through its pretension. What deafness, what stone-blind custom, what overgrown error you behold is there only by sufferance,—by your sufferance. See it to be a lie, and you have already dealt it its mortal blow.

Yes, we are the cowed,—we the trustless. It is a mischievous notion that we are come late into nature; that the world was finished a long time ago. As the world was plastic and fluid in the hands of God, so it is ever to so much of his attributes as we bring to it. To ignorance and sin it is flint. They adapt themselves to it as they may; but in proportion as a man has any thing in him divine, the firmament flows before him and takes his signet[66] and form. Not he is great who can alter matter, but he who can alter my state of mind. They are the kings of the world who give the color of their present thought to all nature and all art, and persuade men, by the cheerful serenity of their carrying the matter, that this thing which they do is the apple which the ages have desired to pluck, now at last ripe, and inviting nations to the harvest. The great man makes the great thing. Wherever Macdonald[67] sits, there is the head of the table. Linnæus[68] makes botany the most alluring of studies, and wins it from the farmer and the herb-woman: Davy,[69] chemistry; and Cuvier,[70] fossils. The day is always his who works in it with serenity and great aims. The unstable estimates of men crowd to him whose mind is filled with a truth, as the heaped waves of the Atlantic follow the moon.[71]

For this self-trust, the reason is deeper than can be fathomed,—darker than can be enlightened. I might not carry with me the feeling of my audience in stating my own belief. But I have already shown the ground of my hope, in adverting to the doctrine that man is one. I believe man has been wronged; he has wronged himself. He has almost lost the light that can lead him back to his prerogatives. Men are become of no account. Men in history, men in the world of to-day, are bugs, are spawn, and are called "the mass" and "the herd." In a century, in a millennium, one or two men;[72] that is to say, one or two approximations to the right state of every man. All the rest behold in the hero or the poet their own green and crude being,—ripened; yes, and are content to be less, so *that* may attain to its full stature. What a testimony, full of grandeur, full of pity, is borne to the demands of his own nature, by the poor clansman, the poor partisan, who rejoices in the glory of his chief! The poor and the low find some amends to their immense moral capacity, for their acquiescence in a political and social inferiority.[73] They are content to be brushed like flies from the path of a great person, so that justice shall be done by him to that common nature which it is the dearest desire of all to see enlarged and glorified. They sun themselves in the great man's light, and feel it to be their own element. They cast the dignity of man from their downtrod selves upon the shoulders of a hero, and will perish to add one drop of blood to make that great heart beat, those giant sinews combat and conquer. He lives for us, and we live in him.

Men such as they[74] are very naturally seek money or power; and power because it is as good as money,—the "spoils," so called, "of office." And why not? For they aspire to the highest, and this, in their sleep-walking, they dream is highest. Wake them and they shall quit the false good and leap to the true, and leave governments to clerks and desks. This revolution is to be wrought by the gradual domestication of the idea of Culture. The main enterprise of the world for splendor, for extent, is the upbuilding of a man. Here are the materials strewn along the ground. The private life of one man shall be a more illustrious monarchy, more formidable to its enemy, more sweet and serene in its influence to its friend, than any kingdom in history. For a man, rightly viewed, comprehendeth[75] the particular natures of all men. Each philosopher, each bard, each actor has only done for me, as by a delegate, what one day I can do for myself. The books which once we valued more than the apple of the eye, we have quite exhausted. What is that but saying that we have come up with the point of view which the universal mind took through the eyes of one scribe; we have been that man, and have passed on. First, one, then another, we drain all cisterns, and waxing greater by all these supplies, we crave a better and a more abundant food. The man has never lived that can feed us ever. The human mind cannot be enshrined in a person who shall set a barrier on any one side to this unbounded, unboundable empire. It is one central fire, which, flaming now out of the lips of Etna, lightens the capes of Sicily, and now out of the throat of Vesuvius, illuminates the towers and vineyards of Naples. It is one light which beams out of a thousand stars. It is one soul which animates all men.

*   *   *   *   *

But I have dwelt perhaps tediously upon this abstraction of the Scholar. I ought not to delay longer to add what I have to say of nearer reference to the time and to this country.

Historically, there is thought to be a difference in the ideas which predominate over successive epochs, and there are data for marking the genius of the Classic, of the Romantic, and now of the Reflective or Philosophical age.[76] With the views I have intimated of the oneness or the identity of the mind through all individuals, I do not much dwell on these differences. In fact, I believe each individual passes through all three. The boy is a Greek; the youth, romantic; the adult, reflective. I deny not, however, that a revolution in the leading idea may be distinctly enough traced.

Our age is bewailed as the age of Introversion.[77] Must that needs be evil? We, it seems, are critical. We are embarrassed with second thoughts.[78] We cannot enjoy anything for hankering to know whereof the pleasure consists. We are lined with eyes. We see with our feet. The time is infected with Hamlet's unhappiness,—"Sicklied o'er with the pale cast of thought."[79]

Is it so bad then? Sight is the last thing to be pitied. Would we be blind? Do we fear lest we should outsee nature and God, and drink truth dry? I look upon the discontent of the literary class as a mere announcement of the fact that they find themselves not in the state of mind of their fathers, and regret the coming state as untried; as a boy dreads the water before he has learned that he can swim. If there is any period one would desire to be born in, is it not the age of Revolution; when the old and the new stand side by side and admit of being compared; when the energies of all men are searched by fear and by hope; when the historic glories of the old can be compensated by the rich possibilities of the new era? This time, like all times, is a very good one, if we but know what to do with it.

I read with some joy of the auspicious signs of the coming days, as they glimmer already through poetry and art, through philosophy and science, through church and state.

One of these signs is the fact that the same movement[80] which effected the elevation of what was called the lowest class in the state assumed in literature a very marked and as benign an aspect. Instead of the sublime and beautiful, the near, the low, the common, was explored and poetized. That which had been negligently trodden under foot by those who were harnessing and provisioning themselves for long journeys into far countries, is suddenly found to be richer than all foreign parts. The literature of the poor, the feelings of the child, the philosophy of the street, the meaning of household life, are the topics of the time. It is a great stride. It is a sign—is it not?—of new vigor when the extremities are made active, when currents of warm life run into the hands and the feet. I ask not for the great, the remote, the romantic; what is doing in Italy or Arabia; what is Greek art, or Provençal minstrelsy; I embrace the common, I explore and sit at the feet of the familiar, the low. Give me insight into to-day, and you may have the antique and future worlds. What would we really know the meaning of? The meal in the firkin; the milk in the pan; the ballad in the street; the news of the boat; the glance of the eye; the form and the gait of the body;—show me the ultimate reason of these matters; show me the sublime presence of the highest spiritual cause lurking, as always it does lurk, in these suburbs and extremities of nature; let me see every trifle bristling with the polarity that ranges it instantly on an eternal law;[81] and the shop, the plow, and the ledger referred to the like cause by which light undulates and poets sing;—and the world lies no longer a dull miscellany and lumber-room, but has form and order: there is no trifle, there is no puzzle, but one design unites and animates the farthest pinnacle and the lowest trench.

This idea has inspired the genius of Goldsmith,[82] Burns,[83] Cowper,[84] and, in a newer time, of Goethe,[85] Wordsworth,[86] and Carlyle.[87] This idea they have differently followed and with various success. In contrast with their writing, the style of Pope,[88] of Johnson,[89] of Gibbon,[90] looks cold and pedantic. This writing is blood-warm. Man is surprised to find that things near are not less beautiful and wondrous than things remote. The near explains the far. The drop is a small ocean. A man is related to all nature. This perception of the worth of the vulgar is fruitful in discoveries. Goethe, in this very thing the most modern of the moderns, has shown us, as none ever did, the genius of the ancients.

There is one man of genius who has done much for this philosophy of life, whose literary value has never yet been rightly estimated:—I mean Emanuel Swedenborg.[91] The most imaginative of men, yet writing with the precision of a mathematician, he endeavored to engraft a purely philosophical Ethics on the popular Christianity of his time. Such an attempt of course must have difficulty which no genius could surmount. But he saw and showed the connexion between nature and the affections of the soul. He pierced the emblematic or spiritual character of the visible, audible, tangible world. Especially did his shade-loving muse hover over and interpret the lower parts of nature; he showed the mysterious bond that allies moral evil to the foul material forms, and has given in epical parables a theory of insanity, of beasts, of unclean and fearful things.

Another sign of our times, also marked by an analogous political movement, is the new importance given to the single person. Everything that tends to insulate the individual—to surround him with barriers of natural respect, so that each man shall feel the world is his, and man shall treat with man as a sovereign state with a sovereign state—tends to true union as well as greatness. "I learned," said the melancholy Pestalozzi,[92] "that no man in God's wide earth is either willing or able to help any other man." Help must come from the bosom alone. The scholar is that man who must take up into himself all the ability of the time, all the contributions of the past, all the hopes of the future. He must be an university of knowledges. If there be one lesson more than another that should pierce his ear, it is—The world is nothing, the man is all; in yourself is the law of all nature, and you know not yet how a globule of sap ascends; in yourself slumbers the whole of Reason; it is for you to know all; it is for you to dare all. Mr. President and Gentlemen, this confidence in the unsearched might of man belongs, by all motives, by all prophecy, by all preparation, to the American Scholar. We have listened too long to the courtly muses of Europe. The spirit of the American freeman is already suspected to be timid, imitative, tame. Public and private avarice make the air we breathe thick and fat. The scholar is decent, indolent, complaisant. See already the tragic consequence. The mind of this country, taught to aim at low objects, eats upon itself. There is no work for any one but the decorous and the complaisant. Young men of the fairest promise, who begin life upon our shores, inflated by the mountain winds, shined upon by all the stars of God, find the earth below not in unison with these, but are hindered from action by the disgust which the principles on which business is managed inspire, and turn drudges, or die of disgust, some of them suicides. What is the remedy? They did not yet see, and thousands of young men as hopeful now crowding to the barriers for the career do not yet see, that if the single man plant himself indomitably on his instincts, and there abide, the huge world will come round to him. Patience,—patience; with the shades of all the good and great for company; and for solace the perspective of your own infinite life; and for work the study and the communication of principles, the making those instincts prevalent, the conversion of the world. Is it not the chief disgrace in the world, not to be an unit; not to be reckoned one character; not to yield that peculiar fruit which each man was created to bear, but to be reckoned in the gross, in the hundred, or the thousand, of the party, the section, to which we belong; and our opinion predicted geographically, as the north, or the south? Not so, brothers and friends,—please God, ours shall not be so. We will walk on our own feet; we will work with our own hands; we will speak our own minds. Then shall man be no longer a name for pity, for doubt, and for sensual indulgence. The dread of man and the love of man shall be a wall of defense and a wreath of joy around all. A nation of men will for the first time exist, because each believes himself inspired by the Divine Soul which also inspires all men.

Regarding the Text

1. If Emerson had given a quick definition of an "American Scholar," how would that definition read?

2. How, does Emerson propose, should the mind of nature and the mind of the past influence the scholar?

3. In section I, what importance does the skill of classification have to Emerson?

Joining the Conversation

4. Emerson describes the mind as being reflected in nature, writing about the scholar that, "He shall see that nature is the opposite of the soul, answering to it part for part." How does "nature" answer the "soul"? What does Emerson mean by these two terms?

5. In speeches and addresses, such as this one, you might find a particular tone set to stir a crowd to feel an emotion or to want to take action. Where precisely in this essay can you locate such a tone? How does it differ from the tone you would expect to see if this were instead a paper written for a college class?

Owning the Idea

6. How do the authors of "Total Eclipse," "The Solace of Open Spaces," and "Havasu" take up Emerson's call to understand their own minds as they understand nature? How do these authors respond to Emerson when he writes, "Nature then becomes to him the measure of his attainments. So much of nature as he is ignorant of, so much of his own mind does he not yet possess"?

7. How similar or different does Emerson's conception of the scholar look compared to your own conception of a student? Do you find Emerson's description of a scholar realistic? Do you think students should attain the qualities Emerson describes, or do today's students have another purpose? Does Emerson speak in particular to his own age, or do his ideas still have relevance?

Joy

Zadie Smith

http://theessayexperiencefall2013.qwriting.qc.cuny.edu/files/2013/09/Joy-by-Zadie-Smith.pdf

Regarding the Text

1. What are the various experiences Smith regards as pleasurable? What do they have in common in bringing her pleasure?

2. What does Smith say, in the end, is an important difference that distinguishes pleasure from joy?

Joining the Conversation

3. What do you think would occasion an essay like this? What evidence can you find in Smith's essay that would shed light on the impetus or motivation for writing about joy as a distinct experience?

4. What do you think about Smith's references to taking drugs for pleasure as a young woman? Do you think she regards her behavior with the fondness with which she appears to remember it in her narrative?

Owning the Idea

5. What can you find about the British TV comedy Smith mentions, "Peep Show," and its character "Super Hans"? What reason would Smith have to remember this show so specifically?

6. In what contexts does joy seem to exist for Smith? Where do you find joy? Is joy a universal feeling, or is it cultivated within the arrangements of culture and social expectations?

Of the Custom of Wearing Clothes

Michel de Montaigne

Whatever I shall say upon this subject, I am of necessity to invade some of the bounds of custom, so careful has she been to shut up all the avenues. I was disputing with myself in this shivering season, whether the fashion of going naked in those nations lately discovered is imposed upon them by the hot temperature of the air, as we say of the Indians and Moors, or whether it be the original fashion of mankind. Men of understanding, forasmuch as all things under the sun, as the Holy Writ declares, are subject to the same laws, were wont in such considerations as these, where we are to distinguish the natural laws from those which have been imposed by man's invention, to have recourse to the general polity of the world, where there can be nothing counterfeit. Now, all other creatures being sufficiently furnished with all things necessary for the support of their being—[Montaigne's expression is, "with needle and thread."— W.C.H.]—it is not to be imagined that we only are brought into the world in a defective and indigent condition, and in such a state as cannot subsist without external aid. Therefore it is that I believe, that as plants, trees, and animals, and all things that have life, are seen to be by nature sufficiently clothed and covered, to defend them from the injuries of weather:

> *Proptereaque fere res omnes ant corio sunt, Aut seta, ant conchis, ant callo, ant cortice tectae,*

> [And that for this reason nearly all things are clothed with skin, or hair, or shells, or bark, or some such thing. —Lucretius, iv. 936.]

so were we: but as those who by artificial light put out that of day, so we by borrowed forms and fashions have destroyed our own. And 'tis plain enough to be seen, that 'tis custom only which renders that impossible that otherwise is nothing so; for of those nations who have no manner of knowledge of clothing, some are situated under the same temperature that we are, and some in much colder climates. And besides, our most tender parts are always exposed to the air, as the eyes, mouth, nose, and ears; and our country labourers, like our ancestors in former times, go with their breasts and bellies open. Had we been born with a necessity upon us of wearing petticoats and breeches, there is no doubt but nature would have fortified those parts she intended should be exposed to the fury of the seasons with a thicker skin, as she has done the finger-ends and the soles of the feet. And why should this seem hard to believe? I observe much greater distance betwixt my habit and that of one of our country boors, than betwixt his and that of a man who has no other covering but his skin. How many men, especially in Turkey, go naked upon the account of devotion? Some one asked a beggar, whom he saw in his shirt in the depth of winter, as brisk and frolic as he who goes muffled up to the ears in furs, how he was able to endure to go so? "Why, sir," he answered, "you go with your face bare: I am all face." The Italians have a story of the Duke of Florence's fool, whom his master asking how, being so thinly clad, he was able to support the cold, when he himself, warmly wrapped up as he was, was hardly able to do it? "Why," replied the fool, "use my receipt to put on all your clothes you have at once, and you'll feel no more cold than I." King Massinissa, to an extreme old age, could never be prevailed upon to go with his head covered, how cold, stormy, or rainy soever the weather might be; which also is reported of the Emperor Severus. Herodotus tells us, that in the battles fought betwixt the Egyptians and the Persians, it was observed both by himself and by others, that of those who were left dead upon the field, the heads of the Egyptians were without comparison harder than those of the Persians, by reason that the last had gone with their heads always covered from their infancy, first with biggins, and then with turbans, and the others always shaved and bare. King Agesilaus continued to a decrepit age to wear always the same clothes in winter that he did in summer. Caesar, says Suetonius, marched always at the head of his army, for the most part on foot, with his head bare, whether it was rain or sunshine, and as much is said of Hannibal:

Tum vertice nudo, Excipere insanos imbres, coelique ruinam.

[Bareheaded he marched in snow, exposed to pouring rain and the utmost rigour of the weather.—*Silius Italicus*, i. 250.]

A Venetian who has long lived in Peru, and has lately returned thence, writes that the men and women of that kingdom, though they cover all their other parts, go always barefoot and ride so too; and Plato very earnestly advises for the health of the whole body, to give the head and the feet no other clothing than what nature has bestowed. He whom the Poles have elected for their king, —[Stephen Bathory]—since ours came thence, who is, indeed, one of the greatest princes of this age, never wears any gloves, and in winter or whatever weather can come, never wears other cap abroad than that he wears at home. Whereas I cannot endure to go unbuttoned or untied; my neighboring labourers would think themselves in chains, if they were so braced. Varro is of opinion, that when it was ordained we should be bare in the presence of the gods and before the magistrate, it was so ordered rather upon the score of health, and to inure us to the injuries of weather, than upon the account of reverence; and since we are now talking of cold, and Frenchmen used to wear variety of colours (not I myself, for I seldom wear other than black or white, in imitation of my father), let us add another story out of Le Capitaine Martin du Bellay, who affirms, that in the march to Luxembourg he saw so great frost, that the munition-wine was cut with hatchets and wedges, and delivered out to the soldiers by weight, and that they carried it away in baskets: and Ovid,

Nudaque consistunt, formam servantia testae, Vina; nec hausta meri, sed data frusta, bibunt.

[The wine when out of the cask retains the form of the cask; and is given out not in cups, but in bits. —Ovid, *Trist.,* iii. 10, 23.]

At the mouth of Lake Maeotis the frosts are so very sharp, that in the very same place where Mithridates' lieutenant had fought the enemy dryfoot and given them a notable defeat, the summer following he obtained over them a naval victory. The Romans fought at a very great disadvantage, in the engagement they had with the Carthaginians near Piacenza, by reason that they went to the charge with their blood congealed and their limbs numbed with cold, whereas Hannibal had caused great fires to be dispersed quite through his camp to warm his soldiers, and oil to be distributed amongst them, to the end that anointing themselves, they might render their nerves more supple and active, and fortify the pores against the violence of the air and freezing wind, which raged in that season.

The retreat the Greeks made from Babylon into their own country is famous for the difficulties and calamities they had to overcome; of which this was one, that being encountered in the mountains of Armenia with a horrible storm of snow, they lost all knowledge of the country and of the ways, and being driven up, were a day and a night without eating or drinking; most of their cattle died, many of themselves were starved to death, several struck blind with the force of the hail and the glare of the snow, many of them maimed in their fingers and toes, and many stiff and motionless with the extremity of the cold, who had yet their understanding entire.

Alexander saw a nation, where they bury their fruit-trees in winter to protect them from being destroyed by the frost, and we also may see the same.

But, so far as clothes go, the King of Mexico changed four times a day his apparel, and never put it on again, employing that he left off in his continual liberalities and rewards; and neither pot, dish, nor other utensil of his kitchen or table was ever served twice.

(1574)

Regarding the Text

1. One of the rudiments of Montaigne's essays *not* to be handed down to us in the present day is the predilection of dropping quotations from ancient literature into his essay. Without much support, either by way of introduction or analysis, Montaigne leaves what he finds fit scattered about in his essay. We call these now "floating quotations" and regard them as indicative of sloppy scholarship. How do you react to them (or their translation) in Montaigne's essay? Do they seem appropriate or oddly placed? Interesting or interruptive?

2. What do Montaigne's references to several conquerors and situations of battle in the essay have to do with clothing?

Joining the Conversation

3. What are the various uses for clothes Montaigne notes in his essay?

4. Do you think in the end that Montaigne finds clothing a custom rather than a basic necessity?

Owning the Idea

5. Montaigne wrote this essay in 1574. Nearly four and a half centuries later, it is still odd to think of people wandering about without clothes. While some nudist colonies exist throughout the world, and some small cultures still go largely naked, what do you think is Montaigne's real issue with wearing clothes?

6. In "The View from 80," Malcolm Cowley catalogs some of the ways the elderly attempt to reclaim their youth. What similarities do you find in Montaigne's essay regarding, rather than those of the elderly, the habits of the wealthy or powerful?

The Republic, Excerpts from "Allegory of the Cave"

Plato

Book VII

Socrates—GLAUCON

And now, I said, let me show in a figure how far our nature is enlightened or unenlightened:—Behold! human beings living in a underground den, which has a mouth open towards the light and reaching all along the den; here they have been from their childhood, and have their legs and necks chained so that they cannot move, and can only see before them, being prevented by the chains from turning round their heads. Above and behind them a fire is blazing at a distance, and between the fire and the prisoners there is a raised way; and you will see, if you look, a low wall built along the way, like the screen which marionette players have in front of them, over which they show the puppets.

I see.

And do you see, I said, men passing along the wall carrying all sorts of vessels, and statues and figures of animals made of wood and stone and various materials, which appear over the wall? Some of them are talking, others silent.

You have shown me a strange image, and they are strange prisoners.

Like ourselves, I replied; and they see only their own shadows, or the shadows of one another, which the fire throws on the opposite wall of the cave?

True, he said; how could they see anything but the shadows if they were never allowed to move their heads?

And of the objects which are being carried in like manner they would only see the shadows?

Yes, he said.

And if they were able to converse with one another, would they not suppose that they were naming what was actually before them?

Very true.

And suppose further that the prison had an echo which came from the other side, would they not be sure to fancy when one of the passers-by spoke that the voice which they heard came from the passing shadow?

No question, he replied.

To them, I said, the truth would be literally nothing but the shadows of the images.

That is certain.

And now look again, and see what will naturally follow it the prisoners are released and disabused of their error. At first, when any of them is liberated and compelled suddenly to stand up and turn his neck round and walk and look towards the light, he will suffer sharp pains; the glare will distress him, and he will be unable to see the realities of which in his former state he had seen the shadows; and then conceive some one saying to him, that what he saw before was an illusion, but that now, when he is approaching nearer to being and his eye is turned towards more real existence, he has a clearer vision,—what will be his reply? And you may further imagine that his instructor is pointing to the objects as they pass and requiring him to name them,—will he not be perplexed? Will he not fancy that the shadows which he formerly saw are truer than the objects which are now shown to him?

Far truer.

And if he is compelled to look straight at the light, will he not have a pain in his eyes which will make him turn away to take in the objects of vision which he can see, and which he will conceive to be in reality clearer than the things which are now being shown to him?

True.

And suppose once more, that he is reluctantly dragged up a steep and rugged ascent, and held fast until he's forced into the presence of the sun himself, is he not likely to be pained and irritated? When he approaches the light his eyes will be dazzled, and he will not be able to see anything at all of what are now called realities.

Not all in a moment, he said.

He will require to grow accustomed to the sight of the upper world. And first he will see the shadows best, next the reflections of men and other objects in the water, and then the objects themselves; then he will gaze upon the light of the moon and the stars and the spangled heaven; and he will see the sky and the stars by night better than the sun or the light of the sun by day?

Certainly.

Last of he will be able to see the sun, and not mere reflections of him in the water, but he will see him in his own proper place, and not in another; and he will contemplate him as he is.

Certainly.

He will then proceed to argue that this is he who gives the season and the years, and is the guardian of all that is in the visible world, and in a certain way the cause of all things which he and his fellows have been accustomed to behold?

Clearly, he said, he would first see the sun and then reason about him.

And when he remembered his old habitation, and the wisdom of the den and his fellow-prisoners, do you not suppose that he would felicitate himself on the change, and pity them?

Certainly, he would.

And if they were in the habit of conferring honours among themselves on those who were quickest to observe the passing shadows and to remark which of them went before, and which followed after, and which were together; and who were therefore best able to draw conclusions as to the future, do you think that he would care for such honours and glories, or envy the possessors of them? Would he not say with Homer,

Better to be the poor servant of a poor master, and to endure anything, rather than think as they do and live after their manner?

Yes, he said, I think that he would rather suffer anything than entertain these false notions and live in this miserable manner.

Imagine once more, I said, such an one coming suddenly out of the sun to be replaced in his old situation; would he not be certain to have his eyes full of darkness?

To be sure, he said.

And if there were a contest, and he had to compete in measuring the shadows with the prisoners who had never moved out of the den, while his sight was still weak, and before his eyes had become steady (and the time which would be needed to acquire this new habit of sight might be very considerable) would he not be ridiculous? Men would say of him that up he went and down he came without his eyes; and that it was better not even to think of ascending; and if any one tried to loose another and lead him up to the light, let them only catch the offender, and they would put him to death.

No question, he said.

This entire allegory, I said, you may now append, dear Glaucon, to the previous argument; the prison-house is the world of sight, the light of the fire is the sun, and you will not misapprehend me if you interpret the journey upwards to be the ascent of the soul into the intellectual world according to my poor belief, which, at your desire, I have expressed whether rightly or wrongly God knows. But, whether true or false, my opinion is that in the world of knowledge the idea of good appears last of all, and is seen only with an effort; and, when seen, is also inferred to be the universal author of all things beautiful and right, parent of light and of the lord of light in this visible world, and the immediate source of reason and truth in the intellectual; and that this is the power upon which he who would act rationally, either in public or private life must have his eye fixed.

I agree, he said, as far as I am able to understand you.

Moreover, I said, you must not wonder that those who attain to this beatific vision are unwilling to descend to human affairs; for their souls are ever hastening into the upper world where they desire to dwell; which desire of theirs is very natural, if our allegory may be trusted.

Yes, very natural.

And is there anything surprising in one who passes from divine contemplations to the evil state of man, misbehaving himself in a ridiculous manner; if, while his eyes are blinking and before he has become accustomed to the surrounding darkness, he is compelled to fight in courts of law, or in other places, about the images or the shadows of images of justice, and is endeavouring to meet the conceptions of those who have never yet seen absolute justice?

Anything but surprising, he replied.

Any one who has common sense will remember that the bewilderments of the eyes are of two kinds, and arise from two causes, either from coming out of the light or from going into the light, which is true of the mind's eye, quite as much as of the bodily eye; and he who remembers this when he sees any one whose vision is perplexed and weak, will not be too ready to laugh; he will first ask whether that soul of man has come out of the brighter light, and is unable to see because unaccustomed to the dark, or having turned from darkness to the day is dazzled by excess of light. And he will count the one happy in his condition and state of being, and he will pity the other; or, if he have a mind to laugh at the soul which comes from below into the light, there will be more reason in this than in the laugh which greets him who returns from above out of the light into the den.

That, he said, is a very just distinction.

But then, if I am right, certain professors of education must be wrong when they say that they can put a knowledge into the soul which was not there before, like sight into blind eyes.

They undoubtedly say this, he replied.

Whereas, our argument shows that the power and capacity of learning exists in the soul already; and that just as the eye was unable to turn from darkness to light without the whole body, so too the instrument of knowledge can only by the movement of the whole soul be turned from the world of becoming into that of being, and learn by degrees to endure the sight of being, and of the brightest and best of being, or in other words, of the good.

Very true.

And must there not be some art which will effect conversion in the easiest and quickest manner; not implanting the faculty of sight, for that exists already, but has been turned in the wrong direction, and is looking away from the truth?

Yes, he said, such an art may be presumed.

And whereas the other so-called virtues of the soul seem to be akin to bodily qualities, for even when they are not originally innate they can be implanted later by habit and exercise, the of wisdom more than anything else contains a divine element which always remains, and by this conversion is rendered useful and profitable; or, on the other hand, hurtful and useless. Did you never observe the narrow intelligence flashing from the keen eye of a clever rogue —how eager he is, how clearly his paltry soul sees the way to his end; he is the reverse of blind, but his keen eyesight is forced into the service of evil, and he is mischievous in proportion to his cleverness.

Very true, he said.

But what if there had been a circumcision of such natures in the days of their youth; and they had been severed from those sensual pleasures, such as eating and drinking, which, like leaden weights, were attached to them at their birth, and which drag them down and turn the vision of their souls upon the things that are below—if, I say, they had been released from these impediments and turned in the opposite direction, the very same faculty in them would have seen the truth as keenly as they see what their eyes are turned to now.

Very likely.

Yes, I said; and there is another thing which is likely, or rather a necessary inference from what has preceded, that neither the uneducated and uninformed of the truth, nor yet those who never make an end of their education, will be able ministers of State; not the former, because they have no single aim of duty which is the rule of all their actions, private as well as public; nor the latter, because they will not act at all except upon compulsion, fancying that they are already dwelling apart in the islands of the blest.

Very true, he replied.

Then, I said, the business of us who are the founders of the State will be to compel the best minds to attain that knowledge which we have already shown to be the greatest of all-they must continue to ascend until they arrive at the good; but when they have ascended and seen enough we must not allow them to do as they do now.

What do you mean?

I mean that they remain in the upper world: but this must not be allowed; they must be made to descend again among the prisoners in the den, and partake of their labours and honours, whether they are worth having or not.

But is not this unjust? he said; ought we to give them a worse life, when they might have a better?

You have again forgotten, my friend, I said, the intention of the legislator, who did not aim at making any one class in the State happy above the rest; the happiness was to be in the whole State, and he held the citizens together by persuasion and necessity, making them benefactors of the State, and therefore benefactors of one another; to this end he created them, not to please themselves, but to be his instruments in binding up the State.

True, he said, I had forgotten.

Observe, Glaucon, that there will be no injustice in compelling our philosophers to have a care and providence of others; we shall explain to them that in other States, men of their class are not obliged to share in the toils of politics: and this is reasonable, for they grow up at their own sweet will, and the government would rather not have them. Being self-taught, they cannot be expected to show any gratitude for a culture which they have never received. But we have brought you into the world to be rulers of the hive, kings of yourselves and of the other citizens, and have educated you far better and more perfectly than they have been educated, and you are better able to share in the double duty. Wherefore each of you, when his turn comes, must go down to the general underground abode, and get the habit of seeing in the dark. When you have acquired the habit, you will see ten thousand times better than the inhabitants of the den, and you will know what the several images are, and what they represent, because you have seen the beautiful and just and good in their truth. And thus our State which is also yours will be a reality, and not a dream only, and will be administered in a spirit unlike that of other States, in which men fight with one another about shadows only and are distracted in the struggle for power, which in their eyes is a great good. Whereas the truth is that the State in which the rulers are most reluctant to govern is always the best and most quietly governed, and the State in which they are most eager, the worst.

Quite true, he replied.

And will our pupils, when they hear this, refuse to take their turn at the toils of State, when they are allowed to spend the greater part of their time with one another in the heavenly light?

Impossible, he answered; for they are just men, and the commands which we impose upon them are just; there can be no doubt that every one of them will take office as a stern necessity, and not after the fashion of our present rulers of State.

Yes, my friend, I said; and there lies the point. You must contrive for your future rulers another and a better life than that of a ruler, and then you may have a well-ordered State; for only in the State which offers this, will they rule who are truly rich, not in silver and gold, but in virtue and wisdom, which are the true blessings of life. Whereas if they go to the administration of public affairs, poor and hungering after the own private advantage, thinking that hence they are to snatch the chief good, order there can never be; for they will be fighting about office, and the civil and domestic broils which thus arise will be the ruin of the rulers themselves and of the whole State.

Regarding the Text

1. Even in the writing of antiquity, Glaucon finds the image Socrates proposes to be "strange," as it most certainly is to us even now. How is the image understandable if it is also strange?

2. The thought experiment is a staple of philosophical explanation. Can you picture the image Socrates proposes? Do you find it helpful to visualize his ideas?

Joining the Conversation

3. In the allegory, Socrates seems to concern himself with where we have come from and where we are headed. What is the "cave" from which we emerge? Where do you think we go if we are able to exit the cave?

4. Do you share Socrates' view that those with intellectual riches should rule rather than those with the most material riches?

Owning the Idea

5. What similarities can you find between Bertrand Russell's ideas in "Political Ideals" and Plato's in "The Allegory of the Cave"?

6. What does Socrates advocate in his allegory? Does he expect people to retreat from the body of the world into the life of the mind or do the enlightened have to enter the cave again among the others?

7. What comment does this text make on your own pursuit of education? What responsibilities do you receive along with new understanding?

ASSIGNMENT: CLOSE READING OF A CHALLENGING PASSAGE

Writing Assignment

Objective

Reading a text closely means attending to a limited array of details in order to expand or dilate the meaning of specific passages. Close reading accounts for the use of specific words or phrasing. It also explains the context of details within passages where they occur and within the work as a whole. Close reading and explication should slow your reading until you feel you have exhausted the meaning of the words.

Assignment

Write a paper in which you examine closely a particularly difficult and/or meaningful passage in one of the essays printed in this textbook. Your objective is to read the passage closely and to show explicitly how to think through what is said in order to understand it clearly and to understand its context within the essay as a whole. When you write your paper, project an audience of other students who would have read the essay you are writing about but who will not have spent the time needed to understand the essay in detail. Focus on a single passage, which may be from a few sentences to an entire paragraph in length in the essay, and explain it carefully, referring to other passages as you need to in order to clarify the context of the writing. Then explain why you think the passage appears in the essay and how it helps you understand the theme or main idea.

To Consider

Try to explain what seems ambiguous about the passage you have chosen to work with. How might it be read or misread? Consider whether your reading or understanding of the passage has changed over the course of re-reading it and thinking about it. What changed your mind about its meaning?

Revision Ideas

1. Revision, which is the process of understanding anew the ideas you are forming about what you have read and what you want to say, begins the moment you approach a task and continues until you no longer work on that task. Not *wanting to* work on a task does not mean you have finished with it. Even some avoidance behaviors and some ways of procrastinating can be considered part of the process of reframing. Reading for pleasure, understanding what you have read, evaluating the ideas you encounter, and evaluating your own writing combined with other recursive and underlying cognitive activities you engage in. That is to say, nearly everything you do helps you to reinvent your understanding of what you see, hear, read, and activities in which you participate. Keep an open mind and observe new meanings or contrary ideas as you find them rather than discard information that appears not to agree with your general understanding.

2. There is no such thing as a true synonym, as language has no need to duplicate words. To understand the distance between synonyms, as you perform a close reading of a passage (1) look up the definitions not only of words you do not know but of *interesting* words or words used in unusual or unfamiliar ways, and (2) consider what other words could have been used in their place. How do those alternative words change the meaning?

Essay Conventions

Writing the Paragraph

Every paragraph makes its own point, but it also welcomes the point that preceded it and ushers in the point that follows in the next paragraph. Paragraph breaks are sometimes arbitrary, but you can learn to get the sense of what at minimum is needed to make a paragraph complete in most cases. When you're reading a paragraph, think about not only what the paragraph says but how it fits into the organization of the essay. What problem does this paragraph help you solve? What would happen to the understandability of your point if you moved this paragraph to a spot earlier or later in your essay?

Making Successful Transitions

With few exceptions, academic writing demands attention to the *development* of your ideas in your essay. As readers, we can follow the development of your ideas only if your paragraphs highlight the transition from one to the next, and only if your sentences do the same. One sentence must have a relation to the next, and that relation must be made evident to the reader. And so also for paragraphs. Transitions are more than words or sentences; they are the result of thinking made manifest. Imagine that the papers you write show your process of understanding an idea. Without meaningful transitions, your writing would not be able to show your thinking or evince the synergy of ideas that comes from thoughtful consideration of your purpose and your motivation to communicate your ideas.

To picture in your mind what transitions do, and why they are necessary, think of the writing process in terms of fishing: reeling in a big catch means winding the reel, letting out some slack so you don't break the line, then winding the reel again and repeating this process until you have the catch in a net or in your hands.

Quoting, Summarizing, Paraphrasing

If you are unsure about the definition of these terms, consult the handbook. When you provide details from a text to support an assertion, you must refer to that text. Referring can mean quoting, but it can also mean summarizing or paraphrasing briefly. Referring to a text situates us, orients us in the text so we know for sure what you want us to see. Quote only when you have to, when the very words themselves are so full of meaning or beauty, or convey a supra-semantic "feel" as with tone or diction. Otherwise make a quick reference by summarizing or paraphrasing.

Sample of Close Reading Student Essay

Below is a student's essay on "Joy" by Zadie Smith. In this Close Reading Essay, the student addresses finding pleasure in the ordinary. Does the student recognize the differences between pleasure and joy as set forth by Smith? Does her paper account for ambiguities and possible readings of Smith's essay?

Fernanda Silva
English 110

Essay on Close Reading: "Joy"

Most people define pleasure and joy as simply being correlated states of happiness. Just as Zadie Smith said in her essay "Joy," "A lot of people seem to feel that joy is only the most intense version of pleasure, arrived at by the same road," and that is just how far the definition goes for people who take ordinary or even special moments in life for granted, imperceptibly blocking further observations on the matter from coming to mind or just experiencing pleasure and joy for the sake of it. However, there are people who still manage to find pleasure in the ordinary, and for those who are able to treasure deeply having that fresh watermelon juice in the morning or receiving a welcoming good morning from their neighbor, joy becomes much more complex than simply a more intense version of pleasure.

I'm not saying pleasure takes a less important role in individuals' lives, but certainly a less complex one. Pleasure can be found in so many situations that it makes it so much easier to handle once the sensation goes away. You know you'll have pleasure again any time soon, whether it be sexual pleasure, tasting a delicious meal or getting a haircut that makes you say: WOW! But the same cannot be said about joy. In the following passage from the essay, it is possible to understand a bit more of the dilemma between defining what is pleasure or joy: "The writer Julian Barnes, considering mourning, once said, 'It hurts just as much as it is worth.' In fact, it was a friend of his who wrote the line in a letter of condolence, and Julian told it to my husband, who told it to me. For months afterward these words stuck with both of us, so clear and so brutal. It hurts just as much as it is worth. What an arrangement. Why would anyone accept such a crazy deal? Surely if we were sane and reasonable we would every time choose a pleasure over a joy, as animals themselves sensibly do. The end of a pleasure brings no great harm to anyone, after all, and can always be replaced with another of more or less equal worth."

This passage refers exactly to the fact that joy is of a broader complexity than pleasure. That being said, joy brings its troubles. The unbalanced weight of carrying the feeling of having that insatiable excitement and happiness defined as joy is balanced out with the loss of that same feeling. Achieving joy is just as fortunate as its loss is unfortunate. Therefore, why would anyone aim for joy if it can hurt just as much as it is worth? What if the extent of a certain joy is found in its peak? Can one handle the fall? Shouldn't pleasure be considered extreme happiness once awakening from it doesn't hurt as much as joy does? As it is hard to find a concrete answer for these matters we must blame our insanity for defining joy as something more fortunate than pleasure.

Furthermore, the majority of people only talk about the bright side of what joy brings, and I for sure belonged to that group of people until I came across this essay. It is really easy for people to think only about the pleasurable aspect of joy and ignore the after effects of it. A common example of joy being possibly destructive is whenever someone is under the influence of ecstasy for instance. It is somewhat difficult to put in words exactly what "popping" ecstasy makes you feel. That euphoria of feeling like you're on top of the world and the happiness that comes with it, the fact that one becomes an extremely loving person, and oh, the way one's senses are so sharp and one is so loose. There's no way all these combinations of amazing sensations can't be defined as joy in its most common definition. However, to feel all of that you need to be strongly prepared physically and mentally to handle any side effects and after effects the drug might bring. Most users of such a drug have to deal with feeling like a loser the next day; some even feel depressed and despondent and unwilling to do anything. In addition to that, ecstasy users have a high tendency to become addicted, for they come to believe that true happiness only exists while they're under the influence of the drug.

Is it an equivalent example of the hardness of joy to look at what happens when one is deeply in love, as love can often be highly dangerous and destructive? Nobody aims for having a broken heart; however, being able to experience the joy true love brings makes the passionate birds in play forget about all the risks and succumb to the strong emotions of love.

It is possible then to assert that human beings are driven by their need to be challenged. As pleasure can be easily found, we seek joy, which is way more challenging. "It hurts just as much as it is worth," Julian Barnes once said. And maybe that's just what we need, happiness and pain tied up together. There's nothing more challenging than that.

CHAPTER 20

Interpreting

FINITUDE AND AMBIGUITY

Ambiguity in language, the lack of clarity over how to interpret certain details we notice, naturally occurs because language is finite. A growing awareness that language itself is to blame for misunderstandings and multiple interpretations visits writers who struggle to clarify their thoughts. Language is finite. We have only a certain number of words in English. Though our language constantly expands and contracts, taking on neologisms with the arrival of new technologies and ideas, shedding archaisms as old views of the world fall away, we can at any moment count up the words in English (an impos-

sible task practically, but estimates in 2013 ran wildly from 600,000 to 1.2 million words). Language must always be finite. If it were infinite, every thought, feeling, and thing would have one word to describe it, and no one would be able to communicate with anyone else—we would never be able to find a common language. Because words describe more than one thing—they have multiple meanings and uses—words are ambiguous. The very existence of language precludes its ultimate clarity. This means that all language requires some degree of interpretation.

INTERPRETIVE ANALYSIS

Writers spend their energies trying to be understood clearly. To interpret is to understand something in its context. We interpret spoken language, facial gestures and body "language," street signs, tones of voice, moods, sounds, advertising images, and art. How we interpret all these signals does not have to be left a mystery, and exploring how we interpret can lead us to insights about how our minds work and where our interpretations are sound or need work.

When you read, you spend some time trying to understand who has your attention and why, and you spend some energy identifying why you are reading. Does the writer want something from you? Are you looking for information to help you perform a task? Does the writer want you to think a certain way or to take a particular action? Are you expected to answer in return? Are you being asked to make a decision? You think through all of these ideas quite naturally. It is also natural that when you read you handle these questions from a particularly defensive position. You don't want to be ripped off or fooled, and you don't want someone to waste your time.

Interpretive analysis builds on the skills employed in response analysis, which focuses on how you respond to details in a text through an analysis of your own experiences, values, beliefs, prior reading, and sense of self. While your response is still important, in interpretive analysis you turn your attention to finding important details that help you address ambiguities you find and lend some insight into the implications of a text. We can make a system of our interpretive strategies by employing a three-step process:

Steps Toward an Interpretive Analysis

1. Catalog the details you notice

2. Associate details that seem to go together

3. Guess at the meaning of the details

To catalog the details you notice, take note of words, phrases, images, and other particulars that stand out, even if you cannot yet explain why you have noticed those details. When you think about what you have read, inevitably you remember at least a handful of details. At this point you should not be concerned with why you remember the details or what they mean. It is significant enough that you remember them (intuition is a wonderful thing), and it is enough to recall them.

After you have catalogued details, you then associate details that seem to go together. This is a kind of classification game. Imagine you step up to a table where someone has left seven items: deodorant, a hairbrush, a camera, a bar of soap, a bag of marbles, toothpaste, and a cocker spaniel. You notice that a few of those items seem to go together (especially if you were in a hurry to get to school this morning), and your association simply ends there. The items needed to get ready in the morning go together. The dog, while probably very cute, the marbles, and the camera do not belong in that grouping. To write briefly about the associations you find, follow the pattern from the example above. If you write that four of the seven items are items used for grooming, or to clean up, or items found in a bathroom, you have written about the association of details.

Only when you arrive at step 3 to address the meaning of the details are you thinking about what the pattern might mean. Usually to arrive at step 3, there needs to be some kind of context. The items on a table have reached their limit. If you had awakened to find that those four items had been left next to the sink in your bathroom and that your roommate had bought them for you, you might be getting a hint about your personal hygiene. (That's just an example of a theme. No one is saying that it is true.)

We interpret information *all the time*. We constantly catalog details we encounter and classify details into groups, and we do this very often without thinking about it. We have to. Walking into a dark alley where shadowy figures emerge slowly, and seeing that no one else appears on the streets around us should be a good enough indication that we need to move along. Our interpretive powers save us from trouble and make our lives livable, but they can deceive us, too, if we are not careful to account for how we arrive at our interpretations.

EXAMPLE: INTERPRETATION OF A REAL WORLD SETTING

1. Catalog the Details

You walk into a room you've never seen before. You notice a drop ceiling, fluorescent lights, chalkboards, a TV hanging from the ceiling, a large table adjacent to the chalk board, a projector screen, rows of smaller one-piece chair/desks, and an American flag.

You already know, when you walk into this room, where you should sit and how you should behave. (That's actually step four. College-level thinking and writing requires accounting for how we arrive at our conclusions.)

2. Associate Details

The chalkboards, projector screen, and chair/desks seem to go together. While fluorescent lighting in a drop ceiling may not indicate your exact environment, it does not draw the picture of a living space. We know we are somewhere else, some place less comfortable than home, with less attention to the luxury of space that we look for in our living spaces. You establish, very, very quickly, that this is a place where the chalkboards belong to someone else, that that one large table at the front is not yours. This is the process of associating details. This place does not look like your living room (or one would hope not), so you sit in one of the small chair/desks (you are making inferences, even without saying, "This is a classroom.")

leungchopan/Shutterstock.com

3. Guess at the Meaning of the Details

This step encompasses thinking about the significance of the details. What does it *mean* that you take the smaller desk, that you face the front, that you keep your desk in the row to which it seems to belong; that you quietly listen to the person at the front of the room who gets to stand and move wherever she pleases while you must stay seated? What does it mean that you are quiet while she speaks, that you are expected to write some detail into a notebook from what she says, that you raise your hand to speak?

The classroom itself is an environment formed by the theories of education we adhere to, which are based on placing value on order, authority, a lack of democracy (it stings, but it is true), inferiority of the student, primacy of the instructor's word, maintaining predictable avenues of interaction, and so on. The way a classroom looks says a lot about what will go on in it. But we all know there are other ways to learn besides to sit in a classroom. Not everything to be learned is learned sitting down, and not all classrooms look alike. Learning also occurs in places far from any kind of classroom, to be sure, but ingrained in our recognition of the place is a closely-held theory of how to behave in that space, and that behavior is itself indicative of a set of values.

And that is the beginning of an interpretation of our classroom.

Total Eclipse

Annie Dillard

from *Teaching a Stone to Talk*

It had been like dying, that sliding down the mountain pass. It had been like the death of someone, irrational, that sliding down the mountain pass and into the region of dread. It was like slipping into fever, or falling down that hole in sleep from which you wake yourself whimpering. We had crossed the mountains that day, and now we were in a strange place—a hotel in central Washington, in a town near Yakima. The eclipse we had traveled here to see would occur early in the next morning.

I lay in bed. My husband, Gary, was reading beside me. I lay in bed and looked at the painting on the hotel room wall. It was a print of a detailed and lifelike painting of a smiling clown's head, made out of vegetables. It was a painting of the sort which you do not intend to look at, and which, alas, you never forget. Some tasteless fate presses it upon you; it becomes part of the complex interior junk you carry with you wherever you go. Two years have passed since the total eclipse of which I write. During those years I have forgotten, I assume, a great many things I wanted to remember–but I have not forgotten that clown painting or its lunatic setting in the old hotel. The clown was bald. Actually, he wore a clown's tight rubber wig, painted white; this stretched over the top of his skull, which was a cabbage. His hair was bunches of baby carrots. Inset in his white clown makeup, and in his cabbage skull, were his small and laughing human eyes. The clown's glance was like the glance of Rembrandt in some of the self-portraits: lively, knowing, deep, and loving. The crinkled shadows around his eyes were string beans. His eyebrows were parsley. Each of his ears was a broad bean. His thin, joyful lips were red chili peppers; between his lips were wet rows of human teeth and a suggestion of a real tongue. The clown print was framed in gilt and glassed.

To put ourselves in the path of the total eclipse, that day we had driven five hours inland from the Washington coast, where we lived. When we tried to cross the Cascades range, an avalanche had blocked the pass.

A slope's worth of snow blocked the road; traffic backed up. Had the avalanche buried any cars that morning? We could not learn. This highway was the only winter road over the mountains. We waited as highway crews bulldozed a passage through the avalanche. With two-by-fours and walls of plywood, they erected a one-way, roofed tunnel through the avalanche. We drove through the avalanche tunnel, crossed the pass, and descended several thousand feet into central Washington and the broad Yakima valley, about which we knew only that it was orchard country. As we lost altitude, the snows disappeared; our ears popped; the trees changed, and in the trees were strange birds. I watched the landscape innocently, like a fool, like a diver in the rapture of the deep who plays on the bottom while his air runs out.

The hotel lobby was a dark, derelict room, narrow as a corridor, and seemingly without air. We waited on a couch while the manager vanished upstairs to do something unknown to our room. Beside us on an overstuffed chair, absolutely motionless, was a platinum-blond woman in her forties wearing a black silk dress and a strand of pearls. Her long legs were crossed; she supported her head on her fist. At the dim far end of the room, their backs toward us, sat six bald old men in their shirtsleeves, around a loud television. Two of them seemed asleep. They were drunks. "Number six!" cried the man on television, "Number six!"

On the broad lobby desk, lighted and bubbling, was a ten-gallon aquarium containing one large fish; the fish tilted up and down in its water. Against the long opposite wall sang a live canary in its cage. Beneath the cage, among spilled millet seeds on the carpet, were a decorated child's sand bucket and matching sand shovel.

Now the alarm was set for six. I lay awake remembering an article I had read downstairs in the lobby, in an engineering magazine. The article was about gold mining.

In South Africa, in India, and in South Dakota, the gold mines extend so deeply into the earth's crust that they are hot. The rock walls burn the miners' hands. The companies have to air--condition the mines; if the air conditioners break, the miners die. The elevators in the mine shafts run very slowly, down, and up, so the miners' ears will not pop in their skulls. When the miners return to the surface, their faces are deathly pale.

Early the next morning we checked out. It was February 26, 1979, a Monday morning. We would drive out of town, find a hilltop, watch the eclipse, and then drive back over the mountains and home to the coast. How familiar things are here; how adept we are; how smoothly and professionally we check out! I had forgotten the clown's smiling head and the hotel lobby as if they had never existed. Gary put the car in gear and off we went, as off we have gone to a hundred other adventures.

It was dawn when we found a highway out of town and drove into the unfamiliar countryside. By the growing light we could see a band of cirrostratus clouds in the sky. Later the rising sun would clear these clouds before the eclipse began. We drove at random until we came to a range of unfenced hills. We pulled off the highway, bundled up, and climbed one of these hills.

II

The hill was five hundred feet high. Long winter-killed grass covered it, as high as our knees. We climbed and rested, sweating in the cold; we passed clumps of bundled people on the hill-side who were setting up telescopes and fiddling with cameras. The top of the hill stuck up in the middle of the sky. We tightened our scarves and looked around.

East of us rose another hill like ours. Between the hills, far below, 13 was the highway which threaded south into the valley. This was the Yakima valley; I had never seen it before. It is justly famous for its beauty, like every planted valley. It extended south into the horizon, a distant dream of a valley, a Shangrila. All its hundreds of low, golden slopes bore orchards. Among the orchards were towns, and roads, and plowed and fallow fields. Through the valley wandered a thin, shining river; from the river extended fine, frozen irrigation ditches. Distance blurred and blued the sight, so that the whole valley looked like a thickness or sediment at the bottom of the sky. Directly behind us was more sky, and empty lowlands blued by distance, and Mount Adams. Mount Adams was an enormous, snow-covered volcanic cone rising flat, like so much scenery.

Now the sun was up. We could not see it; but the sky behind the band of clouds was yellow, and, far down the valley, some hillside orchards had lighted up. More people were parking near the highway and climbing the hills. It was the West. All of us rugged individualists were wearing knit caps and blue nylon parkas. People were climbing the nearby hills and setting up shop in clumps among the dead grasses. It looked as though we had all gathered on hilltops to pray for the world on its last day. It looked as though we had all crawled out of spaceships and were preparing to assault the valley below. It looked as though we were scattered on hilltops at dawn to sacrifice virgins, make rain, set stone stelae in a ring. There was no place out of the wind. The straw grasses banged our legs.

Up in the sky where we stood the air was lusterless yellow. To the west the sky was blue. Now the sun cleared the clouds. We cast rough shadows on the blowing grass; freezing, we waved our arms. Near the sun, the sky was bright and colorless. There was nothing to see.

It began with no ado. It was odd that such a well advertised public event should have no start-ing gun, no overture, no introductory speaker. I should have known right then that I was out of my depth. Without pause or preamble, silent as orbits, a piece of the sun went away. We looked at it through welders' goggles. A piece of the sun was missing; in its place we saw empty sky.

I had seen a partial eclipse in 1970. A partial eclipse is very interesting. It bears almost no rela-tion to a total eclipse. Seeing a partial eclipse bears the same relation to seeing a total eclipse as kissing a man does to marrying him, or as flying in an airplane does to falling out of an air-plane. Although the one experience precedes the other, it in no way prepares you for it. During a partial eclipse the sky does not darken–not even when 94 percent of the sun is hidden. Nor does the sun, seen colorless through protective devices, seem terribly strange. We have all seen a sliver of light in the sky; we have all seen the crescent moon by day. However, during a partial eclipse the air does indeed get cold, precisely as if someone were standing between you and the fire. And blackbirds do fly back to their roosts. I had seen a partial eclipse before, and here was another.

What you see in an eclipse is entirely different from what you know. It is especially different for those of us whose grasp of astronomy is so frail that, given a flashlight, a grapefruit, two oranges, and fifteen years, we still could not figure out which way to set the clocks for Daylight

Saving Time. Usually it is a bit of a trick to keep your knowledge from blinding you. But during an eclipse it is easy. What you see is much more convincing than any wild-eyed theory you may know.

You may read that the moon has something to do with eclipses. I have never seen the moon yet. You do not see the moon. So near the sun, it is as completely invisible as the stars are by day. What you see before your eyes is the sun going through phases. It gets narrower and narrower, as the waning moon does, and, like the ordinary moon, it travels alone in the simple sky. The sky is of course background. It does not appear to eat the sun; it is far behind the sun. The sun simply shaves away; gradually, you see less sun and more sky.

The sky's blue was deepening, but there was no darkness. The sun was a wide crescent, like a segment of tangerine. The wind freshened and blew steadily over the hill. The eastern hill across the highway grew dusky and sharp. The towns and orchards in the valley to the south were dissolving into the blue light. Only the thin river held a trickle of sun.

Now the sky to the west deepened to indigo, a color never seen. A dark sky usually loses color. This was a saturated, deep indigo, up in the air. Stuck up into that unworldly sky was the cone of Mount Adams, and the alpenglow was upon it. The alpenglow is that red light of sunset which holds out on snowy mountain tops long after the valleys and tablelands are dimmed. "Look at Mount Adams," I said, and that was the last sane moment I remember.

I turned back to the sun. It was going. The sun was going, and the world was wrong. The grasses were wrong; they were platinum. Their every detail of stem, head, and blade shone lightless and artificially distinct as an art photographer's platinum print. This color has never been seen on earth. The hues were metallic; their finish was matte. The hillside was a nineteenth-century tinted photograph from which the tints had faded. All the people you see in the photograph, distinct and detailed as their faces look, are now dead. The sky was navy blue. My hands were silver. All the distant hills' grasses were finespun metal which the wind laid down. I was watching a faded color print of a movie filmed in the Middle Ages; I was standing in it, by some mistake. I was standing in a movie of hillside grasses filmed in the Middle Ages. I missed my own century, the people I knew, and the real light of day.

I looked at Gary. He was in the film. Everything was lost. He was a platinum print, a dead artist's version of life. I saw on his skull the darkness of night mixed with the colors of day. My mind was going out; my eyes were receding the way galaxies recede to the rim of space. Gary was lighters away, gesturing inside a circle of darkness, down the wrong end of a telescope. He smiled as if he saw me; the stringy crinkles around his eyes moved. The sight of him, familiar and wrong, was something I was remembering from centuries hence, from the other side of death: yes, that is the way he used to look, when we were living. When it was our generation's turn to be alive. I could not hear him; the wind was too loud. Behind him the sun was going. We had all started down a chute of time. At first it was pleasant; now there was no stopping it. Gary was chuting away across space, moving and talking and catching my eye, chuting down the long corridor of separation. The skin on his face moved like thin bronze plating that would peel.

The grass at our feet was wild barley. It was the wild einkorn wheat which grew on the hilly flanks of the Zagros Mountains, above the Euphrates valley, above the valley of the river we called River. We harvested the grass with stone sickles, I remember. We found the grasses on the hillsides; we built our shelter beside them and cut them down. That is how he used to look then, that one, moving and living and catching my eye, with the sky so dark behind him, and the wind blowing. God save our life.

From all the hills came screams. A piece of sky beside the crescent sun was detaching. It was a loosened circle of evening sky, suddenly lighted from the back. It was an abrupt black body out of nowhere; it was a flat disk; it was almost over the sun. That is when there were screams. At once this disk of sky slid over the sun like a lid. The sky snapped over the sun like a lens cover. The hatch in the brain slammed. Abruptly it was dark night, on the land and in the sky. In the night sky was a tiny ring of light. The hole where the sun belongs is very small. A thin ring of light marked its place. There was no sound. The eyes dried, the arteries drained, the lungs hushed. There was no world. We were the world's dead people rotating and orbiting around and around, embedded in the planet's crust, while the earth rolled down. Our minds were light years distant, forgetful of almost everything. Only an extraordinary act of will could recall to us our former, living selves and our contexts in matter and time. We had, it seems, loved the planet and loved our lives, but could no longer remember the way of them. We got the light wrong. In the sky was something that should not be there. In the black sky was a ring of light. It was a thin ring, an old, thin silver wedding band, an old, worn ring. It was an old wedding band in the sky, or a morsel of bone. There were stars. It was all over.

III

It is now that the temptation is strongest to leave these regions. We have seen enough; let's go. Why burn our hands any more than we have to? But two years have passed; the price of gold has risen. I return to the same buried alluvial beds and pick through the strata again.

I saw, early in the morning, the sun diminish against a backdrop of sky. I saw a circular piece of that sky appear, suddenly detached, blackened, and backlighted; from nowhere it came and overlapped the sun. It did not look like the moon. It was enormous and black If I had not read that it was the moon, I could have seen the sight a hundred times and never thought of the moon once. (If, however, I had not read that it was the moon–if, like most of the world's people throughout time, I had simply glanced up and seen this thing–then I doubtless would not have speculated much, but would have, like Emperor Louis of Bavaria in 840, simply died of fright on the spot.) It did not look like a dragon, although it looked more like a dragon than the moon. It looked like a lens cover, or the lid of a pot. It materialized out of thin air–black, and flat, and sliding, outlined in flame.

Seeing this black body was like seeing a mushroom cloud. The heart screeched. The meaning of the sight overwhelmed its fascination. It obliterated meaning itself. If you were to glance out one day and see a row of mushroom clouds rising on the horizon, you would know at once that what you were seeing, remarkable as it was, was intrinsically not worth remarking. No use running to tell anyone. Significant as it was, it did not matter a whit. For what is significance? It is significance for people. No people, no significance. This is all I have to tell you.

In the deeps are the violence and terror of which psychology has warmed us. But if you ride these monsters deeper down, if you drop with them farther over the world's rim, you find what our sciences cannot locate or name, the substrate, the ocean or matrix or ether which buoys the rest, which gives goodness its power for good, and evil. Its power for evil, the unified field: our complex and inexplicable caring for each other, and for our life together here. This is given. It is not learned.

The world which lay under darkness and stillness following the closing of the lid was not the world we know. The event was over. Its devastation lay around about us. The clamoring mind and heart stilled, almost indifferent, certainly disembodied, frail, and exhausted. The hills were hushed, obliterated. Up in the sky, like a crater from some distant cataclysm, was a hollow ring.

You have seen photographs of the sun taken during a total eclipse. The corona fills the print. All of those photographs were taken through telescopes. The lenses of telescopes and cameras can no more cover the breadth and scale of the visual array than language can cover the breadth and simultaneity of internal experience. Lenses enlarge the sight, omit its context, and make of it a pretty and sensible picture, like something on a Christmas card. I assure you, if you send any shepherds a Christmas card on which is printed a three-by-three photograph of the angel of the Lord, the glory of the Lord, and a multitude of the heavenly host, they will not be sore afraid. More fearsome things can come in envelopes. More moving photographs than those of the sun's corona can appear in magazines. But I pray you will never see anything more awful in the sky.

You see the wide world swaddled in darkness; you see a vast breadth of hilly land, and an enormous, distant, blackened valley; you see towns' lights, a river's path, and blurred portions of your hat and scarf; you see your husband's face looking like an early black-and-white film; and you see a sprawl of black sky and blue sky together, with unfamiliar stars in it, some barely visible bands of cloud, and over there, a small white ring. The ring is as small as one goose in a flock of migrating geese–if you happen to notice a flock of migrating geese. It is one 360th part of the visible sky. The sun we see is less than half the diameter of a dime held at arm's length.

The Crab Nebula, in the constellation Taurus, looks, through binoculars, like a smoke ring. It is a star in the process of exploding. Light from its explosion first reached the earth in 1054; it was a supernova then, and so bright it shone in the daytime. Now it is not so bright, but it is still exploding. It expands at the rate of seventy million miles a day. It is interesting to look through binoculars at something expanding seventy million miles a day. It does not budge. Its apparent size does not increase. Photographs of the Crab Nebula taken fifteen years ago seem identical to photographs of it taken yesterday. Some lichens are similar. Botanists have measured some ordinary lichens twice, at fifty-year intervals, without detecting any growth at all. And yet their cells divide; they live.

The small ring of light was like these things—like a ridiculous lichen up in the sky, like a perfectly still explosion 4,200 light-years away: it was interesting, and lovely, and in witless motion, and it had nothing to do with anything.

It had nothing to do with anything. The sun was too small, and too cold, and too far away, to keep the world alive. The white ring was not enough. It was feeble and worthless. It was as useless as a memory; it was as off-kilter and hollow and wretched as a memory.

When you try your hardest to recall someone's face, or the look of a place, you see in your mind's eye some vague and terrible sight such as this. It is dark; it is insubstantial; it is all wrong.

The white ring and the saturated darkness made the earth and the sky look as they must look in the memories of the careless dead. What I saw, what I seemed to be standing in, was all the wrecked light that the memories of the dead could shed upon the living world. We had all died in our boots on the hilltops of Yakima, and were alone in eternity. Empty space stoppered our eyes and mouths; we cared for nothing. We remembered our living days wrong. With great effort we had remembered some sort of circular light in the sky—but only the outline. Oh, and then the orchard trees withered, the ground froze, the glaciers slid down the valleys and overlapped the towns. If there had ever been people on earth, nobody knew it. The dead had forgotten those they had loved. The dead were parted one from the other and could no longer remember the faces and lands they had loved in the light. They seemed to stand on darkened hilltops, looking down.

IV

We teach our children one thing only, as we were taught: to wake up. We teach our children to look alive there, to join by words and activities the life of human culture on the planet's crust. As adults we are almost all adept at waking up. We have so mastered the transition we have forgotten we ever learned it. Yet it is a transition we make a hundred times a day, as, like so many will-less dolphins, we plunge and surface, lapse and emerge. We live half our waking lives and all of our sleeping lives in some private, useless, and insensible waters we never mention or recall. Useless, I say. Valueless, I might add—until someone hauls their wealth up to the surface and into the wide-awake city, in a form that people can use.

I do not know how we got to the restaurant. Like Roethke, "I take my waking slow." Gradually I seemed more or less alive, and already forgetful. It was now almost nine in the morning. It was the day of a solar eclipse in central Washington, and a fine adventure for everyone. The sky was clear; there was a fresh breeze out of the north.

The restaurant was a roadside place with tables and booths. The other eclipsewatchers were there. From our booth we could see their cars' California license plates, their University of Washington parking stickers. Inside the restaurant we were all eating eggs or waffles; people were fairly shouting and exchanging enthusiasms, like fans after a World Series game. Did you see . . . ? Did you see . . . ? Then somebody said something which knocked me for a loop.

A college student, a boy in a blue parka who carried a Hasselblad, said to us, "Did you see that little white ring? It looked like a Life Saver. It looked like a Life Saver up in the Sky."

And so it did. The boy spoke well. He was a walking alarm clock. I myself had at that time no access to such a word. He could write a sentence, and I could not. I grabbed that Life Saver and rode it to the surface. And I had to laugh. I had been dumbstruck on the Euphrates River, I had been dead and gone and grieving, all over the sight of something which, if you could claw your way up to that level, you would grant looked very much like a Life Saver. It was good to be back among people so clever; it was good to have all the world's words at the mind's disposal, so the mind could begin its task. All those things for which we have no words are lost. The mind—the culture—has two little tools, grammar and lexicon: a decorated sand bucket and a matching shovel. With these we bluster about the continents and do all the world's work. With these we try to save our very lives.

There are a few more things to tell from this level, the level of the restaurant. One is the old joke about breakfast. "It can never be satisfied, the mind, never." Wallace Stevens wrote that, and in the long run he was right. The mind wants to live forever, or to learn a very good reason why not. The mind wants the world to return its love, or its awareness; the mind wants to know all the world, and all eternity, and God. The mind's sidekick, however, will settle for two eggs over easy.

The dear, stupid body is as easily satisfied as a spaniel. And, incredibly, the simple spaniel can lure the brawling mind to its dish. It is everlastingly funny that the proud, metaphysically ambitious, clamoring mind will hush if you give it an egg.

Further: while the mind reels in deep space, while the mind grieves or fears or exults, the workaday senses, in ignorance or idiocy, like so many computer terminals printing out market prices while the world blows up, still transcribe their little data and transmit them to the warehouse in the skull. Later, under the tranquilizing influence of fried eggs, the mind can sort through this data. The restaurant was a halfway house, a decompression chamber. There I remembered a few things more.

The deepest, and most terrifying, was this: I have said that I heard screams. (I have since read that screaming, with hysteria, is a common reaction even to expected total eclipses.) People on all the hillsides, including, I think, myself, screamed when the black body of the moon detached from the sky and rolled over the sun. But something else was happening at that same instant, and it was this, I believe, which made us scream.

The second before the sun went out we saw a wall of dark shadow come speeding at us. We no sooner saw it than it was upon us, like thunder. It roared up the valley. It slammed our hill and knocked us out. It was the monstrous swift shadow cone of the moon. I have since read that this wave of shadow moves 1,800 miles an hour. Language can give no sense of this sort of speed—1,800 miles an hour. It was 195 miles wide. No end was in sight—you saw only the edge.

It rolled at you across the land at 1,800 miles an hour, hauling darkness like plague behind it. Seeing it, and knowing it was coming straight for you, was like feeling a slug of anesthetic shoot up your arm. If you think very fast, you may have time to think, "Soon it will hit my brain." You can feel the deadness race up your arm; you can feel the appalling, inhuman speed of your own blood. We saw the wall of shadow coming, and screamed before it hit.

This was the universe about which we have read so much and never before felt: the universe as a clockwork of loose spheres flung at stupefying, unauthorized speeds. How could anything moving so fast not crash, not veer from its orbit amok like a car out of control on a turn?

Less than two minutes later, when the sun emerged, the trailing edge of the shadow cone sped away. It coursed down our hill and raced eastward over the plain, faster than the eye could believe; it swept over the plain and dropped over the planet's rim in a twinkling It had clobbered us, and now it roared away. We blinked in the light It was as though an enormous, loping god in the sky had reached down and slapped the earth's face.

Something else, something more ordinary, came back to me along about the third cup of coffee. During the moments of totality, it was so dark that drivers on the highway below turned on their cars' headlights. We could see the highway's route as a strand of lights. It was bumper-to-bumper down there. It was eight-fifteen in the morning, Monday morning, and people were driving into Yakima to work. That it was as dark as night, and eerie as hell, an hour after dawn, apparently meant that in order to see to drive to work, people had to use their headlights. Four or five cars pulled off the road. The rest, in a line at least five miles long, drove to town. The highway ran between hills; the people could not have seen any of the eclipsed sun at all. Yakima will have another total eclipse in 2086. Perhaps, in 2086, businesses will give their employees an hour off.

From the restaurant we drove back to the coast. The highway crossing the Cascades range was open. We drove over the mountain like old pros. We joined our places on the planet's thin crust; it held. For the time being, we were home free.

Early that morning at six, when we had checked out, the six bald men were sitting on folding chairs in the dim hotel lobby. The television was on. Most of them were awake. You might drown in your own spittle, God knows, at any time; you might wake up dead in a small hotel, a cabbage head watching TV while snows pile up in the passes, watching TV while the chili peppers smile and the moon passes over the sun and nothing changes and nothing is learned because you have lost your bucket and shovel and no longer care. What if you regain the surface and open your sack and find, instead of treasure, a beast which jumps at you? Or you may not come back at all. The winches may jam, the scaffolding buckle, the air conditioning collapse. You may glance up one day and see by your headlamp the canary keeled over in its cage. You may reach into a cranny for pearls and touch a moray eel. You yank on your rope; it is too late.

Apparently people share a sense of these hazards, for when the total eclipse ended, an odd thing happened.

When the sun appeared as a blinding bead on the ring's side, the eclipse was over. The black lens cover appeared again, back-lighted, and slid away. At once the yellow light made the sky blue again; the black lid dissolved and vanished. The real world began there. I remember now: we all hurried away. We were born and bored at a stroke. We rushed down the hill. We found our car; we saw the other people streaming down the hillsides; we joined the highway traffic and drove away.

We never looked back. It was a general vamoose, and an odd one, for when we left the hill, the sun was still partially eclipsed–a sight rare enough, and one which, in itself, we would probably have driven five hours to see. But enough is enough. One turns at last even from glory itself with a sigh of relief. From the depths of mystery, and even from the heights of splendor, we bounce back and hurry for the latitudes of home.

Regarding the Text

1. It is common to find this essay strange. Do you think Dillard herself finds the essay strange? Why do you think it took her two years after the experience before she wrote about it?

2. What is the effect of having the essay split into four sections marked by Roman numerals?

3. Make a list of details you recall from the essay without yet looking back through the pages. See if you can include twenty to thirty details in your list from memory. Draw connection lines between any details that seem like they somehow go together.

4. What does the title mean? Obviously it refers to a celestial phenomenon, but few would argue that Dillard's essay is an astronomy lesson. What does it mean to eclipse something or someone? What does it mean to be eclipsed?

Joining the Conversation

5. Students invariably comment that Dillard seems to be losing her mind in the essay. How would you describe what the author experiences in the essay? Why do you think it took her two years after the eclipse, as she says, until she would write this essay?

Owning the Idea

6. Dillard uses a variety of metaphors to describe our ability to pay attention, how we "lapse" and "emerge." Why do you think Dillard finds the idea of paying attention so urgent? What does Dillard think is gained by looking at an eclipse as if we did not have the science to understand what is happening objectively?

7. Like several of the essays in this book, the subject in "Total Eclipse" is existential (in philosophy, a way of understanding what is known by experience rather than by reason) and portrays this understanding as a journey undertaken alone. What about understanding the world by experience requires these authors to do so alone?

The Solace of Open Spaces

Gretel Ehrlich

It's May and I've just awakened from a nap, curled against sagebrush the way my dog taught me to sleep—sheltered from wind. A front is pulling the huge sky over me, and from the dark a hailstone has hit me on the head. I'm trailing a band of two thousand sheep across a stretch of Wyoming badlands, a fifty-mile trip that takes five days because sheep shade up in hot sun and won't budge until it's cool. Bunched together now, and excited into a run by the storm, they drift across dry land, tumbling into draws like water and surge out again onto the rugged, choppy plateaus that are the building blocks of this state.

The name Wyoming comes from an Indian word meaning "at the great plains," but the plains are really valleys, great arid valleys, sixteen hundred square miles, with the horizon bending up on all sides into mountain ranges. This gives the vastness a sheltering look.

Winter lasts six months here. Prevailing winds spill snowdrifts to the east, and new storms from the northwest replenish them. This white hulk is sometimes dizzying, even nauseating, to look at. At twenty, thirty, and forty degrees below zero, not only does your car not work, but neither do your mind and body. The landscape hardens into a dungeon of space. During the winter, while I was riding to find a new calf, my jeans froze to the saddle, and in the silence that such cold creates I felt like the first person on earth, or the last.

Today the sun is out—only a few clouds billowing. In the east, where the sheep have started off without me, the benchland tilts up in a series of eroded red-earthed mesas, planed flat on top by a million years of water: behind them, a bold line of muscular scarps rears up ten thousand feet to become the Big Horn Mountains. A tidal pattern is engraved into the ground, as if left by the sea that once covered this state. Canyons curve down like galaxies to meet the oncoming rush of flat land.

To live and work in this kind of open country, with its hundred-mile views, is to lose the distinction between background and foreground. When I asked an older ranch hand to describe Wyoming's openness, he said, "It's all a bunch of nothing—wind and rattlesnakes—and so much of it you can't tell where you're going or where you've been and it don't make much difference." John, a sheepman I know, is tall and handsome and has an explosive temperament. He has a perfect intuition about people and sheep. They call him "Highpockets," because he's so long-legged: his graceful stride matches the distances he has to cover. He says, "Open space hasn't affected me at all. It's all the people moving in on it." The huge ranch he was born on takes up much of one county and spreads into another state: to put 100,000 miles on his pickup in three years and never leave home is not unusual. A friend of mine has an aunt who ranched on Powder River and didn't go off her place for eleven years. When her husband died, she quickly moved to town, bought a car, and drove around the States to see what she'd been missing.

Most people tell me they've simply driven through Wyoming, as if there were nothing to stop for. Or else they've skied in Jackson Hole, a place Wyomingites acknowledge uncomfortably because its green beauty and chic affluence are mismatched with the rest of the state. Most of Wyoming has a "lean-to" look. Instead of big, roomy barns and Victorian houses, there are dugouts, low sheds, log cabins, sheep camps, and fence lines that look like driftwood blown haphazardly into place. People here still feel pride because they live in such a harsh place, part of the glamorous cowboy past, and they are determined not to be the victims of a mining-dominated future.

Most characteristic of the state's landscape is what a developer euphemistically describes as "indigenous growth right up to your front door"—a reference to waterless stands of salt sage, snakes, jackrabbits, deerflies, red dust, a brief respite of wildflowers, dry washes, and no trees. In the Great Plains the vistas look like music, like Kyries⁰ of grass, but Wyoming seems to be the doing of a mad architect—tumbled and twisted, ribboned with faded, deathbed colors, thrust up and pulled down as if the place had been startled out of a deep sleep and thrown into a pure light.

I came here four years ago. I had not planned to stay, but I couldn't make myself leave. John, the sheepman, put me to work immediately. It was spring, and shearing time. For fourteen days of fourteen hours each, we moved thousands of sheep through sorting corrals to be sheared, branded, and deloused. I suspect that my original motive for coming here was to "lose myself" in new and unpopulated territory, instead of producing the numbness I thought I wanted, life on the sheep

---

⁰**Kyries** Short prayers, beginning *Kyrie eleison* ("Lord, have mercy"), often sung or chanted.

ranch woke me up. The vitality of the people I was working with flushed out what had become a hallucinatory rawness inside me. I threw away my clothes and bought new ones; I cut my hair. The arid country was a clean slate. Its absolute indifference steadied me.

Sagebrush covers fifty-eight thousand square miles of Wyoming. The biggest city has a population of fifty thousand, and there are only five settlements that could be called cities in the whole state. The rest are towns, scattered across the expanse with as much as sixty miles between them, their populations two thousand, fifty, or ten. They are fugitive-looking, perched on a barren, windblown bench, or tagged onto a river or a railroad, or laid out straight in a farming valley with implement stores and a block-long Mormon church. In the eastern part of the state, which slides down into the Great Plains, the new mining settlements are boomtowns, trailer cities, metal knots on flat land.

Despite the desolate look, there's a coziness to living in this state. There are so few people (only 470,000) that ranchers who buy and sell cattle know one another statewide; the kids who choose to go to college usually go to the state's one university, in Laramie; hired hands work their way around Wyoming in a lifetime of hirings and firings. And despite the physical separation, people stay in touch, often driving two or three hours to another ranch for dinner.

Seventy-five years ago, when travel was by buckboard or horseback, cowboys who were temporarily out of work rode the grub line—drifting from ranch to ranch, mending fences or milking cows, and receiving in exchange a bed and meals. Gossip and messages traveled this slow circuit with them, creating an intimacy between ranchers who were three and four weeks' ride apart. One old-time couple I know, whose turn-of-the-century homestead was used by an outlaw gang as a relay station for stolen horses, recall that if you were traveling, desperado or not, any lighted ranch house was a welcome sign. Even now, for someone who lives in a remote spot, arriving at a ranch or coming to town for supplies is cause for celebration. To emerge from isolation can be disorienting. Everything looks bright, new, vivid. After I had been herding sheep for only three days, the sound of the camp tender's pickup flustered me. Longing for human company, I felt a foolish grin take over my face; yet I had to resist an urgent temptation to run and hide.

Things happen suddenly in Wyoming, the change of seasons and weather; for people, the violent swings in and out of isolation. But good-naturedness is concomitant with severity. Friendliness is a tradition. Strangers passing on the road wave hello. A common sight is two pickups stopped side by side far out on a range, on a dirt track winding through the sage. The drivers will share a cigarette, uncap their Thermos bottles, and pass a battered cup, steaming with coffee, between windows. These meetings summon up the details of several generations, because, in Wyoming, private histories are largely public knowledge.

Because ranch work is a physical and, these days, economic strain, being "at home on the range" is a matter of vigor, self-reliance, and common sense. A person's life is not a series of dramatic events for which he or she is applauded or exiled but a slow accumulation of days, seasons, years, fleshed out by the generational weight of one's family and anchored by a landbound sense of place.

In most parts of Wyoming, the human population is visibly outnumbered by the animal. Not far from my town of fifty, I rode into a narrow valley and startled a herd of two hundred elk. Eagles look like small people as they eat car-killed deer by the road. Antelope, moving in small, graceful bands, travel at sixty miles an hour, their mouths open as if drinking in the space.

The solitude in which westerners live makes them quiet. They telegraph thoughts and feelings by the way they tilt their heads and listen; pulling their Stetsons into a steep dive over their eyes, or pigeon-toeing one boot over the other, they lean against a fence with a fat wedge of Copenhagen beneath their lower lips and take in the whole scene. These detached looks of quiet amusement are sometimes cynical, but they can also come from a dry-eyed humility as lucid as the air is clear.

Conversation goes on in what sounds like a private code; a few phrases imply a complex of meanings. Asking directions, you get a curious list of details. While trailing sheep I was told to "ride up to that kinda upturned rock, follow the pink wash, turn left at the dump, and then you'll see the water hole." One friend told his wife on roundup to "turn at the salt lick and the dead cow," which turned out to be a scattering of bones and no salt lick at all.

Sentence structure is shortened to the skin and bones of a thought. Descriptive words are dropped, even verbs; a cowboy looking over a corral full of horses will say to a wrangler, "Which one needs rode?" People hold back their thoughts in what seems to be a dumbfounded silence, then erupt with an excoriating perceptive remark. Language, so compressed, becomes metaphorical. A rancher ended a relationship with one remark: "You're a bad check," meaning bouncing in and out was intolerable, and even coming back would be no good.

What's behind this laconic style is shyness. There is no vocabulary for the subject of feelings. It's not a hangdog shyness, or anything coy—always there's a robust spirit in evidence behind the restraint, as it the earth-dredging wind that pulls across Wyoming had carried its people's voices away but everything else in them had shouldered confidently into the breeze.

I've spent hours riding to sheep camp at dawn in a pickup when nothing was said; eaten meals in the cookhouse when the only words spoken were a mumbled "Thank you, ma'am" at the end of dinner. The silence is profound. Instead of talking, we seem to share one eye. Keenly observed, the world is transformed. The landscape is engorged with detail, every movement on it chillingly sharp. The air between people is charged. Days unfold, bathed in their own music. Nights become hallucinatory; dreams, prescient.

Spring weather is capricious and mean. It snows, then blisters with heat. There have been tornadoes. They lay their elephant trunks out in the sage until they find houses, then slurp everything up and leave. I've noticed that melting snowbanks hiss and rot, viperous, then drip into calm pools where ducklings hatch and livestock, being trailed to summer range, drink. With the ice cover gone, rivers churn a milkshake brown, taking culverts and small bridges with them. Water in such an arid place (the average annual rainfall where I live is less than eight inches) is like blood. It festoons drab land with green veins; a line of cottonwoods following a stream; a strip of alfalfa; and, on ditch banks, wild asparagus growing.

I've moved to a small cattle ranch owned by friends. It's at the foot of the Big Horn Mountains. A few weeks ago, I helped them deliver a calf who was stuck halfway out of his mother's body. By the time he was freed, we could see a heartbeat, but he was straining against a swollen tongue for air. Mary and I held him upside down by his back feet, while Stan, on his hands and knees in the blood, gave the calf mouth-to-mouth resuscitation. I have a vague memory of being pneumonia-choked as a child, my mother giving me her air, which may account for my romance with this windswept state.

If anything is endemic to Wyoming, it is wind. This big room of space is swept out daily, leaving a bone yard of fossils, agates, and carcasses in every stage of decay. Though it was water that initially shaped the state, wind is the meticulous gardener, raising dust and pruning the sage.

I try to imagine a world in which I could ride my horse across uncharted land. There is no wilderness left; wildness, yes, but true wilderness has been gone on this continent since the time of Lewis and Clark's overland journey.

Two hundred years ago, the Crow, Shoshone, Arapaho, Cheyenne, and Sioux roamed the intermountain West, orchestrating their movements according to hunger, season, and warfare. Once they acquired horses, they traversed the spines of all the big Wyoming ranges—

the Absarokas, the Wind Rivers, the Tetons, the Big Horns—and wintered on the unprotected plains that fan out from them. Space was life. The world was their home.

What was life-giving to Native Americans was often nightmarish to sodbusters who had arrived encumbered with families and ethnic pasts to be transplanted in nearly uninhabitable land. The great distances, the shortage of water and trees, and the loneliness created unexpected hardships for them. In her book *O Pioneers!,* Willa Cather gives a settler's version of the bleak landscape:

> The little town behind them had vanished as if it had never been, had fallen behind the swell of the prairie, and the stern frozen country received them into its bosom. The homesteads were few and far apart; here and there a windmill gaunt against the sky, a sod house crouching in a hollow.

The emptiness of the West was for others a geography of possibility. Men and women who amassed great chunks of land and struggled to preserve unfenced empires were, despite their self-serving motives, unwitting geographers. They understood the lay of the land. But by the 1850s the Oregon and Mormon trails sported bumper-to-bumper traffic. Wealthy landowners, many of them aristocratic absentee landlords, known as remittance men because they were paid to come West and get out of their families' hair, overstocked the range with more than a million head of cattle. By 1885 the feed and water were desperately short, and the winter of 1886 laid out the gaunt bodies of dead animals so closely together that when the thaw came, one rancher from Kaycee claimed to have walked on cowhide all the way to Crazy Woman Creek, twenty miles away.

Territorial Wyoming was a boy's world. The land was generous with everything but water. At first there was room enough, food enough, for everyone. And, as with all beginnings, an expansive mood set in. The young cowboys, drifters, shopkeepers, schoolteachers, were heroic, lawless, generous, rowdy, and tenacious. The individualism and optimism generated during those times have endured.

John Tisdale rode north with the trail herds from Texas. He was a college-educated man with enough money to buy a small outfit near the Powder River. While driving home from the town of Buffalo with a buckboard full of Christmas toys for his family and a winter's supply of food, he was shot in the back by an agent of the cattle barons who resented the encroachment of small-time stockmen like him. The wealthy cattlemen tried to control all the public grazing land by restricting membership in the Wyoming Stock Growers Association, as if it were a country club. They ostracized from roundups and brandings cowboys and ranchers who were not members, then denounced them as rustlers. Tisdale's death, the second such cold-blooded murder, kicked off the Johnson County cattle war, which was no simple good-guy-bad-guy shoot-out but a complicated class struggle between landed gentry and less affluent settlers—a shocking reminder that the West was not an egalitarian sanctuary after all.

Fencing ultimately enforced boundaries, but barbed wire abrogated space. It was stretched across the beautiful valleys, into the mountains, over desert badlands, through buffalo grass. The "anything is possible" fever—the lure of any new place—was constricted. The integrity of the land as a geographical body, and the freedom to ride anywhere on it, were lost.

I punched cows with a young man named Martin, who is the great-grandson of John Tisdale. His inheritance is not the open land that Tisdale knew and prematurely lost but a rage against restraint.

Wyoming tips down as you head northeast; the highest ground—the Laramie Plains—is on the Colorado border. Up where I live, the Big Horn River leaks into difficult, arid terrain. In the basin where it's dammed, sandhill cranes gather and, with delicate legwork, slice through the stilled water. I was driving by with a rancher one morning when he commented that cranes are "old-fashioned." When I asked why, he said, "Because they mate for life." Then he looked at me with a twinkle in his eyes, as if to say he really did believe in such things but also understood why we break our own rules.

In all this open space, values crystalize quickly. People are strong on scruples but tender-hearted about quirky behavior. A friend and I found one ranch hand, who's "not quite right in the head," sitting in front of the badly decayed carcass of a cow, shaking his finger and saying, "Now, I don't want you to do this ever again!" When I asked what was wrong with him, I was told, "He's goofier than hell, just like the rest of us." Perhaps because the West is historically new, conventional morality is still felt to be less important than rock-bottom truths. Though there's always a lot of teasing and sparring, people are blunt with one another, sometimes even cruel, believing honesty is stronger medicine than sympathy, which may console but often conceals.

The formality that goes hand in hand with the rowdiness is known as the Western Code. It's a list of practical do's and don'ts, faithfully observed. A friend, Cliff, who runs a trapline in the winter, cut off half his foot while chopping a hole in the ice. Alone, he dragged himself to his pickup and headed for town, stopping to open the ranch gate as he left, and getting out to close it again, thus losing, in his observance of rules, precious time and blood. Later, he commented, "How would it look, them having to come to the hospital to tell me their cows had gotten out?"

Accustomed to emergencies, my friends doctor each other from the vet's bag with relish. When one old-timer suffered a heart attack in hunting camp, his partner quickly stirred up a brew of red horse liniment and hot water and made the half-conscious victim drink it, then tied him onto a horse and led him twenty miles to town. He regained consciousness and lived.

The roominess of the state has affected political attitudes as well. Ranchers keep up with world politics and the convulsions of the economy but are basically isolationists. Being used to running their own small empires of land and livestock, they're suspicious of big government. It's a "don't fence me in" holdover from a century ago. They still want the elbow room their grandfathers had, so they're strongly conservative, but with a populist twist.

Summer is the season when we get our "cowboy tans"—on the lower parts of our faces and on three fourths of our arms. Excessive heat, in the nineties and higher, sends us outside with the mosquitoes. In winter we're tucked inside our houses, and the white wasteland outside appears to be expanding, but in summer all the greenery abridges space. Summer is a go-ahead season. Every living thing is off the block and in the race: battalions of bugs in flight and biting; bats swinging around my log cabin as if the bases were loaded and someone had hit a home run. Some of summer's high-speed growth is ominous: Larkspur, death camas, and green grease wood can kill sheep—an ironic idea, dying in this desert from eating what is too verdant. With sixteen hours of daylight, farmers and ranchers irrigate feverishly. There are first, second, and third cuttings of hay, some crews averaging only four hours of sleep a night for weeks. And, like the cowboys who in summer ride the night rodeo circuit, nighthawks make daredevil dives at dusk with an eerie whirring sound like a plane going down on the shimmering horizon.

In the town where I live, they've had to board up the dance-hall windows because there have been so many fights. There's so little to do except work that people wind up in a state of idle agitation that becomes fatalistic, as if there were nothing to be done about all this untapped energy. So the dark side to the grandeur of these spaces is the small-mindedness that seals people in. Men become hermits; women go mad. Cabin fever explodes into suicides, or into grudges and lifelong family feuds. Two sisters in my area inherited a ranch but found they couldn't get along. They fenced the place in half. When one's cows got out and mixed with the other's, the women went at each other with shovels. They ended up in the same hospital room but never spoke a word to each other for the rest of their lives.

After the brief lushness of summer, the sun moves south. The range grass is brown. Livestock is trailed back down from the mountains. Water holes begin to frost over at night. Last fall Martin asked me to accompany him on a pack trip. With five horses, we followed a river into the mountains behind the tiny Wyoming town of Meeteetse. Groves of aspen, red and orange, gave off a light that made us look toasted. Our hunting camp was so high that clouds skidded across our foreheads, then slowed to sail out across the warm valleys. Except for a bull moose who wandered into our camp and mistook our black gelding for a rival, we shot at nothing.

One of our evening entertainments was to watch the night sky. My dog, a dingo bred to herd sheep, also came on the trip. He is so used to the silence and empty skies that when an airplane flies over he always looks up and eyes the distant intruder quizzically. The sky, lately, seems to be much more crowded than it used to be. Satellites make their silent passes in the dark with great regularity. We counted eighteen in one hour's viewing. How odd to think that while they circumnavigated the planet, Martin and I had moved only six miles into our local wilderness and had seen no other human for the two weeks we stayed there.

At night, by moonlight, the land is whittled to slivers—a ridge, a river, a strip of grassland stretching to the mountains, then the huge sky. One morning a full moon was setting in the west just as the sun was rising. I felt precariously balanced between the two as I loped across a meadow. For a moment, I could believe that the stars, which were still visible, work like cooper's bands, holding together everything above Wyoming.

Space has a spiritual equivalent and can heal what is divided and burdensome in us. My grandchildren will probably use space shuttles for a honeymoon trip or to recover from heart attacks, but closer to home we might also learn how to carry space inside ourselves in the effortless way we carry our skins. Space represents sanity, not a life purified, dull, or "spaced out" but one that might accommodate intelligently any idea or situation.

From the clayey soil of northern Wyoming is mined bentonite, which is used as a filler in candy, gum, and lipstick. We Americans are great on fillers, as if what we have, what we are, is not enough. We have a cultural tendency toward denial, but, being affluent, we strangle ourselves with what we can buy. We have only to look at the houses we build to see how we build *against* space, the way we drink against pain and loneliness. We fill up space as if it were a pie shell, with things whose opacity further obstructs our ability to see what is already there.

Regarding the Text

1. Describe the opening image of the essay. Why do you think Ehrlich tells us about getting hit in the head with a hailstone?

2. The essay appears to have several sections separated by editorial breaks—those extra line spaces that occur before some paragraphs. How many sections do you count? Do these sections have to remain in this order? What would happen to your understanding of the essay if they were rearranged?

3. If the essay focuses on open spaces, what by contrast are closed spaces? Where do we normally imagine we spend most of our time?

4. The last two paragraphs of Ehrlich's essay depart from the author merely describing her experience. What do you think Ehrlich wants to accomplish with these final paragraphs? How do these paragraphs capitalize on the writing that precedes them in the essay?

Joining the Conversation

5. How do you think you might regard the essay differently if it were written by an author named Gerhard Ehrlich? Would your attitudes about a man having these experiences differ from your attitudes toward this woman's experience? How do you suppose men and women would have reacted to the essay differently had it been written in the early twentieth century?

6. Ehrlich writes, "Instead of the numbness I thought I wanted…," which indicates that something different than numbness came to her, and that numbness is not after all what she was after. It is understandable for people feeling pain or loss to say they feel or want to feel numb, but Ehrlich says she did not want that numbness. Why did she think she wanted to be numb in the first place? And how and why did "life on the sheep ranch [wake her] up"?

Owning the Idea

7. Is it true that Americans have a tendency toward asceticism or denial, as Ehrlich writes, and yet crave "fillers"? In what ways do you see Americans denying themselves comforts, benefits, or luxuries? What sorts of fillers do Americans find—or even look for—in their lives? What does Ehrlich think should take the place of those fillers? Would Annie Dillard agree?

8. Is America still the land of open spaces? Homesteaders were urged to populate the territory west of the Mississippi River. Is there any longer a call to populate unsettled areas? What has happened to those spaces that are left undeveloped?

On Lying in Bed

G. K. Chesterton

Lying in bed would be an altogether perfect and supreme experience if only one had a coloured pencil long enough to draw on the ceiling. This, however, is not generally a part of the domestic apparatus on the premises. I think myself that the thing might be managed with several pails of Aspinall and a broom. Only if one worked in a really sweeping and masterly way, and laid on the colour in great washes, it might drip down again on one's face in floods of rich and mingled colour like some strange fairy rain; and that would have its disadvantages. I am afraid it would be necessary to stick to black and white in this form of artistic composition. To that purpose, indeed, the white ceiling would be of the greatest possible use; in fact, it is the only use I think of a white ceiling being put to.

But for the beautiful experiment of lying in bed I might never have discovered it. For years I have been looking for some blank spaces in a modern house to draw on. Paper is much too small for any really allegorical design; as Cyrano de Bergerac says, "*Il me faut des géants*" ["I need giants"]. But when I tried to find these fine clear spaces in the modern rooms such as we all live in I was continually disappointed. I found an endless pattern and complication of small objects hung like a curtain of fine links between me and my desire. I examined the walls; I found them to my surprise to be already covered with wallpaper, and I found the wallpaper to be already covered with uninteresting images, all bearing a ridiculous resemblance to each other. I could not understand why one arbitrary symbol (a symbol apparently entirely devoid of any religious or philosophical significance) should thus be sprinkled all over my nice walls like a sort of small-pox. The Bible must be referring to wallpapers, I think, when it says, "Use not vain repetitions, as the Gentiles do." I found the Turkey carpet a mass of unmeaning colours, rather like the Turkish Empire, or like the sweetmeat called Turkish Delight. I do not exactly know what Turkish Delight really is; but I suppose it is Macedonian Massacres. Everywhere that I went forlornly, with my pencil or my paint brush, I found that others had unaccountably been before me, spoiling the walls, the curtains, and the furniture with their childish and barbaric designs.

*   *   *   *   *

Nowhere did I find a really clear space for sketching until this occasion when I prolonged beyond the proper limit the process of lying on my back in bed. Then the light of that white heaven broke upon my vision, that breadth of mere white which is indeed almost the definition of Paradise, since it means purity and also means freedom. But alas! like all heavens, now that it is seen it is found to be unattainable; it looks more austere and more distant than the blue sky outside the window. For my proposal to paint on it with the bristly end of a broom has been discouraged— never mind by whom; by a person debarred from all political rights—and even my minor proposal to put the other end of the broom into the kitchen fire and turn it to charcoal has not been conceded. Yet I am certain that it was from persons in my position that all the original inspiration came for covering the ceilings of palaces and cathedrals with a riot of fallen angels or victorious gods. I am sure that it was only because Michael Angelo was engaged in the ancient and honourable occupation of lying in bed that he ever realized how the roof of the Sistine Chapel might be made into an awful imitation of a divine drama that could only be acted in the heavens.

The tone now commonly taken toward the practice of lying in bed is hypocritical and unhealthy. Of all the marks of modernity that seem to mean a kind of decadence, there is none more menacing and dangerous than the exultation of very small and secondary matters of conduct at the expense of very great and primary ones, at the expense of eternal ties and tragic human morality. If there is one thing worse than the modern weakening of major morals, it is the modern strengthening of minor morals. Thus it is considered more withering to accuse a man of bad taste than of bad ethics. Cleanliness is not next to godliness nowadays, for cleanliness is made essential and godliness is regarded as an offence. A playwright can attack the institution of marriage so long as he does not misrepresent the manners of society, and I have met Ibsenite pessimists who thought it wrong to take beer but right to take prussic acid. Especially this is so in matters of hygiene; notably such matters as lying in bed. Instead of being regarded, as it ought to be, as a matter of personal convenience and adjustment, it has come to be regarded by many as if it were a part of essential morals to get up early in the morning. It is upon the whole part of practical wisdom; but there is nothing good about it or bad about its opposite.

*   *   *   *   *

Misers get up early in the morning; and burglars, I am informed, get up the night before. It is the great peril of our society that all its mechanisms may grow more fixed while its spirit grows more fickle. A man's minor actions and arrangements ought to be free, flexible, creative; the things that should be unchangeable are his principles, his ideals. But with us the reverse is true; our views change constantly; but our lunch does not change. Now, I should like men to have strong and rooted conceptions, but as for their lunch, let them have it sometimes in the garden, sometimes in bed, sometimes on the roof, sometimes in the top of a tree. Let them argue from the same first principles, but let them do it in a bed, or a boat, or a balloon. This alarming growth of good habits really means a too great emphasis on those virtues which mere custom can ensure, it means too little emphasis on those virtues which custom can never quite ensure, sudden and splendid virtues of inspired pity or of inspired candour. If ever that abrupt appeal is made to us we may fail. A man can get used to getting up at five o'clock in the morning. A man cannot very well get used to being burnt for his opinions; the first experiment is commonly fatal. Let us pay a little more attention to these possibilities of the heroic and unexpected. I dare say that when I get out of this bed I shall do some deed of an almost terrible virtue.

For those who study the great art of lying in bed there is one emphatic caution to be added. Even for those who can do their work in bed (like journalists), still more for those whose work cannot be done in bed (as, for example, the professional harpooners of whales), it is obvious that the indulgence must be very occasional. But that is not the caution I mean. The caution is this: if you do lie in bed, be sure you do it without any reason or justification at all. I do not speak, of course, of the seriously sick. But if a healthy man lies in bed, let him do it without a rag of excuse; then he will get up a healthy man. If he does it for some secondary hygienic reason, if he has some scientific explanation, he may get up a hypochondriac.

(1909)

Regarding the Text

1. Writing on walls was quite common in ancient Rome, though not in the way graffiti is written in bathroom stalls, which we now encounter endlessly. Why do you think Chesterton is looking for a place to draw on the walls and ceiling?

Joining the Conversation

2. While journalists and harpooners of whales, as Chesterton points out, cannot do their work in bed, what benefit might lying in bed prove even to people who have those jobs, according to the author?

3. Why do you think people of Chesterton's time regarded lying about as a kind of immoral laziness? Do people of our time and place hold the same value on work and lassitude?

Owning the Idea

4. How do you think Chesterton might react to Plato's "Allegory of the Cave"?

5. Can you find ideas in Chesterton's humorous essay with which Bertrand Russell might be content to align himself?

Life Without Principle

Henry David Thoreau

AT A LYCEUM, not long since, I felt that the lecturer had chosen a theme too foreign to himself, and so failed to interest me as much as he might have done. He described things not in or near to his heart, but toward his extremities and superficies. There was, in this sense, no truly central or centralizing thought in the lecture. I would have had him deal with his privatest experience, as the poet does. The greatest compliment that was ever paid me was when one asked me what I thought, and attended to my answer. I am surprised, as well as delighted, when this happens, it is such a rare use he would make of me, as if he were acquainted with the tool. Commonly, if men want anything of me, it is only to know how many acres I make of their land- since I am a surveyor- or, at most, what trivial news I have burdened myself with. They never will go to law for my meat; they prefer the shell. A man once came a considerable distance to ask me to lecture on Slavery; but on conversing with him, I found that he and his clique expected seven eighths of the lecture to be theirs, and only one eighth mine; so I declined. I take it for granted, when I am invited to lecture anywhere—for I have had a little experience in that business- that there is a desire to hear what I think on some subject, though I may be the greatest fool in the country—and not that I should say pleasant things merely, or such as the audience will assent to; and I resolve, accordingly, that I will give them a strong dose of myself. They have sent for me, and engaged to pay for me, and I am determined that they shall have me, though I bore them beyond all precedent.

So now I would say something similar to you, my readers. Since you are my readers, and I have not been much of a traveller, I will not talk about people a thousand miles off, but come as near home as I can. As the time is short, I will leave out all the flattery, and retain all the criticism.

Let us consider the way in which we spend our lives.

This world is a place of business. What an infinite bustle! I am awaked almost every night by the panting of the locomotive. It interrupts my dreams. There is no sabbath. It would be glorious to see mankind at leisure for once. It is nothing but work, work, work. I cannot easily buy a blank-book to write thoughts in; they are commonly ruled for dollars and cents. An Irishman, seeing me making a minute in the fields, took it for granted that I was calculating my wages. If a man was tossed out of a window when an infant, and so made a cripple for life, or seared out of his wits by the Indians, it is regretted chiefly because he was thus incapacitated for business! I think that there is nothing, not even crime, more opposed to poetry, to philosophy, ay, to life itself, than this incessant business.

There is a coarse and boisterous money-making fellow in the outskirts of our town, who is going to build a bank-wall under the hill along the edge of his meadow. The powers have put this into his head to keep him out of mischief, and he wishes me to spend three weeks digging there with him. The result will be that he will perhaps get some more money to board, and leave for his heirs to spend foolishly. If I do this, most will commend me as an industrious and hard-working man; but if I choose to devote myself to certain labors which yield more real profit, though but little money, they may be inclined to look on me as an idler. Nevertheless, as I do not need the police of meaningless labor to regulate me, and do not see anything abso-lutely praiseworthy in this fellow's undertaking any more than in many an enterprise of our own or foreign governments, however amusing it may be to him or them, I prefer to finish my education at a different school.

If a man walk in the woods for love of them half of each day, he is in danger of being regarded as a loafer; but if he spends his whole day as a speculator, shearing off those woods and mak-ing earth bald before her time, he is esteemed an industrious and enterprising citizen. As if a town had no interest in its forests but to cut them down!

Most men would feel insulted if it were proposed to employ them in throwing stones over a wall, and then in throwing them back, merely that they might earn their wages. But many are no more worthily employed now. For instance: just after sunrise, one summer morning, I noticed one of my neighbors walking beside his team, which was slowly drawing a heavy hewn stone swung under the axle, surrounded by an atmosphere of industry—his day's work begun—his brow commenced to sweat—a reproach to all sluggards and idlers—pausing abreast the shoulders of his oxen, and half turning round with a flourish of his merciful whip, while they gained their length on him. And I thought, Such is the labor which the American Congress exists to protect—honest, manly toil—honest as the day is long—that makes his bread taste sweet, and keeps society sweet—which all men respect and have consecrated; one of the sacred band, doing the needful but irksome drudgery. Indeed, I felt a slight reproach, because I observed this from a window, and was not abroad and stirring about a similar busi-ness. The day went by, and at evening I passed the yard of another neighbor, who keeps many servants, and spends much money foolishly, while he adds nothing to the common stock, and there I saw the stone of the morning lying beside a whimsical structure intended to adorn this Lord Timothy Dexter's premises, and the dignity forthwith departed from the teamster's labor, in my eyes. In my opinion, the sun was made to light worthier toil than this. I may add that his employer has since run off, in debt to a good part of the town, and, after passing through Chancery, has settled somewhere else, there to become once more a patron of the arts.

The ways by which you may get money almost without exception lead downward. To have done anything by which you earned money merely is to have been truly idle or worse. If the laborer gets no more than the wages which his employer pays him, he is cheated, he cheats himself. If you would get money as a writer or lecturer, you must be popular, which is to go down perpendicularly. Those services which the community will most readily pay for, it is most disagreeable to render. You are paid for being something less than a man. The State does not commonly reward a genius any more wisely. Even the poet laureate would rather not have to celebrate the accidents of royalty. He must be bribed with a pipe of wine; and perhaps another poet is called away from his muse to gauge that very pipe. As for my own business, even that kind of surveying which I could do with most satisfaction my employers do not want. They would prefer that I should do my work coarsely and not too well, ay, not well enough. When I observe that there are different ways of surveying, my employer commonly asks which will give him the most land, not which is most correct. I once invented a rule for measuring cord-wood, and tried to introduce it in Boston; but the measurer there told me that the sellers did not wish to have their wood measured correctly—that he was already too accurate for them, and therefore they commonly got their wood measured in Charlestown before crossing the bridge.

The aim of the laborer should be, not to get his living, to get "a good job," but to perform well a certain work; and, even in a pecuniary sense, it would be economy for a town to pay its laborers so well that they would not feel that they were working for low ends, as for a livelihood merely, but for scientific, or even moral ends. Do not hire a man who does your work for money, but him who does it for love of it.

It is remarkable that there are few men so well employed, so much to their minds, but that a little money or fame would commonly buy them off from their present pursuit. I see advertisements for active young men, as if activity were the whole of a young man's capital. Yet I have been surprised when one has with confidence proposed to me, a grown man, to embark in some enterprise of his, as if I had absolutely nothing to do, my life having been a complete failure hitherto. What a doubtful compliment this to pay me! As if he had met me half-way across the ocean beating up against the wind, but bound nowhere, and proposed to me to go along with him! If I did, what do you think the underwriters would say? No, no! I am not without employment at this stage of the voyage. To tell the truth, I saw an advertisement for able-bodied seamen, when I was a boy, sauntering in my native port, and as soon as I came of age I embarked.

The community has no bribe that will tempt a wise man. You may raise money enough to tunnel a mountain, but you cannot raise money enough to hire a man who is minding his own business. An efficient and valuable man does what he can, whether the community pay him for it or not. The inefficient offer their inefficiency to the highest bidder, and are forever expecting to be put into office. One would suppose that they were rarely disappointed.

Perhaps I am more than usually jealous with respect to my freedom. I feel that my connection with and obligation to society are still very slight and transient. Those slight labors which afford me a livelihood, and by which it is allowed that I am to some extent serviceable to my contemporaries, are as yet commonly a pleasure to me, and I am not often reminded that they are a necessity. So far I am successful. But I foresee that if my wants should be much increased, the labor required to supply them would become a drudgery. If I should sell both my forenoons and afternoons to society, as most appear to do, I am sure that for me there would be nothing left worth living for. I trust that I shall never thus sell my birthright for a mess of pottage. I wish to suggest that a man may be very industrious, and yet not spend his time well. There is no more fatal blunderer than he who consumes the greater part of his life getting his living. All great enterprises are self-supporting. The poet, for instance, must sustain his body by his poetry, as a steam planing-mill feeds its boilers with the shavings it makes. You must get your living by loving. But as it is said of the merchants that ninety-seven in a hundred fail, so the life of men generally, tried by this standard, is a failure, and bankruptcy may be surely prophesied.

Merely to come into the world the heir of a fortune is not to be born, but to be still-born, rather. To be supported by the charity of friends, or a government pension—provided you continue to breathe—by whatever fine synonyms you describe these relations, is to go into the almshouse. On Sundays the poor debtor goes to church to take an account of stock, and finds, of course, that his outgoes have been greater than his income. In the Catholic Church, especially, they go into chancery, make a clean confession, give up all, and think to start again. Thus men will lie on their backs, talking about the fall of man, and never make an effort to get up.

As for the comparative demand which men make on life, it is an important difference between two, that the one is satisfied with a level success, that his marks can all be hit by point-blank shots, but the other, however low and unsuccessful his life may be, constantly elevates his aim, though at a very slight angle to the horizon. I should much rather be the last man—though, as the Orientals say, "Greatness doth not approach him who is forever looking down; and all those who are looking high are growing poor."

It is remarkable that there is little or nothing to be remembered written on the subject of getting a living; how to make getting a living not merely holiest and honorable, but altogether inviting and glorious; for if getting a living is not so, then living is not. One would think, from looking at literature, that this question had never disturbed a solitary individual's musings. Is it that men are too much disgusted with their experience to speak of it? The lesson of value which money teaches, which the Author of the Universe has taken so much pains to teach us, we are inclined to skip altogether. As for the means of living, it is wonderful how indifferent men of all classes are about it, even reformers, so called—whether they inherit, or earn, or steal it. I think that Society has done nothing for us in this respect, or at least has undone what she has done. Cold and hunger seem more friendly to my nature than those methods which men have adopted and advise to ward them off.

The title wise is, for the most part, falsely applied. How can one be a wise man, if he does not know any better how to live than other men?—if he is only more cunning and intellectually subtle? Does Wisdom work in a tread-mill? or does she teach how to succeed by her example? Is there any such thing as wisdom not applied to life? Is she merely the miller who grinds the finest logic? It is pertinent to ask if Plato got his living in a better way or more successfully than his contemporaries—or did he succumb to the difficulties of life like other men? Did he seem to prevail over some of them merely by indifference, or by assuming grand airs? or find it easier to live, because his aunt remembered him in her will? The ways in which most men get their living, that is, live, are mere makeshifts, and a shirking of the real business of life—chiefly because they do not know, but partly because they do not mean, any better.

The rush to California, for instance, and the attitude, not merely of merchants, but of philosophers and prophets, so called, in relation to it, reflect the greatest disgrace on mankind. That so many are ready to live by luck, and so get the means of commanding the labor of others less lucky, without contributing any value to society! And that is called enterprise! I know of no more startling development of the immorality of trade, and all the common modes of getting a living. The philosophy and poetry and religion of such a mankind are not worth the dust of a puffball. The hog that gets his living by rooting, stirring up the soil so, would be ashamed of such company. If I could command the wealth of all the worlds by lifting my finger, I would not pay such a price for it. Even Mahomet knew that God did not make this world in jest. It makes God to be a moneyed gentleman who scatters a handful of pennies in order to see mankind scramble for them. The world's raffle! A subsistence in the domains of Nature a thing to be raffled for! What a comment, what a satire, on our institutions! The conclusion will be, that mankind will hang itself upon a tree. And have all the precepts in all the Bibles taught men only this? and is the last and most admirable invention of the human race only an improved muck-rake? Is this the ground on which Orientals and Occidentals meet? Did God direct us so to get our living, digging where we never planted—and He would, perchance, reward us with lumps of gold?

God gave the righteous man a certificate entitling him to food and raiment, but the unrighteous man found a facsimile of the same in God's coffers, and appropriated it, and obtained food and raiment like the former. It is one of the most extensive systems of counterfeiting that the world has seen. I did not know that mankind was suffering for want of old. I have seen a little of it. I know that it is very malleable, but not so malleable as wit. A grain of gold gild a great surface, but not so much as a grain of wisdom.

The gold-digger in the ravines of the mountains is as much a gambler as his fellow in the saloons of San Francisco. What difference does it make whether you shake dirt or shake dice? If you win, society is the loser. The gold-digger is the enemy of the honest laborer, whatever checks and compensations there may be. It is not enough to tell me that you worked hard to get your gold. So does the Devil work hard. The way of transgressors may be hard in many respects. The humblest observer who goes to the mines sees and says that gold-digging is of the character of a lottery; the gold thus obtained is not the same thing with the wages of honest toil. But, practically, he forgets what he has seen, for he has seen only the fact, not the principle, and goes into trade there, that is, buys a ticket in what commonly proves another lottery, where the fact is not so obvious.

After reading Howitt's account of the Australian gold-diggings one evening, I had in my mind's eye, all night, the numerous valleys, with their streams, all cut up with foul pits, from ten to one hundred feet deep, and half a dozen feet across, as close as they can be dug, and partly filled with water—the locality to which men furiously rush to probe for their fortunes—uncertain where they shall break ground—not knowing but the gold is under their camp itself—sometimes digging one hundred and sixty feet before they strike the vein, or then missing it by a foot—turned into demons, and regardless of each others' rights, in their thirst for riches—whole valleys, for thirty miles, suddenly honeycombed by the pits of the miners, so that even hundreds are drowned in them—standing in water, and covered with mud and clay, they work night and day, dying of exposure and disease. Having read this, and partly forgotten it, I was thinking, accidentally, of my own unsatisfactory life, doing as others do; and with that vision of the diggings still before me, I asked myself why I might not be washing some gold daily, though it were only the finest particles—why I might not sink a shaft down to the gold within me, and work that mine. There is a Ballarat, a Bendigo for you—what though it were a sulky-gully? At any rate, I might pursue some path, however solitary and narrow and crooked, in which I could walk with love and reverence. Wherever a man separates from the multitude, and goes his own way in this mood, there indeed is a fork in the road, though ordinary travellers may see only a gap in the paling. His solitary path across lots will turn out the higher way of the two.

Men rush to California and Australia as if the true gold were to be found in that direction; but that is to go to the very opposite extreme to where it lies. They go prospecting farther and farther away from the true lead, and are most unfortunate when they think themselves most successful. Is not our native soil auriferous? Does not a stream from the golden mountains flow through our native valley? and has not this for more than geologic ages been bringing down the shining particles and forming the nuggets for us? Yet, strange to tell, if a digger steal away, prospecting for this true gold, into the unexplored solitudes around us, there is no danger that any will dog his steps, and endeavor to supplant him. He may claim and undermine the whole valley even, both the cultivated and the uncultivated portions, his whole life long in peace, for no one will ever dispute his claim. They will not mind his cradles or his toms. He is not confined to a claim twelve feet square, as at Ballarat, but may mine anywhere, and wash the whole wide world in his tom.

Howitt says of the man who found the great nugget which weighed twenty-eight pounds, at the Bendigo diggings in Australia: "He soon began to drink; got a horse, and rode all about, generally at full gallop, and, when he met people, called out to inquire if they knew who he was, and then kindly informed them that he was 'the bloody wretch that had found the nugget.' At last he rode full speed against a tree, and nearly knocked his brains out." I think, however, there was no danger of that, for he had already knocked his brains out against the nugget. Howitt adds, "He is a hopelessly ruined man." But he is a type of the class. They are all fast men. Hear some of the names of the places where they dig: "Jackass Flat"—"Sheep's-Head Gully"—"Murderer's Bar," etc. Is there no satire in these names? Let them carry their ill-gotten wealth where they will, I am thinking it will still be "Jackass Flat," if not "Murderer's Bar," where they live.

The last resource of our energy has been the robbing of graveyards on the Isthmus of Darien, an enterprise which appears to be but in its infancy; for, according to late accounts, an act has passed its second reading in the legislature of New Granada, regulating this kind of mining; and a correspondent of the "Tribune" writes: "In the dry season, when the weather will permit of the country being properly prospected, no doubt other rich guacas [that is, graveyards] will be found." To emigrants he says: "do not come before December; take the Isthmus route in preference to the Boca del Toro one; bring no useless baggage, and do not cumber yourself with a tent; but a good pair of blankets will be necessary; a pick, shovel, and axe of good material will be almost all that is required": advice which might have been taken from the "Burker's Guide." And he concludes with this line in Italics and small capitals: "If you are doing well at home, STAY THERE," which may fairly be interpreted to mean, "If you are getting a good living by robbing graveyards at home, stay there."

But why go to California for a text? She is the child of New England, bred at her own school and church.

It is remarkable that among all the preachers there are so few moral teachers. The prophets are employed in excusing the ways of men. Most reverend seniors, the illuminati of the age, tell me, with a gracious, reminiscent smile, betwixt an aspiration and a shudder, not to be too tender about these things—to lump all that, that is, make a lump of gold of it. The highest advice I have heard on these subjects was grovelling. The burden of it was—It is not worth your while to undertake to reform the world in this particular. Do not ask how your bread is buttered; it will make you sick, if you do—and the like. A man had better starve at once than lose his innocence in the process of getting his bread. If within the sophisticated man there is not an unsophisticated one, then he is but one of the devil's angels. As we grow old, we live more coarsely, we relax a little in our disciplines, and, to some extent, cease to obey our finest instincts. But we should be fastidious to the extreme of sanity, disregarding the gibes of those who are more unfortunate than ourselves.

In our science and philosophy, even, there is commonly no true and absolute account of things. The spirit of sect and bigotry has planted its hoof amid the stars. You have only to discuss the problem, whether the stars are inhabited or not, in order to discover it. Why must we daub the heavens as well as the earth? It was an unfortunate discovery that Dr. Kane was a Mason, and that Sir John Franklin was another. But it was a more cruel suggestion that possibly that was the reason why the former went in search of the latter. There is not a popular magazine in this country that would dare to print a child's thought on important subjects without comment. It must be submitted to the D.D.'s. I would it were the chickadee-dees.

You come from attending the funeral of mankind to attend to a natural phenomenon. A little thought is sexton to all the world.

I hardly know an intellectual man, even, who is so broad and truly liberal that you can think aloud in his society. Most with whom you endeavor to talk soon come to a stand against some institution in which they appear to hold stock—that is, some particular, not universal, way of viewing things. They will continually thrust their own low roof, with its narrow skylight, between you and the sky, when it is the unobstructed heavens you would view. Get out of the way with your cobwebs; wash your windows, I say! In some lyceums they tell me that they have voted to exclude the subject of religion. But how do I know what their religion is, and when I am near to or far from it? I have walked into such an arena and done my best to make a clean breast of what religion I have experienced, and the audience never suspected what I was about. The lecture was as harmless as moonshine to them. Whereas, if I had read to them the biography of the greatest scamps in history, they might have thought that I had written the lives of the deacons of their church. Ordinarily, the inquiry is, Where did you come from? or, Where are you going? That was a more pertinent question which I overheard one of my auditors put to another one—"What does he lecture for?" It made me quake in my shoes.

To speak impartially, the best men that I know are not serene, a world in themselves. For the most part, they dwell in forms, and flatter and study effect only more finely than the rest. We select granite for the underpinning of our houses and barns; we build fences of stone; but we do not ourselves rest on an underpinning of granitic truth, the lowest primitive rock. Our sills are rotten. What stuff is the man made of who is not coexistent in our thought with the purest and subtilest truth? I often accuse my finest acquaintances of an immense frivolity; for, while there are manners and compliments we do not meet, we do not teach one another the lessons of honesty and sincerity that the brutes do, or of steadiness and solidity that the rocks do. The fault is commonly mutual, however; for we do not habitually demand any more of each other.

That excitement about Kossuth, consider how characteristic, but superficial, it was!—only another kind of politics or dancing. Men were making speeches to him all over the country, but each expressed only the thought, or the want of thought, of the multitude. No man stood on truth. They were merely banded together, as usual one leaning on another, and all together on nothing; as the Hindoos made the world rest on an elephant, the elephant on a tortoise, and the tortoise on a serpent, and had nothing to put under the serpent. For all fruit of that stir we have the Kossuth hat.

Just so hollow and ineffectual, for the most part, is our ordinary conversation. Surface meets surface. When our life ceases to be inward and private, conversation degenerates into mere gossip. We rarely meet a man who can tell us any news which he has not read in a newspaper, or been told by his neighbor; and, for the most part, the only difference between us and our fellow is that he has seen the newspaper, or been out to tea, and we have not. In proportion as our inward life fails, we go more constantly and desperately to the post-office. You may depend on it, that the poor fellow who walks away with the greatest number of letters, proud of his extensive correspondence, has not heard from himself this long while.

I do not know but it is too much to read one newspaper a week. I have tried it recently, and for so long it seems to me that I have not dwelt in my native region. The sun, the clouds, the snow, the trees say not so much to me. You cannot serve two masters. It requires more than a day's devotion to know and to possess the wealth of a day.

We may well be ashamed to tell what things we have read or heard in our day. I did not know why my news should be so trivial—considering what one's dreams and expectations are, why the developments should be so paltry. The news we hear, for the most part, is not news to our genius. It is the stalest repetition. You are often tempted to ask why such stress is laid on a particular experience which you have had—that, after twenty-five years, you should meet

Hobbins, Registrar of Deeds, again on the sidewalk. Have you not budged an inch, then? Such is the daily news. Its facts appear to float in the atmosphere, insignificant as the sporules of fungi, and impinge on some neglected thallus, or surface of our minds, which affords a basis for them, and hence a parasitic growth. We should wash ourselves clean of such news. Of what consequence, though our planet explode, if there is no character involved in the explosion? In health we have not the least curiosity about such events. We do not live for idle amusement. I would not run round a corner to see the world blow up.

All summer, and far into the autumn, perchance, you unconsciously went by the newspapers and the news, and now you find it was because the morning and the evening were full of news to you. Your walks were full of incidents. You attended, not to the affairs of Europe, but to your own affairs in Massachusetts fields. If you chance to live and move and have your being in that thin stratum in which the events that make the news transpire—thinner than the paper on which it is printed—then these things will fill the world for you; but if you soar above or dive below that plane, you cannot remember nor be reminded of them. Really to see the sun rise or go down every day, so to relate ourselves to a universal fact, would preserve us sane forever. Nations! What are nations? Tartars, and Huns, and Chinamen! Like insects, they swarm. The historian strives in vain to make them memorable. It is for want of a man that there are so many men. It is individuals that populate the world. Any man thinking may say with the Spirit of Lodin—"I look down from my height on nations, And they become ashes before me;—Calm is my dwelling in the clouds; Pleasant are the great fields of my rest."

Pray, let us live without being drawn by dogs, Esquimaux-fashion, tearing over hill and dale, and biting each other's ears.

Not without a slight shudder at the danger, I often perceive how near I had come to admitting into my mind the details of some trivial affair—the news of the street; and I am astonished to observe how willing men are to lumber their minds with such rubbish—to permit idle rumors and incidents of the most insignificant kind to intrude on ground which should be sacred to thought. Shall the mind be a public arena, where the affairs of the street and the gossip of the tea-table chiefly are discussed? Or shall it be a quarter of heaven itself—an hypaethral temple, consecrated to the service of the gods? I find it so difficult to dispose of the few facts which to me are significant, that I hesitate to burden my attention with those which are insignificant, which only a divine mind could illustrate. Such is, for the most part, the news in newspapers and conversation. It is important to preserve the mind's chastity in this respect. Think of admitting the details of a single case of the criminal court into our thoughts, to stalk profanely through their very sanctum sanctorum for an hour, ay, for many hours! to make a very bar-room of the mind's inmost apartment, as if for so long the dust of the street had occupied us—the very street itself, with all its travel, its bustle, and filth, had passed through our thoughts' shrine! Would it not be an intellectual and moral suicide? When I have been compelled to sit spectator and auditor in a court-room for some hours, and have seen my neighbors, who were not compelled, stealing in from time to time, and tiptoeing about with washed hands and faces, it has appeared to my mind's eye, that, when they took off their hats, their ears suddenly expanded into vast hoppers for sound, between which even their narrow heads were crowded. Like the vanes of windmills, they caught the broad but shallow stream of sound, which, after a few titillating gyrations in their coggy brains, passed out the other side. I wondered if, when they got home, they were as careful to wash their ears as before their hands and faces. It has seemed to me, at such a time, that the auditors and the witnesses, the jury and the counsel, the judge and the criminal at the bar—if I may presume him guilty before he is convicted—were all equally criminal, and a thunderbolt might be expected to descend and consume them all together.

By all kinds of traps and signboards, threatening the extreme penalty of the divine law, exclude such trespassers from the only ground which can be sacred to you. It is so hard to forget what it is worse than useless to remember! If I am to be a thoroughfare, I prefer that it be of the mountain brooks, the Parnassian streams, and not the town sewers. There is inspiration, that gossip which comes to the ear of the attentive mind from the courts of heaven. There is the profane and stale revelation of the bar-room and the police court. The same ear is fitted to receive both communications. Only the character of the hearer determines to which it shall be open, and to which closed. I believe that the mind can be permanently profaned by the habit of attending to trivial things, so that all our thoughts shall be tinged with triviality. Our very intellect shall be macadamized, as it were—its foundation broken into fragments for the wheels of travel to roll over; and if you would know what will make the most durable pavement, surpassing rolled stones, spruce blocks, and asphaltum, you have only to look into some of our minds which have been subjected to this treatment so long.

If we have thus desecrated ourselves—as who has not?—the remedy will be by wariness and devotion to reconsecrate ourselves, and make once more a fane of the mind. We should treat our minds, that is, ourselves, as innocent and ingenuous children, whose guardians we are, and be careful what objects and what subjects we thrust on their attention. Read not the Times. Read the Eternities.

Conventionalities are at length as had as impurities. Even the facts of science may dust the mind by their dryness, unless they are in a sense effaced each morning, or rather rendered fertile by the dews of fresh and living truth. Knowledge does not come to us by details, but in flashes of light from heaven. Yes, every thought that passes through the mind helps to wear and tear it, and to deepen the ruts, which, as in the streets of Pompeii, evince how much it has been used. How many things there are concerning which we might well deliberate whether we had better know them—had better let their peddling-carts be driven, even at the slowest trot or walk, over that bride of glorious span by which we trust to pass at last from the farthest brink of time to the nearest shore of eternity! Have we no culture, no refinement—but skill only to live coarsely and serve the Devil?—to acquire a little worldly wealth, or fame, or liberty, and make a false show with it, as if we were all husk and shell, with no tender and living kernel to us? Shall our institutions be like those chestnut burs which contain abortive nuts, perfect only to prick the fingers?

America is said to be the arena on which the battle of freedom is to be fought; but surely it cannot be freedom in a merely political sense that is meant. Even if we grant that the American has freed himself from a political tyrant, he is still the slave of an economical and moral tyrant. Now that the republic—the respublica—has been settled, it is time to look after the res-privata—the private state—to see, as the Roman senate charged its consuls, "ne quid res-PRIVATA detrimenti caperet," that the private state receive no detriment.

Do we call this the land of the free? What is it to be free from King George and continue the slaves of King Prejudice? What is it to be born free and not to live free? What is the value of any political freedom, but as a means to moral freedom? Is it a freedom to be slaves, or a freedom to be free, of which we boast? We are a nation of politicians, concerned about the outmost defences only of freedom. It is our children's children who may perchance be really free. We tax ourselves unjustly. There is a part of us which is not represented. It is taxation without representation. We quarter troops, we quarter fools and cattle of all sorts upon ourselves. We quarter our gross bodies on our poor souls, till the former eat up all the latter's substance.

With respect to a true culture and manhood, we are essentially provincial still, not metropolitan—mere Jonathans. We are provincial, because we do not find at home our standards; because we do not worship truth, but the reflection of truth; because we are warped and narrowed by an exclusive devotion to trade and commerce and manufactures and agriculture and the like, which are but means, and not the end.

So is the English Parliament provincial. Mere country bumpkins, they betray themselves, when any more important question arises for them to settle, the Irish question, for instance—the

English question why did I not say? Their natures are subdued to what they work in. Their "good breeding" respects only secondary objects. The finest manners in the world are awkwardness and fatuity when contrasted with a finer intelligence. They appear but as the fashions of past days—mere courtliness, knee-buckles and small-clothes, out of date. It is the vice, but not the excellence of manners, that they are continually being deserted by the character; they are cast-off-clothes or shells, claiming the respect which belonged to the living creature. You are presented with the shells instead of the meat, and it is no excuse generally, that, in the case of some fishes, the shells are of more worth than the meat. The man who thrusts his manners upon me does as if he were to insist on introducing me to his cabinet of curiosities, when I wished to see himself. It was not in this sense that the poet Decker called Christ "the first true gentleman that ever breathed." I repeat that in this sense the most splendid court in Christendom is provincial, having authority to consult about Transalpine interests only, and not the affairs of Rome. A praetor or proconsul would suffice to settle the questions which absorb the attention of the English Parliament and the American Congress.

Government and legislation! these I thought were respectable professions. We have heard of heaven-born Numas, Lycurguses, and Solons, in the history of the world, whose names at least may stand for ideal legislators; but think of legislating to regulate the breeding of slaves, or the exportation of tobacco! What have divine legislators to do with the exportation or the importation of tobacco? what humane ones with the breeding of slaves? Suppose you were to submit the question to any son of God—and has He no children in the Nineteenth Century? is it a family which is extinct?—in what condition would you get it again? What shall a State like Virginia say for itself at the last day, in which these have been the principal, the staple productions? What ground is there for patriotism in such a State? I derive my facts from statistical tables which the States themselves have published.

A commerce that whitens every sea in quest of nuts and raisins, and makes slaves of its sailors for this purpose! I saw, the other day, a vessel which had been wrecked, and many lives lost, and her cargo of rags, juniper berries, and bitter almonds were strewn along the shore. It seemed hardly worth the while to tempt the dangers of the sea between Leghorn and New York for the sake of a cargo of juniper berries and bitter almonds. America sending to the Old World for her bitters! Is not the sea-brine, is not shipwreck, bitter enough to make the cup of life go down here? Yet such, to a great extent, is our boasted commerce; and there are those who style themselves statesmen and philosophers who are so blind as to think that progress and civilization depend on precisely this kind of interchange and activity—the activity of flies about a molasses—hogshead. Very well, observes one, if men were oysters. And very well, answer I, if men were mosquitoes.

Lieutenant Herndon, whom our government sent to explore the Amazon, and, it is said, to extend the area of slavery, observed that there was wanting there "an industrious and active population, who know what the comforts of life are, and who have artificial wants to draw out the great resources of the country." But what are the "artificial wants" to be encouraged? Not the love of luxuries, like the tobacco and slaves of, I believe, his native Virginia, nor the ice and granite and other material wealth of our native New England; nor are "the great resources of a country" that fertility or barrenness of soil which produces these. The chief want, in every State that I have been into, was a high and earnest purpose in its inhabitants. This alone draws out "the great resources" of Nature, and at last taxes her beyond her resources; for man naturally dies out of her. When we want culture more than potatoes, and illumination more than sugar-plums, then the great resources of a world are taxed and drawn out, and the result, or staple production, is, not slaves, nor operatives, but men—those rare fruits called heroes, saints, poets, philosophers, and redeemers.

In short, as a snow-drift is formed where there is a lull in the wind, so, one would say, where there is a lull of truth, an institution springs up. But the truth blows right on over it, nevertheless, and at length blows it down.

What is called politics is comparatively something so superficial and inhuman, that practically I have never fairly recognized that it concerns me at all. The newspapers, I perceive, devote some of their columns specially to politics or government without charge; and this, one would say, is all that saves it; but as I love literature and to some extent the truth also, I never read those columns at any rate. I do not wish to blunt my sense of right so much. I have not got to answer for having read a single President's Message. A strange age of the world this, when empires, kingdoms, and republics come a-begging to a private man's door, and utter their complaints at his elbow! I cannot take up a newspaper but I find that some wretched government or other, hard pushed and on its last legs, is interceding with me, the reader, to vote for it—more importunate than an Italian beggar; and if I have a mind to look at its certificate, made, perchance, by some benevolent merchant's clerk, or the skipper that brought it over, for it cannot speak a word of English itself, I shall probably read of the eruption of some Vesuvius, or the overflowing of some Po, true or forged, which brought it into this condition. I do not hesitate, in such a case, to suggest work, or the almshouse; or why not keep its castle in silence, as I do commonly? The poor President, what with preserving his popularity and doing his duty, is completely bewildered. The newspapers are the ruling power. Any other government is reduced to a few marines at Fort Independence. If a man neglects to read the Daily Times, government will go down on its knees to him, for this is the only treason in these days.

Those things which now most engage the attention of men, as politics and the daily routine, are, it is true, vital functions of human society, but should be unconsciously performed, like the corresponding functions of the physical body. They are infrahuman, a kind of vegetation. I sometimes awake to a half-consciousness of them going on about me, as a man may become conscious of some of the processes of digestion in a morbid state, and so have the dyspepsia, as it is called. It is as if a thinker submitted himself to be rasped by the great gizzard of creation. Politics is, as it were, the gizzard of society, full of grit and gravel, and the two political parties are its two opposite halves—sometimes split into quarters, it may be, which grind on each other. Not only individuals, but states, have thus a confirmed dyspepsia, which expresses itself, you can imagine by what sort of eloquence. Thus our life is not altogether a forgetting, but also, alas! to a great extent, a remembering, of that which we should never have been conscious of, certainly not in our waking hours. Why should we not meet, not always as dyspeptics, to tell our had dreams, but sometimes as eupeptics, to congratulate each other on the ever-glorious morning? I do not make an exorbitant demand, surely.

Regarding the Text

1. What comments does Thoreau make about leisure time? What does he want to do with his time?

2. In paragraph 8, why does Thoreau have disdain for most jobs?

3. What is the principle by which the author believes life should be lived?

Joining the Conversation

4. What impressions of Thoreau do you have when you first meet him in this essay?

5. Thoreau gets to sounding as if were on a rant by the midpoint of his essay. How would you describe his tone? What does he intend to accomplish with this tone?

Owning the Idea

6.   The counter-culture of the 1960s and 1970s in America appreciated Thoreau. What can you find in common between Thoreau's attitudes and that of the counter-culture?

Short Assignments on Interpretive Analysis

1.   A student once made the surprising argument that "Total Eclipse" is an essay about Annie Dillard's dissolving marriage. Why would the student come to this conclusion? It is important to note that Dillard's essay is not about this at all. In fact, the student's paper was immaturely written. Explain where the student went wrong in her approach, as the logic is quite telling. In two to three paragraphs, examine the details in Dillard's essay that could lead to such an interpretation. Find four to five details from "Total Eclipse" that could be construed as addressing the subject of marriage. Then, using the 3-step method, determine where the student went wrong with the interpretation. What does it mean that there are details in the essay that conceivably could address Dillard's marriage? On the other hand, what makes this student's interpretation weak or invalid?

2.   Choose a passage from "The Solace of Open Spaces" that seems representative of the theme or ideas Ehrlich formulates in her essay. In other words, find a block of text from one or two sentences to a paragraph that sounds to you like this must be what Ehrlich is getting at. The passage you choose will help you to find solid connections with other parts of the essay, but it will be brief enough for you to address it fully without leaving out any important details.

Interpret the passage by writing one or two paragraphs. What is Ehrlich saying? What are the *implications*—or what is the *significance*—of what she is saying? Do not merely summarize what you have read, but instead look for explanations as to why Ehrlich's point might matter to someone reading her essay. Do not neglect the power of looking up terms or words that are used in unusual contexts. Then, in another paragraph, explain how the passage you interpreted is representative of the larger scope of the essay, accounting for how the part fits into the whole.

ASSIGNMENT: INTERPRETIVE ANALYSIS ESSAY

Writing Assignment

Objective

Context gives writing meaning. When you can apply a piece of writing to a variety of contexts, you demonstrate an ability to synthesize ideas and engage in symbolic thinking, two very important skills in academics. You will write an interpretive analysis by focusing on several short passages in one essay and show what that essay has to say about an issue or idea.

Assignment

The essays in this chapter have a variety of themes that intersect. Write an interpretative analysis of one of these essays in which you consider that essay's ultimate reason for being. What purpose does the author have in writing it? How does it make its point? To whom is the essay relevant? In what context(s) might the essay make the most sense or be most interesting to read? (Consider that any of these essays would read much differently, for instance, immediately after a national disaster, or after the birth of the reader's first child. What makes this essay important or particularly interesting?) Use specific references to the original text to identify important details that help support your conclusions about the essay.

To Consider

Use the instructions for the *Short Assignments on Interpretive Analysis* as a guide for preparing to write your essay. Spending time thinking about meaningful passages will help give your paper coherence. Close reading and careful explanation of significant details will help anchor your analysis.

SAMPLE OF INTERPRETIVE ANALYSIS STUDENT ESSAY

Below is a student's essay, an interpretive analysis on Gretel Ehrlich's essay, "The Solace of Open Spaces." Look for the context the student offers for reading Ehrlich's essay. Where does the student find relevance in the writing?

Kailey Burke

English 110—Composition

Interpretive Analysis of "The Solace of Open Spaces"

"The Solace of Open Spaces" is an anthem for the lover of the natural world. People who have experienced the brilliance of living in sync with nature are able to connect with the descriptions and feelings of Gretel Ehrlich's words. Shaped by weather, natural patterns, and what it costs to survive, the inhabitants of Wyoming strip their lives of the frills that consume "modern" areas of society.

The people of Wyoming are not enchanted by false beauty that creates a seemingly perfect person or culture, yet they hold deep appreciation for the ragged beauty of the natural world with all of its flaws and imperfections. Gretel Ehrlich's personal back-to-the-land movement through her lifestyle change exemplifies her transition into self reflection and happiness derived from simplicity. Ehrlich came to Wyoming with the intention of leaving after a few months but was soon captivated by the vastly unfamiliar lifestyle which, in turn, she "could not make [herself] leave." She was in search of numbness to contemplate the truth in her life and to take time away from her previous home that was overtaken by death.

What she found was vitality in the land and the people living within their means. Living every day so close to nature and the reality of death pulls away the inconspicuous veil over perception so that life and truth are immediately accessible. They need no searching out. In Wyoming Ehrlich is able to find purpose in her daily life as she can connect with the sources of devastation and creation and understand that her energy is recycled into a greater force. The land and the work of the people create a simple complexity that aligns with human nature. The tangibility of progress creates honest work that is directly correlated to sustaining their bodies and the meaning of their lives. Ehrlich shares that, "...being 'at home on the range' is a matter of vigor, self-reliance, and common sense. A person's life is not a series of dramatic events for which he or she is applauded or exiled but a slow accumulation of days, seasons, years, fleshed out by the generational weight of one's family and anchored by a land-bound sense of place."

It is this sense of place that has evolved greatly for Ehrlich and has become much more meaningful to her than previously she experienced it. Over time she is able to create an understanding of all kinds of relationships, between people, nature, animals, and work—discovering that they are all connected and bound together. Ehrlich shares the notion that our country had lost its "true wilderness" since the exploration of Lewis and Clark.

She relates that this "true wilderness" holds mystery, endless possibility, and wildness that supplies genuine enigma. Unlike the colonists, the natives of the land, inhabiting centuries before, lived at the mercy of its fluctuations and respected the natural ecological cycles, for they knew they were not rulers of the land but a piece of its puzzle.

Ehrlich finds deep connection with the Native American way of life, saying, "Space was life. The world was their home." Both Ehrlich and the Native Americans have a spiritual connection with space and nature, allowing spirituality and righteousness to dictate the work in their lives. Others held a different respect for the land, seeing it as a great opportunity for self-serving motives rather than a sacred area that would shape their way of life. She writes, "Wealthy landowners, many of them aristocratic absentee landlords, known as remittance men because they were paid to come West and get out of their families' hair, overstocked the range with more than a million head of cattle." These men did not know the land; they were merely reaping the space for all that it had, the very same space that is so sacred to the soul of Ehrlich's experience and the original natives of the land. But, as time went on, fences were put up, boundaries were created, and freedom was slowly being lost.

On a two week pack trip Ehrlich further feels the encroachment of humans onto the natural world as she star gazes atop a mountain in a small Wyoming town. Though she is far away from civilization, merged into wild nature, and has not encountered another person besides her hiking partner, the reminder of space developed by humans is still readily visible. The once out of reach space, the night sky, is now filled with satellites that circumnavigate the earth with an unnatural regularity. Similar to the way that the sparsely populated land of Wyoming had provided a sense of vastness, the paradigm of conversation and encounter is greatly contrasting to that of contemporary exchange. Silence is not translated as awkward or empty but it is filled with a shared underlying language of continents, "silence is profound." Sentences are shortened and language becomes metaphorical. "Instead of talking, we seem to share one eye."

The lifestyle of Wyoming is understood between residence, bound by siblings, parents, grandparents, and friends. They share experiences and struggles that do not need to be explained, for they have all felt them. They are one of the same breed that can relate complex emotions though simple words. As the world's population is steadily growing and the movement towards metropolitan areas escalates. Ehrlich's new affection for isolation is thought provoking and contrary to life dictated by majority vote.

The culture of cities is often commercially and economically based, creating abstracts of life that simulate a happiness people are directed to achieve. Ehrlich writes, "We Americans are great on fillers, as if what we have, what we are is not enough. We have a cultural tendency toward denial, but being affluent, we strangle ourselves with what we can buy." The people of Wyoming live and work for things that are true, according to Ehrlich, things that will make them richer than industry.

Stitching Ideas

One method for synthesizing and focusing analysis that you may find helpful is this method of "stitching." When you write analysis, you are explaining the implications of the patterns you observe. When you have finished your analysis of one detail and need to turn your attention to another detail, you need some way of transitioning smoothly to that next segment of analysis. Stitching is applying your ideas about one detail to another detail so that your analysis coheres and stays focused.

Here is an example first of a brief analysis written by a student writer, Angie Karter:

In "The Solace of Open Spaces," Ehrlich writes about surprising herself with what she finds during her time in Wyoming. She had intended to become numb, to keep herself from becoming introspective, to stay on the surface of things, not looking for meaning in her life at that point. As we all have masks we wear when we interact in various situations, so Ehrlich also has more than one self, and it is a self that is new to her, one she has never explored, that she finds in Wyoming and that comes as a surprise to her after a hailstone strikes her in the head. The power of her discovery is the surprise, the fact that finding anything at all about herself is unexpected—unwanted, at least initially.

The student eventually continues this paragraph by explaining the relevance of her point. Prior to that time, however, the student looked for a way to transition into more analysis that would address the implications of what she had written so far without losing focus. She decided the best way to continue was to find another passage that seems relevant to the one she just analyzed. She remembered the detail from Ehrlich's essay where the author has gone a few days without speaking to anyone and someone drives by. She says that she fights the impulse to run and hide. The student asks herself, why would Ehrlich want to hide when she has been alone all this time? So the analysis continues:

> What Ehrlich attempts to flee instead finds her. She maintains she wants to forget, writing, "I threw away my clothes and bought new ones. I cut my hair," yet her essay is full of discoveries that drive her toward—as she explains about Wyomingites—"a laconic shyness." This phenomenon occurs as the result of Ehrlich becoming part of a place. She takes great pains to explain she has not arrived in Jackson Hole ready for a vacation, but rather that she has come to the wilderness. Yet what seems to escape her initially greets us full force as we read, which is that we go to the wilderness when we want to be alone with ourselves, when we want to experience ourselves in our environment, not merely experience our environment. Ehrlich at one point, after working for days without human contact, blanches at the approach of a vehicle, so much not wanting to break her silent retreat that she entertains the idea of hiding. It is clear she has taken hold of something she cannot yet let go, and that specifically is her solitude.

In this paragraph, the student has examined one small detail from Ehrlich's essay that came to mind as the result of her initial analysis. The analysis of that new detail in turn has taken her to the subject of solitude.

Might she be able to find a passage in which Ehrlich addresses solitude in Wyoming? Sure, on every page. She decides to pursue that direction. Her paper will never lose its focus because she keeps stitching one bit of analysis to another bit of analysis, and pretty soon she has written more than she can use in a paper because by repeating this process she can make a chain of associations that go on indefinitely.

REVISION IDEAS

1. How many assertions (statements that require some kind of support) do you make in this paragraph? How many statements of support do you give to each assertion? How many statements of support are themselves assertions? This last question addresses the proverbial can of worms, which at first can seem daunting but is every writer's best friend. If you simply satisfy every assertion you make with multiple statements of support, you will find that you are faced with the constant challenge of cutting words from your papers rather than looking for something to say. If you imagine someone interested in what you have to say standing over your shoulder as you review what you have written, asking you, "What do you mean by that exactly?"—you will have reason to explain yourself without feeling like you are constantly being evaluated for every word you utter, and this realization can lead you to a breakthrough in your writing. That is all that is involved in offering support for assertions.

2. Before you write a draft of your assignment, paraphrase the assignment. Your paraphrase should equal the length of the assignment but should be entirely in your own words. Don't borrow any phrases, and especially don't copy any direction words (explain, propose, observe, etc.). Take your paraphrase to class

or to your teacher and ask if it is accurate. Look at it yourself and decide what are the major differences between the assignment and your paraphrase of the assignment.

3. Write a draft of your paper as a dialogue between you and anyone else: your teacher, a parent, a family doctor, someone serving time in prison. What kinds of questions, comments, resistance, and agreement occur? How might you anticipate these reactions in your paper?

4. Incorporate your notes from a class discussion or lecture into your paper. Make a seamless transition from your draft to your notes and back to your draft. Expand your writing by finding connections between your notes and your thoughts about your topic in your paper.

5. Students generally say writing "flows" when writing includes important transitions from paragraph to paragraph, idea to idea. You might think your writing is choppy if these transitions are missing. Transitions are more than simply key words or sentences. They help your readers understand how and why you are getting from one point to the next. You can take your readers anywhere in your discussion— to Mars if you want—but you cannot let go of their hand. If your writing is missing transitions, find those places in your writing that seem choppy. Try explaining out loud your *reasoning* behind moving from one paragraph to another, or even from one sentence to another. That reasoning will also give you clues about your thesis. The thesis (or answer to "why") is ever present in transitions.

6. Without looking at your paper, say into a voice recorder on your computer or smartphone or type into a word processor what your paper is about, what point you make, and how you chose your points of support. If you can do that successfully, you're probably in good stead. If you cannot do it? Make adjustments to your paper until you're satisfied with your ability to explain it without looking at the paper. (Is your explanation clearer than your paper? Write your explanation in your paper.)

APPENDICES

Seven Style Tips

CREATE ACTIVE SENTENCES WITH SUBJECTS AND VERBS SIDE BY SIDE

In an active sentence, the subject is the actor, performing the action of the verb. In a passive sentence, the subject is not the actor, and in fact *receives* the action of the verb.

	(Subject/Actor)	(Verb/Action)	
ACTIVE:	The cat	chased	the rat.

	(Subject/Receiver)	(Verb/Action)	
PASSIVE:	The rat	was chased	by the cat.

Because the active approach requires fewer words, it's usually preferable. Of course, there are situations in which you may choose to use the passive approach—for emphasis or variety, perhaps. Or you may want to "hide" the actor, when writing about a situation in which some mistake or controversial decision has been made. Here's an example:

	(Subject/Actor)	(Verb/Action)	
ACTIVE:	Linda Fraser	decided	that the class should complain to the Dean.

	(Subject/Receiver)	(Verb/Action)	
PASSIVE:	A decision	was made	that the class should complain to the Dean.

Obviously, the passive would probably be better in a case like this. There is no reason to bring Linda Fraser's identity to the attention of anyone who may later wish to retaliate against her. But use the passive only with good cause; every use of the passive should be purposefully deliberate rather than accidental.

The heart of any sentence, whether active or passive, is the main verb and its subject. Therefore, English sentences are easiest to understand when subjects and verbs are as close together as possible. For example, both of the following sentences are grammatical, but the second is smoother because the first creates an interruption between the main subject and verb.

From *College English: The Basics, 2nd Edition* by George J. Searles. © 2017 by George J. Searles.
Reprinted by permission of Kendall Hunt Publishing Company.

(Subject)   (Verb)

Food servers, because kitchen doors always open to the right, should learn to carry trays left-handed.

(Subject)   (Verb)

Because kitchen doors always open to the right, food servers should learn to carry trays left-handed.

Whenever possible, try to keep subjects and verbs side by side. This will not only ensure maximum clarity, but will also help you avoid grammatical errors involving subject/verb agreement. (See Appendix B, page 218.)

POSITION MODIFIERS NEAR WHAT THEY MODIFY

A modifier is a word or phrase that makes another word or phrase more specific by limiting or qualifying its sense. For example, in the phrase *my English book,* the words *my* and *English* modify the word *book.* In the sentence, *Exhausted, he fell asleep at the wheel,* the word *Exhausted* modifies the word *he,* the word *asleep* modifies the word *fell,* and the phrase *at the wheel* modifies the word *asleep.* That sentence is easy to understand partly because all the modifiers are where they belong. But consider this rather different example:

Growing in the garden, Lisa's mother found marijuana.

Certainly Lisa's mother was not growing in the garden. But that's what the sentence says, because the modifying phrase *growing in the garden* is misplaced, "dangling" off the front of the sentence. Really it should be alongside what it modifies (*marijuana*), like this:

Lisa's mother found marijuana growing in the garden.

Of course, nobody would be likely to misinterpret the original version of that sentence, but misplaced modifiers can indeed create confusion when more than one interpretation is possible. Just as subjects and verbs work best when side-by-side, modifiers should always be positioned as close as possible to what they modify.

NOTE: The modifier *only* is nearly always misplaced, as in this sentence:

I only have two dollars.

Certainly the sentence should be revised as follows, because *only* modifies *two,* not *have*:

I have only two dollars.

USE TRANSITIONS EFFECTIVELY

Transitional words or phrases serve as links between sentence parts, whole sentences, or paragraphs, clarifying the relationships among ideas. In effect, they serve as "bridges" from idea to idea within a piece of writing and are therefore quite helpful to the reader. In general, longer transitions—words such as *therefore* and *consequently* and clusters of words like *on the other hand* or *in conclusion*—tend to appear at the beginning of a sentence, followed by a comma, while short transitions—like *and, but,* and *so*—tend to appear within sentences, often with a comma before them. Transitions can be loosely categorized according to the kinds of relationships they signal. This chart will help you choose a correct transition in each situation.

Signal	Transition
Additional Information	and, also, furthermore, in addition, moreover
Example	for example, for instance, to illustrate
Explanation	in other words, simply stated, that is
Similarity	in like manner, likewise, similarly
Contrast	but, yet, conversely, however, nevertheless, on the other hand
Cause and Effect	accordingly, as a result, because, consequently, hence, so, therefore, thus
Emphasis	clearly, indeed, in fact, obviously
Summary	finally, in conclusion, in short, to sum up

HANDLE NUMBERS CORRECTLY

Frequently we must decide whether to spell out a number or use a numeral (for example, *three hundred* or *300*). This issue is somewhat complicated, because several different systems exist. Usually, however, words are used for amounts from zero to nine, and sometimes for other amounts that can be expressed in one or two words, such as thirty-one or fifty. (Note that two-word numbers under 100 require a hyphen.)

Here are a few guidelines that may help:

▶ Never begin a sentence with a numeral. Either spell it out or, if the number is large, reorder the sentence so the numeral appears elsewhere.

ORIGINAL: 781 students have bought concert tickets so far.

REVISION: So far, 781 students have bought concert tickets.

▶ For very large numbers, combine numerals and words, as in "100 million."

▶ Combine numerals and words whenever such an approach will prevent misreading, as in this example:

ORIGINAL: You will need 3 6 inch screws and 10 4 inch nails.

REVISION: You will need three 6-inch screws and ten 4-inch nails.

Note that a hyphen is required when a number is used with a word to modify another word.

▶ Be consistent about how you deal with numbers in a given piece of writing. Pick one approach and stick with it, as in this example:

ORIGINAL: She took five courses in the spring and 2 in the summer.

REVISION: She took five courses in the spring and two in the summer.

▶ Use numerals for all statistical data, such as the following:

ages and addresses

dates

exact amounts of money

fractions and decimals

identification numbers

measurements (including height and weight)

page numbers

percentages, ratios, proportions

scores

When dealing with statistics, it often makes sense to combine numerals with other symbols rather than with words (*e.g.*, 6′1″ rather than 6 feet, 1 inch and $375 rather than 375 dollars).

USE FAMILIAR VOCABULARY—NOTHING FANCY

Most readers do not respond well to fancy wording. Therefore, you should use ordinary terms your reader will immediately recognize and understand. This is true even when your reader is your professor, who is almost certainly well-educated and equipped with a larger than average vocabulary. Your professor will *understand* inflated diction, but will probably regard it as an irritating (because transparent) attempt to hide weak content beneath the camouflage of ornate language. Keep it simple.

Of course, there's no reason to avoid *technical* terms—specialized words for which there are no satisfactory substitutes—if your reader can be expected to know them. An electrode is an electrode, a condenser is a condenser, and an isometric drawing is an isometric drawing. If you're writing in a technical context, most of your readers (and certainly your professor) will share your knowledge of the subject area. If you're not sure whether your reader is familiar with the vocabulary of the field, provide a glossary (a list of words with their definitions) somewhere within the document. If there are only a few potentially troublesome terms, you can insert parenthesized definitions—as in the previous sentence, where *glossary* is defined.

Generally, however, the best policy is to use the simplest word available, provided it's accurate: *Pay* rather than *remunerate; transparent* rather than *pellucid; steal* rather than *pilfer.* Another advantage of using every-day language is that your spelling will improve, especially when handwriting without the benefit of an electronic spell-checker. You're far more likely to misspell words you're unaccustomed to seeing in print, because you won't know whether they "look right" on the page.

WRITE SHORT SENTENCES

A sentence can be very long and still be grammatical. Many highly-regarded writers—the prize-winning American novelist William Faulkner, for example—have favored highly elaborate sentence structure. But most of us are not trying to become the next Faulkner. We write for a different purpose—usually to convey information, rather than to dazzle or impress. And the longer a sentence becomes, the harder it is for the reader to process. If a sentence goes much beyond twenty-five or thirty words, the reader's comprehension decreases.

To ensure maximum readability, therefore, limit your sentence length to an *average* of no more than twenty words. This can be inhibiting during the actual composing process, so make such adjustments afterwards, when revising.

It's usually fairly easy to see where the breaks should be (after each main idea), as in this example:

ORIGINAL

Athletes who gripe during practice or play practical jokes in the locker room may think they're relieving tension on the team, but in fact they may only be contributing to it, because a really good team is composed of players who rarely argue, seldom complain, and never criticize one another, understanding that a good team is like any efficient organization, in which every individual has a specific role to play, so players should submerge their individual egos for the sake of fostering team unity.

(One 83-word sentence)

REVISION

Athletes who gripe during practice or play practical jokes in the locker room may think they're relieving tension on the team. But in fact they may only be contributing to it. A really good team is composed of players who rarely argue, seldom complain, and never criticize one another. They understand that a good team is like any efficient organization, in which every individual has a specific role. Players should submerge their individual egos for the sake of fostering team unity.

(Five sentences, 16-word average)

Judging whether a sentence is too long, however, depends on context: What comes before it and what comes after. An occasional long sentence is acceptable, especially before or after a short one.

EDIT FOR CONCISION AND ECONOMY

Although everything already discussed in this chapter is crucial to developing a clear, easily readable style, the most important principle of all is to avoid wordiness and strive for concision and economy. Good writing is simple and direct. Of course, achieving a plainspoken, reader-friendly style is far easier said than done. But it becomes somewhat easier if you learn to recognize the five main sources of verbal clutter.

Unnecessary Introductions

Practically all writers waste words, especially in a first draft. But excess verbiage interferes with communication by inflating sentence length and tiring the reader. The unnecessary introduction, for example, is among the most common kinds of verbal clutter.

It's perfectly acceptable—and sometimes necessary—to open a sentence with an introductory phrase that leads into the main idea. But this depends on who the reader is, what the circumstances are, and other factors. Check your writing for *needless* introductions—phrases in which you're simply "clearing your throat," as in these examples:

As I look back on what I have said in this essay, it seems that…

Though this might not seem very important, you should remember that…

Because all of us attended last Friday's lecture, there is no need to summarize that presentation, in which the speaker said that…

Instead, get right to the point:

> It seems that…

> You should remember that…

> In last Friday's lecture, the speaker said that…

Submerged Verbs

Like unnecessary introductions, submerged verbs are a major source of verbal clutter. Too often we use a verb plus another verb (hidden or "submerged" within a noun) when one verb (the submerged one) would do, as in phrases like the following:

> (Verb)   (Noun)   (Verb)
> Come to a conclusion = conclude

> (Verb) (Noun)   (Verb)
> <u>reach</u> a <u>decision</u> = <u>decide</u>

> (Verb) (Noun)   (Verb)
> <u>give</u> a <u>summary</u> = <u>summarize</u>

Instead, simply use the "submerged" verb: *Conclude, decide,* and *summarize*. This approach is far better because it reduces sentence length by expressing ideas more directly.

Self-Evident Modifiers

Sometimes we use words quite unnecessarily, expressing already self-evident ideas, as in these redundant modifiers:

> (Modifier)
> my <u>personal</u> opinion   *All* opinions are "personal."

> (Modifier)
> Visible <u>to the eye</u>   Anything visible *must be* visible "to the eye."

> (Modifier)
> <u>Past</u> history   *All* history is "past."

In each case, it would be better to omit the modifier and use a single word: *Opinion, visible,* and *history*.

The American Psychological Association (APA) *Publication Manual* includes more than a dozen excellent examples of redundancy, including the following. In each, the underlining identifies unnecessary words.

they were <u>both</u> alike	<u>one and</u> the same
<u>a total of</u> 68 participants	in <u>close</u> proximity
four <u>different</u> groups	<u>completely</u> unanimous
<u>exactly</u> the same	<u>just</u> the same
<u>absolutely</u> essential	small <u>in size</u>

Long-Winded Expressions

As we have seen, unnecessary introductions and submerged verbs create bothersome clutter, but any long-winded expression using more words than necessary wastes the reader's time and energy. Here are ten familiar examples:

ORIGINAL	REVISION
at this point in time	now
despite the fact that	although
due to the fact that	because
during the time that	while
in many instances	often
in order to	to
in the course of	during
in the event that	if
in the near future	soon
on two occasions	twice

A great many common clichés also fall into this category. Try to cultivate the habit of boiling down several words into one whenever possible.

Repetitious Wording

As we've seen, several short sentences are usually preferable to one long one. But sometimes it's better to combine two or three short sentences to avoid unnecessarily repeating ourselves. If this is done correctly, the resulting sentence is significantly shorter than the total length of the several sentences that went into it, as in this example:

ORIGINAL

The electric drill is easier to use than the hand drill. The electric drill is faster than the hand drill. The electric drill is a very useful tool. (28 words)

REVISION

Easier and faster to use than the hand drill, the electric drill is a very useful tool. (17 words)

In the original, "the electric drill" appears three times and "the hand drill" twice. By using each of these phrases only once, the revision conveys the same information much more efficiently. Always strive for this level of economy.

Review of Mechanics:
Spelling, Punctuation, and Grammar

SPELLING

Most of us experience at least some difficulty with spelling. You can become a better speller, however, simply by observing the following basic guidelines:

1. Do not concern yourself with spelling while you're composing. Concentrate on content, clarity, and organization instead. But at the rewriting stage, carefully check for obvious errors—words you know how to spell but got wrong through carelessness. Do not permit such blunders to slip past you. When in doubt, consult the dictionary. And correct the words highlighted by your computer's spell-checker. But understand that electronic aids are not foolproof. Although quite helpful in spotting typos, spelling checkers are no substitute for vigilance on the part of the writer.

2. Certain pairs of homonyms—words that sound alike but are spelled differently—give nearly everyone trouble, especially since electronic spell-checkers will not catch the error if you pick the wrong homonym. Memorize this list of commonly confused words:

    accept: to receive willingly   He cannot **accept** criticism.
    except: with the exception of   I like everyone **except** Roger.

    affect: to produce an effect upon   Humidity will always **affect** you.
    effect: that which is produced, a result   That film had an **effect** upon me.

    alot: [no such word]
    a lot: a great many   **A lot** of people fear snakes.

    a while: for a period of time   He studied for **a while**.
    awhile: *for* a while   He studied **awhile**.

    cite: to quote or mention   Always **cite** your sources.
    site: a physical location   The job **site** is on Route 12.
    sight: something seen   It was a **sight** to behold!

From *College English: The Basics, 2nd Edition* by George J. Searles. © 2017 by George J. Searles.
Reprinted by permission of Kendall Hunt Publishing Company.

its: possessive form of *it*
it's: contraction (*it is*)

The cat ate **its** food.
It's raining hard today.

loose: not tight
lose: to misplace

He prefers **loose** clothing.
I hate to **lose** my keys.

passed: past tense of *to pass*
past: gone by in time

She **passed** the test with a 98%.
Try not to repeat **past** mistakes.

their: possessive form of *they*
there: in or at that place
they're: contraction (*they are*)

Their car
is over **there**,
but **they're** over here.

to: expresses movement toward
too: also, more than enough
two: 2

We've sent astronauts **to** the moon.
Me **too**!   **Too** much crime.
She has **two** brothers.

whose: possessive form of *who*
who's: contraction (*who is* or *who has*)

Whose hat is this?
Who's going to the movie tonight?
Who's already seen this movie?

your: possessive form of *you*
you're: contraction (*you are*)

Your mother always praises you
because **you're** a good son.

3. We all have certain words we nearly always misspell, a handful of terms we repeatedly get wrong. Identify your own "problem" words, make a list of them, and consult it whenever you must use one of these words. Eventually you'll no longer need the list as the correct spellings imprint themselves on your memory.

4. As mentioned in Appendix A, pg. 204, you should avoid fancy words you're unaccustomed to seeing in print. Use ordinary, everyday vocabulary instead. Not only will your reader understand more easily, but you'll be more likely to notice if anything "looks wrong" because of misspelling.

5. For the spelling of specialized or technical terms, check manuals and the indexes of textbooks in your field of study.

6. Memorize some basic rules. English spelling is highly inconsistent and filled with exceptions, but there are some generally reliable patterns:

   ► *i* before *e*, as in

      achieve, belief, cashier
      except after *c*, as in
      conceit, deceive, receipt

   Notice that in all the above examples, the two letters *i* and *e* combine to sound like a long *e*. If they combine to sound like anything else, the "*i* before *e* except after *c*" rule no longer applies, as in

      height [long *i* sound] and **weight** [long *a* sound]

   ► When adding a suffix (an ending) to a word that ends in *e*, keep the *e* if the suffix begins with a consonant, as in

arrange, arrange<u>ment</u>
extreme, extreme<u>ly</u>
hope, hope<u>less</u>

Drop the *e* if the suffix begins with a vowel, as in

advertise, advertis<u>ing</u>
debate, debat<u>ed</u>
elevate, eleva<u>tion</u>

► When adding a suffix to a word that ends in a consonant followed by *y*, change the *y* to *i* unless the suffix begins with *i*, as in

angry, angri<u>er</u>
funny, funni<u>est</u>
worry, worri<u>ed</u>

► When adding a suffix to a word that ends in a consonant, double the consonant only if

the consonant is preceded by a vowel;
the word is one syllable, or accented on the last syllable;
the suffix begins with a vowel, as in

cram, cram<u>med</u>
scan, scan<u>ning</u>
spam, spam<u>med</u>

► When choosing between the suffixes *–able* and *–ible*, remember that most of the *–able* words are "able" to stand alone without the suffix, as in **afford<u>able</u>** and **remark<u>able</u>**, while most of the *–ible* words cannot, such as **elig<u>ible</u>** and **leg<u>ible</u>**.

► To make a word plural, add *–es* if the pluralizing creates an additional syllable, unless the word already ends in *-e*; otherwise just add an *–s*.

1 class, 2 class<u>es</u>
1 house, 2 house<u>s</u>
1 section, 2 section<u>s</u>

But if the word ends in a consonant followed by *o,* add *–es* even if the pluralizing does not create an extra syllable

1 hero, 2 hero<u>es</u>
1 motto, 2 motto<u>es</u>

Remember that some words are made plural by changes *within* those words.

1 goose, 2 g<u>ee</u>se
1 man, 2 m<u>e</u>n
1 mouse, 2 m<u>ice</u>

And some words are the same in both the singular and the plural.

1 deer, 2 deer
1 fish, 2 fish

Lastly, remember <u>never</u> to pluralize a word by using an apostrophe. The apostrophe is used only in contractions and to indicate possession. (See Appendix B, pg. 216.)

PUNCTUATION

Punctuation exists not to make writers' lives more difficult but to make readers' lives easier. A punctuation mark is simply a symbol, like a road sign on a highway. It tells readers when to slow down, when to stop, and how to anticipate and respond to what appears before them on the page. This brings us to a basic principle: Trust your ear; listen to the sentence and insert punctuation marks wherever you can hear them.

Be careful not to punctuate excessively. As on a highway, an incorrect sign is even more misleading than a missing one. Consider this sentence, for example:

Shakespeare is revered, of course, as a playwright, but he also authored some of the most outstanding sonnets in the English language.

No real harm would result if those commas were removed, because the reader would probably pause at the appropriate points instinctively and the missing commas would in no way obscure the meaning. But look at this version:

Shakespeare, is revered, of course, as a, playwright, but, he also authored, some, of the most, outstanding, sonnets, in the English, language.

See how much harder it is to read the sentence? All those unnecessary commas cause the reader to hesitate repeatedly, thereby derailing the train of thought. And the reader *will* keep pausing, because we automatically respond to symbols whether we want to or not. Admittedly, few writers would over-punctuate the sentence to that degree, but a second basic principle emerges: *Do not punctuate at all unless you're pretty sure you should; when in doubt, leave it out.*

Of course, there's more to punctuation than these two principles. As you know, there are hundreds of punctuation rules. But the good news is that—unless you plan to become a professional writer or editor—you need to know only a small percentage of them. This section of the Appendix covers the basics everyone must know to punctuate adequately.

End Punctuation: Period, Question Mark, and Exclamation Mark

Practically everyone knows how to use periods, question marks, and exclamation marks at the ends of sentences. Sometimes, however, we simply forget to insert end punctuation because the mind is faster than the hand. As we write, we tend to think ahead a sentence or two, and it's easy to overlook end punctuation in our rush to express the next thought. This is something to watch for at the rewriting stage. Make sure that every sentence ends with punctuation. Be especially vigilant about question marks. A common error is to hastily insert a period even though the sentence is actually a question. As for exclamation marks, use them rarely. If used too often, they lose their impact, much like "four letter words" in conversation. Use exclamation marks only when necessary to signal emphasis.

Comma

The comma is probably the most difficult of all punctuation marks to use correctly because it's required in such a wide range of situations. But if you study the following rules you'll notice that it's also the easiest punctuation mark to "hear." As mentioned earlier, trust your ear in determining where to insert commas. And when in doubt, leave it out. The following guidelines will help:

▶ Use commas to separate words or phrases in a sequence, as in these examples:

> There are five teams in the American League East: Baltimore, Boston, New York, Tampa Bay, and Toronto.

> The mayor met with the city council, reassuring them about the budget crisis, addressing their fears about escalating crime, and promising to investigate recent school board controversies.

Notice that there's a comma before the *and* in both of these sentences. Sometimes called "the Oxford comma," it's optional in sequences of nouns (as in the first example), but is required in sequences of *phrases* (as in the second example). Play it safe: Always use it.

▶ Use a comma after an introductory word or phrase, as in these examples:

> Obviously, everyone should quit smoking.

> Despite the team's best efforts, we lost the basketball game by two points.

▶ Use commas before "linking" words such as *and, but,* or *so* if the word is linking two complete sentences, as in these examples:

> Appetizers usually appear at the beginning of a menu, and desserts usually appear at the end.

> The risks involved in mountain climbing are many, but so are the rewards.

> Most high-performance cars do not get good gas mileage, so they are expensive to take on long trips.

▶ Use commas between two or more adjectives in a row, but only if those adjectives would make sense in any order, as in this example:

> Solving a difficult mathematical equation can be a long, slow process.

In the following example, there are no commas between the adjectives (*three, more,* and *full*) because they make sense only in the order given:

> The senator served three more full terms in office.

▶ Use commas to surround words or phrases that are not essential to the sense of the sentence—words or phrases that could just as easily appear in parentheses, as in these examples:

> Bananas, which are rich in potassium, are a healthy snack food.

> James Joyce, the famous Irish novelist, was a very influential writer.

> La Sagrada Familia, a basilica located in Barcelona, is an amazing architectural achievement.

▶ Use a comma before an afterthought—a word or phrase "tacked on" at the end of a sentence—as in these examples:

> Global warming is a major problem, despite some misinformed people's refusal to take it seriously.

> Self-help books are very popular, although most have little new to say.

> The first hockey goalie to wear a protective mask was Jacques Plante, who starred for Montreal in the 1950s.

▶ Use a comma before a direct quote, as in these examples:

> Nathan Hale said, "I only regret that I have but one life to give for my country."

> The professor asked, "How many people have finished the assignment?"

> What famous writer said, "The reports of my death have been greatly exaggerated"?

Colon and Semicolon

The colon and the semicolon are obviously related, but they serve different purposes and should not be used interchangeably.

The three main uses of the colon are after the salutation of a business letter, to introduce a complicated list, and to introduce a long quote, as in these examples:

> There are several advantages to operating a franchise such as McDonald's or Arby's rather than attempting to open your own business: management training and assistance; a recognized name, product, and operating concept; and financial assistance during start-up.

> All Boy Scouts are required to learn the Scout Oath: "On my honor I will do my best to do my duty to God and my country and to obey the Scout Law; to help other people at all times; to keep myself physically strong, mentally awake and morally straight."

Other uses of the colon are in denoting time of day (3:05 a.m.) and "stopwatch" time (1:07:31), in Biblical citations (Corinthians 3:22), in two-part book and article titles (*A Woman in Charge: The Life of Hillary Rodham Clinton*), and in various locations within bibliography entries (see Chapter 17). It can also be used to serve a "stop/go" function, as in *Some coaches care about only one thing: winning.*

▶ There are really only two uses for the semicolon: to link two complete sentences that are closely related, and to separate the items in a complicated list, as in the *franchise* and *Scout Oath* examples above. The semicolon should generally be avoided, however, because there's usually a better alternative. When linking closely related sentences, for example, a comma along with a transition word like *and*, *but*, or *so* will not only establish the connection but also clarify the relationship between the ideas. Compare these examples:

> She didn't study; she failed the test.

> She didn't study, so she failed the test.

Clearly, the second version is better. It not only connects the two sentences but plainly shows that the second fact is the result of the first.

As for separating the items in a complicated list, simply arrange the items vertically, perhaps with bullets, like this:

There are several advantages to operating a franchise such as McDonald's or Arby's rather than attempting to open your own business:

▶ management training and assistance
▶ a recognized name, product, and operating concept
▶ financial assistance during start-up

Again, the second version is obviously preferable. It enables the reader to differentiate more easily among the separate items.

Quotation Marks

Quotation marks are used to surround the title of a short work (e.g., a newspaper or magazine article, a story, or a poem), a direct quotation (someone else's exact words) or to show that a word or phrase is being used sarcastically, ironically, or in some other non-literal way. Here are examples:

TITLE:	Thomas Paine wrote "Common Sense."
DIRECT QUOTE:	The Nike motto is, "Just do it."
NONLITERAL USE:	No student wants to "bomb" on an exam.

Quotation marks must be positioned correctly in relation to other punctuation, especially end punctuation. Follow these guidelines:

▶ A period at the end of a sentence always goes inside the quotation marks.

  A well-known proverb is, "There's no free lunch."

▶ A question mark at the end of a sentence goes inside the quotation marks if the quote itself is a question.

  Juliet cries, "Wherefore art thou Romeo?"

▶ A question mark at the end of a sentence goes outside the quotation marks if the whole sentence (rather than the quote) is a question. Notice that in such a situation there is no period within the final quotation mark.

  Have you ever heard the proverb, "There's no free lunch"?

▶ A question mark at the end of a sentence goes inside the quotation marks if the quote and the whole sentence are both questions.

  Does Juliet cry, "Wherefore art thou Romeo?"

▶ If an attributing phrase (or anything else) follows the quote, the comma goes inside the quotation marks.

  "There's no free lunch," said my uncle.

▶ If an attributing phrase follows a quote that is a question, omit the comma but leave the question mark inside the quotation marks.

  "Wherefore art thou Romeo?" cries Juliet.

► For exclamation marks, simply follow the same pattern as for question marks.

Paul yelled, "No way!"	(Quote is emphatic.)
Don't you dare say, "Maybe"!	(Sentence is emphatic, quote is not.)
Don't you dare yell, "No way!"	(Quote and sentence are both emphatic.)
"No way!" yelled Paul.	(Emphatic quote is followed by attribution.)

Apostrophe

The apostrophe is often misused, partly because it can't be heard, but the rules governing this punctuation mark are actually quite simple.

1. *Never* use the apostrophe to make a word plural.

   INCORRECT: College student's must master many subject's.

   CORRECT: College students must master many subjects.

2. Use the apostrophe to make a word possessive, as follows:

   ► If the word is singular, add 's

   > one child's hat
   > one man's hat
   > one woman's hat
   > John Jones's hat
   > Jane Smith's hat

   ► If the word is plural and does not already end in –s, add 's

   > the children's hats
   > the men's hats
   > the women's hats

   ► If the word is plural and ends in –s, add an apostrophe

   > the boys' hats
   > the girls' hats
   > the Joneses' house
   > the Smiths' house

3. Use an apostrophe to replace the missing letter(s) in a contraction.

I am, I'm	I will, I'll
should have, should've	could have, could've
should not, shouldn't	could not, couldn't
would have, would've	do not, don't
would not, wouldn't	does not, doesn't
she is, she's	has not, hasn't
is not, isn't	will not, won't

GRAMMAR

As with spelling and punctuation, there are a great many grammar rules. For practical purposes, however, you really need to know relatively few. This section focuses only on the basics—the rules governing sentence fragments, run-ons, and agreement.

Sentence Fragments

As the term itself denotes, a sentence fragment is an incomplete sentence. Most fragments are actually the result of faulty punctuation—when a writer inserts end punctuation too soon, thereby "stranding" part of the sentence. Consider these examples:

> Rabies has been a problem since the 1950s throughout New York State.
>
> (Fragment)
> <u>Including Long Island and New York City</u>.

[The first period should have been a comma.]

> (Fragment)
> <u>If you fail to cite your sources in your research paper.</u> You are guilty of plagiarizing.

[Again, the first period should have been a comma.]

You can usually avoid sentence fragments if you remember three basic rules:

1. To be complete, a sentence must include a subject (actor) and a verb (action).

    > (Subject)　　　　　(Verb)
    > <u>Snowmobilers</u> sometimes <u>take</u> unnecessary risks.

2. If a sentence begins with a word or phrase that seems to point toward a two-part idea (for example, "if this, then that"), the second part must be included within the sentence, because the first part is a fragment and therefore cannot stand alone. For an example, see the "**If** you fail to cite" sentence above. Here are some other words that signal a two-part idea:

after	although	because
before	for	since
unless	until	when

3. Certain verb forms (some *-ed* forms, *-ing* forms, and *to* forms) cannot serve as the main verb in a sentence unless their subjects are expressed.

    > (Fragment)
    > <u>Opened in 1939.</u> The Merritt Parkway in Connecticut was one of America's first freeways.

    > (Fragment)
    > <u>Winding from Chicago to Los Angeles.</u> Route 66 covers 42,000 miles.

    > (Fragment)
    > <u>To succeed in your own business.</u> You need both energy and luck.

Notice that the *–ed, -ing,* and *to* forms frequently appear in introductory phrases. Learn to recognize these for what they are—not sentences in themselves but *beginnings* of sentences—and punctuate each with a comma, not a period. (See the second rule in the section on commas.)

Run-On Sentences

While the sentence fragment is something to avoid, even worse is a sentence that goes on and on after it should've stopped. A run-on sentence spills over into the following sentence with no break in between. When that happens, the writing takes on a rushed, headlong quality, and ideas become jumbled together.

There are two ways that a sentence can overflow into the next: either with a comma weakly separating the two sentences or with nothing at all in between. Here's an example of each:

> A surveyor's measurements must be precise, there is no room for error.

> A surveyor's measurements must be precise there is no room for error.

Technically, only the second example is a true run-on. The first is really an instance of what grammarians call a comma splice. For practical purposes, however, the problem is the same. In both cases, the first sentence has collided with the second. Obviously, the two sentences must be separated.

> A surveyor's measurements must be precise. There is no room for error.

Another option would be to use a linking word to join the two sentences, thereby clarifying the relationship between them.

> A surveyor's measurements must be precise, because there is no room for error.

Or you may prefer to turn one of the sentences into a fragment and use it as an introductory construction.

> Because there is no room for error, a surveyor's measurements must be precise.

It should be clear by now that fragments and run-ons alike are usually the result of faulty punctuation. Certain patterns are correct, while others are not, as the following list indicates:

Correct Patterns	Incorrect Patterns
Sentence.	Fragment.
Sentence. Sentence.	Fragment. Fragment.
Sentence, link + sentence.	Sentence, sentence.
Fragment, sentence.	Fragment. Sentence.
Sentence, fragment.	Sentence. Fragment.
Fragment, sentence, fragment.	Fragment. Sentence. Fragment.

Subject-Verb Agreement

Another common grammar error is to use a plural verb with a singular subject, or vice versa. Remember that a singular subject requires a singular verb, while a plural subject requires a plural verb.

(Singular Subject)	(Singular Verb)	(Plural Subject)	(Plural Verb)
A singer	sings.	Singers	sing.

Note that singular subjects rarely end in *–s*, while singular verbs usually do. Conversely, plural subjects usually do end in *–s*, but plural verbs never do.

Although the subject-verb agreement rules may seem obvious, many writers commit agreement errors simply because they fail to distinguish between singular and plural subjects. This sometimes occurs when the subject is an indefinite pronoun, most of which are singular. Here's a chart of the most common such pronouns, indicating which ones are singular, which plural, and which can function as either:

Singular			Plural	Either
anybody	everybody	no one	few	all
anyone	everyone	nothing	many	any
anything	everything	somebody	several	more
each	neither	someone		most
either	nobody	something		none
				some

Agreement errors can also result when there's a cluster of words between the subject and its verb, thereby creating a misleading sound pattern.

INCORRECT   A pile of tools **are** on the workbench.
CORRECT   A pile of tools **is** on the workbench.

Even though *tools are* sounds correct, the first sentence is incorrect because *pile*—not *tools*—is the (singular) subject, and therefore requires the singular verb *is*.

Pronoun-Antecedent Agreement

Just as subjects and verbs must agree, so too must pronouns and their antecedents (the words that the pronouns refer back to).

(Singular   (Plural
Antecedent)   Pronoun)
For <u>a woman</u> to succeed as an umpire, <u>they</u> must overcome much prejudice.

(Singular   (Singular
Antecedent)   Pronoun)
For <u>a woman</u> to succeed as an umpire, <u>she</u> must overcome much prejudice.

The first sentence is incorrect because *a woman*, which is singular, disagrees with *they*, which is plural. (Although *they* is often used as a singular in speech, it must always be treated as a plural in writing.) The second sentence is correct because both *a woman* and *she* are singular and therefore agree.

Once again, indefinite pronouns can create agreement problems.

(Singular   (Plural
Antecedent)   Pronoun)
<u>Everyone</u> on the men's soccer team should be proud of <u>themselves</u>.

(Singular   (Singular
Antecedent)   Pronoun)
<u>Everyone</u> on the men's soccer team should be proud of <u>himself</u>.

The first sentence is incorrect because *everyone*, which is singular, disagrees with *themselves*, which is plural. The second sentence is correct because both *everyone* and *himself* are singular and therefore agree. Of course, an even better revision would simply delete the last two words, in keeping with the "less is more" principle.

Let's consider one more aspect of agreement, using this sentence as a starting point:

(Singular   (Plural
Antecedent)   Pronoun)
<u>Everybody</u> should mind <u>their</u> own business.

Clearly, there's disagreement between *Everybody*, which is singular, and *their*, which is plural, even though this is how the sentence would probably be worded in speech. But writing is more formal than speech, so the problem must be corrected. There are two ways to do so: Either the pronoun and its antecedent can both be singular, or both can be plural. Here are two singular versions:

(Singular   (Singular
Antecedent)   Pronoun)   This sentence is correct, but
<u>Everybody</u> should mind <u>his</u> own business.   is guilty of gender bias.

(Singular   (Singular
Antecedent)   Pronoun)
<u>Everybody</u> should mind <u>his or her</u> own business.   Better.

Here are two plural versions: The plural approach is almost always best of all, because it avoids gender-bias without resorting to the wordy *his or her* phrasing.

(Plural   (Plural
Antecedent)   Pronoun)
<u>People</u> should mind <u>their</u> own business.

(Plural   (Plural
Antecedent)   Pronoun)
<u>We</u> should all mind <u>our</u> own business.

INDEX